Cruise Operations Management

Cruise Operations Management: Hospitality Perspectives provides a comprehensive and contextualized overview of hospitality services for the cruise industry. As well as providing a background to the cruise industry, it also looks deeper into the management issues, providing a practical guide for both students and professionals alike.

Since the first edition of this book there have been many important developments in the industry and this new edition features revised chapters on

- Contemporary cruise operations
- Cruise geography
- Itinerary planning
- Health, safety and security
- Maritime issues and legislation

In addition there is a new chapter on cruise management resources, intended to be of benefit to research students. *Cruise Operations Management* presents a range of issues illustrated by a number of case studies that encourage the reader to examine the often complex circumstances that surround problems or events associated with cruise operations. The case studies are contemporary and are constructed from first-hand research with a number of international cruise companies, providing a real world insight into this industry. They include roles and responsibilities on a cruise ship, customer service systems and passenger profiles and managing food and drink operations onboard. Some case studies are followed by questions that are intended to illuminate issues and stimulate discussion.

The structure of the book is designed so the reader can either build knowledge cumulatively for an in-depth understanding of managerial practices and procedures onboard a cruise ship, or they can 'dip in' and take advantage of specific material and case studies for use within a more generic hospitality or tourism learning context.

Philip Gibson is Programme Lead for Hospitality and Cruise Management at the University of P

Cruise Operations Management: Hospitality Perspectives

Second Edition

Philip Gibson

Routledge
Taylor & Francis Group

LONDON AND NEW YORK

First published 2012
by Routledge
2 Park Square, Milton Park, Abingdon, Oxon OX14 4RN

Simultaneously published in the USA and Canada
by Routledge
711 Third Avenue, New York, NY 10017

Routledge is an imprint of the Taylor & Francis Group, an informa business

© 2012 Philip Gibson

Previous edition published by Butterworth-Heinemann
First edition 2006

British Library Cataloguing in Publication Data
A catalogue record for this book is available from the British Library

Library of Congress Cataloging-in-Publication Data
Gibson, Philip, 1955-
    Cruise operations management / Philip Gibson.
        p. cm.
    Includes bibliographical references and index.
    1. Ocean travel—Management. 2. Cruise lines—Management. I. Title.
    G550.G53 2012
    387.5'42068—dc23

ISBN: 978-0-415-69940-2 (hbk)
ISBN: 978-0-415-69953-2 (pbk)
ISBN: 978-0-203-12927-2 (ebk)

Typeset in Times New Roman
by Swales & Willis Ltd, Exeter, Devon

MIX
Paper from
responsible sources
FSC
www.fsc.org   FSC® C004839

Printed and bound in Great Britain by
TJ International Ltd, Padstow, Cornwall

Contents

Contemporary cruise operations

1

SUMMARY

The first chapter launches this highly specialized textbook. In this introductory chapter, an overview of the cruise industry is presented in order that the reader can understand issues concerning the way the industry has grown and the types of cruise vacations that are available. In addition, by charting the historical growth, a timeline is created which highlights milestones and can go some way to help explain why some of the developments have occurred. In its current state the market is dominated by cruise corporations and cruise brands, and the final part of this introductory chapter provides an overview of the economical realities that are a feature of cruise business in the early part of the twenty-first century.

Key phrases: cruise industry; elements of cruising; history of cruising; cruise economics.

INTRODUCTION

According to Mancini [1], the definition of a cruise, is, 'a vacation trip by ship'. This brief and unassuming phrase demonstrates that the cruise industry encompasses a broad range of options including: contemporary cruises, traditional cruises, adventure or expedition cruises, world cruises, coastal cruises, repositioning cruises, ferry cruises, river cruises and cruise conferences (see Chapter 3 for more explanation). There are universities at sea for people with motivation to learn, cruise ships fitted out with apartments, themed cruises, cruises to nowhere, short-break cruises – the variations are seemingly extremely diverse and also apparently infinite. Recently, the author observed a father and son on a cruise where the adult son was actively networking with other guests at social events onboard in order to establish clients for his business, so for some it could be said that cruises are business opportunities. A more appropriate definition of today's cruise industry is a vacation by ship involving a voyage by sea, on a lake or on a river.

The cruise industry has grown and continues to grow enormously in scale. It is frequently regarded as being a small but significant sector of the tourism industry [2], but this description fails to recognize the inherent qualities and attributes that support the claim that this is an industry in its own right. In many respects it is helpful to consider, in general terms, some of the evidence for this claim within this introduction, although readers will be able to make a more informed judgement having read the whole book.

Gibson [3] believes that the time is right for those involved in the cruise business – and particularly the professionals in the hotel department onboard – to be more vocal in identifying their status within what is a unique industry. This is stated to be appropriate because, while it is reasonable to categorize the cruise business as being related to tourism, leisure, hospitality and/or maritime industries, the maritime context modifies the way that tourism and hospitality are practised. The ships are travelling internationally, people live onboard for lengthy contracts, maritime culture pervades with resultant strengths and challenges because of the notion of a community at sea [4], and safety at sea is critical. The business of operating what is virtually often a large-scale mobile tourist destination at sea is unique and the complexities support the claim that this world is best referred to as the International Cruise Industry.

According to the Cruise Line International Association [5], 14.3 million people took a cruise in 2010. A sizeable figure but not enormous, when taken in context and comparing to other studies during the same year; e.g. 14.5 million tourists were predicted to visit Thailand [6] and 20 million tourists were expected in Venice [7]. However the CLIA data refers to the numbers of clients catered for by member cruise brands and places a distinct North American and European bias on the analysis. In contrast, Ward [8] believed that the cruise industry attracted 20 million passengers in 2009 and Bayley [9] stated that 18 million people were carried worldwide.

Charlier and McCalla [10] suggest the discrepancy in identifying the true scale of the market demonstrates a lack of 'comprehensive, reliable worldwide statistics' (p.19) in general terms, and considering that the majority of statistics underestimate total figures, both Ward [8] and Bayley [9] agree that the industry has experienced compound aggregate growth of 7% over the last 40 years compared to the long-term average growth worldwide for tourism, which is said to be 4% [11].

The industry employs approximately half a million officers and crew, as well as an estimated 75,000 employees ashore, operating 281 ships worldwide, achieving in excess of 90% occupancy and generating $26.6 billion a year [12]. Indirectly, the industry provides employment for other third-party businesses, including food suppliers, engineering services, manufacturers, port agents and authorities, transport companies, tourist companies, hotels, destination companies, and car-hire and employment agencies. In relation to the growth of the industry in marketing terms, Bayley identifies that total bed-days sold in 2010 were almost 137 million compared to 64 million bed-days sold in 2002 and 35 million bed-days sold in 1997 [9, 13].

In the last ten years, construction of new vessels has been an important feature, with a period of rapid growth fuelled by new orders at shipyards peaking in 2007 [14]. This period saw the emergence of increasingly large vessels, culminating with two giant 220,000 gross registered tonnage (GRT) vessels built for Royal Caribbean Cruise Ltd, each carrying up to 6,000 guests and over 2,000 crew; the *Oasis of the Seas* and the *Allure of the Seas*. Smaller ships are also in production, with Seabourn Cruises leading the way in focusing on vessels carrying around 450 guests and Oceania and MSC constructing ships catering for 1,250 guests.

The Cruise Lines International Association (CLIA, [5]), an organization that represents 25 of the world's major cruise companies, reports that the industry has never been stronger. They state that satisfaction rates are unparalleled, noting that cruising is an important way for passengers to sample destinations and then return at a later stage. The potential market is strong, with only 3.1% of North Americans and 1% of Europeans having cruised before and, because of the array of choice in terms of cruise brands and ships, the market is very diverse [15]. The changing demographic profile of cruising, in terms of the market segment, social status and age, is also of significance [16].

According to Bayley [9], there has been a distinct shift in the pattern of growth, which has resulted in an increase in numbers of passengers emanating from European markets. Bayley [9] suggests that while all regions remain under-penetrated, European markets are showing buoyant growth and, as a result, increasing numbers of vessels are being deployed in order to capitalize on this potential. With 330 million people in North America and 500 million in Europe, there is an obvious opportunity in targeting this large emerging market. The Asian, Pacific and Latin American markets are also on the radar for potential growth, with vast populations, growing economies and very low levels of market penetration.

THE ELEMENTS OF CRUISING

It could be argued that our planet Earth is, in one significant sense, misnamed. This is because 71% of the surface is covered by water [17]. Air travel has been cited as a major influence in supporting changing leisure activities, yet even a novice can recognize the opportunities for considering sea- and water-based vacations using ships as floating resorts. According to Day and McRae [18], a cruise ship provides easy access to some of the world's most popular destinations and this simple statement holds the key to the current success that the industry enjoys. This can be exemplified by examining Table 1.1 and completing the task that is described.

For many tourists, the cruise experience embodies a series of powerful motivators; it is often perceived to be safe, social, customer friendly and service oriented [20]. The ship provides a mobile, consistent, easily accessible base to act as a home from home while the tourist samples the port of call. The tourist adapts to the

Table 1.1 *Tourists' favourite destinations [19]*

Using Viator's [19] favourite travel destinations, identify those that can, in theory, be visited by a cruise ship.

1. Paris, France	18. Athens, Greece	35. Perth, Australia
2. Las Vegas, Nevada	19. Orlando, Florida	36. Kuala Lumpur, Malaysia
3. Rome, Italy	20. Vienna, Austria	37. Montreal, Canada
4. New York City, New York	21. Cairns, Australia	38. Costa del Sol, Spain
5. London, England	22. Zurich, Switzerland	39. Brisbane, Australia
6. Florence, Italy	23. Washington, D.C., USA	40. Dubai, United Arab Emirates
7. Tokyo, Japan	24. Singapore	41. Reykjavik, Iceland
8. Sydney, Australia	25. Dublin, Ireland	42. Auckland, New Zealand
9. San Francisco, California	26. Edinburgh, Scotland	43. Franz Josef & Fox Glacier, New Zealand
10. Melbourne, Australia	27. Hong Kong	44. Cancun, Mexico
11. Venice, Italy	28. Vancouver, Canada	45. Nice, France
12. Munich, Germany	29. Naples, Italy	46. Miami, Florida
13. Barcelona, Spain	30. Oahu, Hawaii	47. Bangkok, Thailand
14. Madrid, Spain	31. Cairo, Egypt	48. Brussels, Belgium
15. Milan, Italy	32. Uluru, Australia	49. Maui, Hawaii
16. Los Angeles, California	33. Salzburg, Austria	50. Boston, Massachusetts
17. Amsterdam, the Netherlands	34. Christchurch, New Zealand	

shipboard life and learns to relax into a holiday routine [21]: a routine that can be interspersed with a choreographed range of ship or land activities.

As travel expert Douglas Ward says:

> Over 10 million people can't be wrong (that's how many people took a cruise last year)! Cruising is popular today because it takes you away from the pressures and strains of contemporary life by offering an escape from reality. Cruise ships are really self-contained resorts, without the crime, which can take you to several destinations in the space of just a few days. [22]

However, the notion of 'cruising' also generates negative perceptions. Dickinson and Vladimir [23] conducted interviews with people who either hadn't considered or didn't want to go on a cruise. They revealed five specific factors that demotivated the potential tourist (see Table 1.2).

Ward [8] counters this list by highlighting emerging patterns. Cruising is presented as being both cost effective and value high. Types of cruises have expanded with opportunities for all sorts of people. In this way, cruising can be socially inclusive and socially exclusive: families can be catered for as a specialist market, as can single tourists, conference delegates, older travellers, active tourists, groups, etc. – the list is endless. Ward recognizes that this type of vacation is appealing to older customers but also notes that the age of first-time cruisers is now well under 40.

A HISTORY OF CRUISING

Considerable insight can be gained when charting the history of cruising in terms of identifying not only where and how the concept of cruising arose, but also in trying to predict where it is going. Table 1.3 [22, 24–29] is not

Table 1.2 *Factors that demotivate potential cruisers (adapted from Dickinson and Vladimir [23])*

Factor	Reason
Cost:	cruising is perceived to be expensive
Exclusivity:	cruising is thought to be a domain for the wealthy, and elitist in terms of social groupings
Family prohibitive:	cruising not felt to be for people with children but rather oriented towards older couples
Claustrophobic:	the ship is thought of as a constraint, with quiet space at a premium
Seasickness:	concerns about coping with seasickness influence decision-making

Table 1.3 *A history of cruising (various sources: [22, 24–29])*

Year	Event
1801	The tug *Charlotte Dundas* goes into service and becomes the first practical steam-driven vessel.
1818	Black Ball Line introduces the *Savannah* 424 GRT or Gross Registered Tonnage (see Table 1.4 for an explanation of this term), carrying 8 customers, and this ship becomes the first to cross the Atlantic from New York to Liverpool. The journey takes 28 days.
1835	First advertised cruise around the Shetland and Orkney islands. This was a cruise that never occurred and it wasn't until 1886 that the North of Scotland and Orkney and Shetland Shipping Company operated short-break cruises.
1837	Peninsular Steam Navigation Company founded (later to become the Peninsular and Oriental Steam and Navigation Company, with the familiar name of P&O Cruises).
1840	Sam Cunard establishes the first transatlantic steamship.
1843	Isambard Kingdom Brunel's ship the *Great Britain*, 3270 GRT, is launched. This ship is the first iron-hulled, propeller-driven customer vessel.
1844	P&O cruises from London to Vigo, Lisbon, Malta, Istanbul and Alexandria aboard the SS *Iberia*.
1858	Customers pay to join the *Ceylon*, a P&O vessel, for what is considered the first cruise.
1867	Author Mark Twain features a P&O voyage from London to the Black Sea in his novel *The Innocents Abroad*.
1881	The *Ceylon* is refitted to become a purpose-built customer ship.
1910	White Star introduces the *Olympic* 46,329 GRT and, the year after, the *Titanic*, which sinks after colliding with an iceberg on 12 April 1912.
1911	*Victoria Louise* becomes the first vessel to be built exclusively for cruising.
1912	Cunard introduces the *Laconia* and *Franconia* as custom-built cruise and line voyagers.
1920–33	In the USA during prohibition, 'booze cruises' from US ports allow customers to drink and gamble while visiting ports such as Cuba, Bermuda and the Bahamas.
1922	Cunard's *Laconia* sails on a world cruise. The ship is relatively small – 20,000 GRT and 2,000 customers in three-class accommodation.

Table 1.3 *Continued*

1929	P&O's *Viceroy of India* is introduced. It is the most impressive ship of its time, featuring the first use of turbo-electric power and the first onboard swimming pool. It is a dual-purpose liner (UK to India) and luxury cruiser.
1930s	Union Castle offers holiday tours to South Africa at highly competitive rates of £30 third class, £60 second class and £90 first class.
1934	The luxury cruise liner RMS *Queen Mary* is launched. With 1,174 officers and crew and 2,000 customers, the ratio is less than 2:1.
1934	United States Lines builds the SS *America*, an oil-fired liner capable of speeds up to 25 knots. This vessel is commissioned as a troop carrier in 1941.
1938	SS *Normandie* 83,000 GRT undertakes a 21-day cruise: New York–Rio de Janeiro–New York. Cost per customer from $395 to $8,600.
1939	World War II is declared. Cruise ships such as *Queen Mary* and *Queen Elizabeth* are converted as troop carriers.
1958	First transatlantic commercial jet aircraft crossing leads to the demise of the liner market and the downturn of business for many cruise companies.
1966	Cruise industry recovers – mainly centred on the UK.
1970s	New cruise companies established – 1% of holidaymakers take cruise holidays. Cruise companies work closely with airlines to develop combined products – fly-cruise. *Love Boat* airs in 1977.
1979	Onboard revenue represents 5% of total revenues.
1984	Carnival Cruises first TV commercial.
1986	*Windstar*, a vessel with computerized sails, is introduced, marrying the romance of sail with modern comforts.
1990s	Consolidation and globalization: leading to mergers and acquisitions.
1999	'Eagle' type vessels such as *Voyager of the Sea* and *Grand Princess* are introduced, bringing higher levels of sophistication, economy of scale and the concept of the vessel as a destination.
2000s	Segmentation and lifestyle cruising. Sustained growth for the North American market (8% annually) from 1980 to 2000.

Table 1.3 *Continued*

2000	Royal Caribbean International's (RCI) *Explorer of the Sea* is introduced (137,308 GRT).
2002	There are an estimated 700 million tourists worldwide, of whom 10.3 million are cruise tourists; 2.4% of the US population, 1.3% of the UK population and less than 1% of Europe's population cruise annually.
2003	Cunard's *Queen Mary 2* launched (150,000 GRT).
2003	Carnival Corporation becomes the largest cruise operator when they merge with P&O Princess Cruises.
2009	Royal Caribbean's Oasis class ship, *Oasis of the Seas*, enters service – at 220,000 GRT she is the world's largest cruise ship.
2006	NCL launches freestyle concept.
2010	Total worldwide cruise market estimated to be almost $30 billion, with Carnival Corporation in control of a 51.6% share of worldwide revenue and Royal Caribbean 25.6%.
2011	Carnival Corporation announces 100th ship.

intended to be inclusive but rather to flag up significant moments over the last 200 years.

Much is said about the size of contemporary super-cruisers. The example in Table 1.3, with the introduction of 'Oasis' and 'Eagle' class cruise ships, leading up to the launch of the *Queen Mary 2* (*QM2*) and then the *Oasis of the Seas* are cases in point. The ship as a destination with sophisticated onboard facilities and a much enhanced product is linked to economies of scale achieved through the construction of larger vessels [26]. This aspect of cruising has captured the public's attention and the implications are, of course, important in terms of the political, economic, social, technological, legal and environmental issues. These aspects will be examined later in this book. However, in basic terms, the sizes of cruise ships provide interesting comparison.

Currently, the largest vessels can carry around 6,000 customers and the smallest fewer than 100 customers. Cunard-Lines' *Queen Mary 2,* is 150,000 GRT. Princess Cruises' *Grand Princess*, weighs in at 108,806 GRT, while Hebridean Island Cruises' the *Hebridean Princess* is 2,112 GRT. Royal Caribbean's *Allure of the Sea* (220,000 GRT) is marginally the largest cruise ship at sea; the ship is 5 centimetres longer than sister ship *Oasis of the Seas* [30].

How do you measure the size of a ship?

Ships can be described by referring to capacity, dimensions or tonnage.

Capacity
A cruise ship's capacity is expressed in terms of the total numbers of officers, crew and customers. Cruise companies frequently plan using lower-berth capacity (referring to the number of beds in a cabin), implying that capacity for some ships could be increased if capacity included upper berths (some cabins can have bunk-beds or two-tier bedding arrangements).

Dimensions
The length is measured from the bows or forward end (fore) to the stern or after end (aft) – fore and aft are commonly used terms.
The beam is the width at the widest point (amidships).
The draft or draught of a ship measures the depth of a ship as the vessel sits in the water.

Tonnage
Ships tend to be described and compared in terms of gross registered tonnage (GRT). According to Branch[24] GRT is calculated by dividing the volume in cubic feet of a vessel's closed-in spaces by 100. A vessel ton is 100ft^3. Tonnage is frequently made use of by port authorities when calculating charges when a ship requires a pilot and for harbour fees. The word 'tonnage' is derived from 'tun', a medieval term meaning barrel.

Speed
Speed is measured in knots. 1 Knot equates to 1 nautical mile per hour. A nautical mile is the equivalent to 1,852 metres or 1.15 land miles.

Figure 1.1 *Ship measurements*

Scale varies depending on purpose. Large vessels such as the 'Eagle' class ships that were discussed previously accommodate larger numbers and can provide opportunities for greater diversity onboard. 'Oasis' class ships and their smaller cousins, the 'Freedom' class ships, are destinations in their own rights. Smaller vessels can be more intimate and provide access to ports, which larger ships cannot visit because of the depth of the ship's keel, the length of the vessel or the constraints of manoeuvrability at the destination. The relationships in terms of ratios (crew to customers, customer space per customer, size of cabin, public areas) all play a part, depending on the type of cruise tourist. The passenger–space ratio is calculated by dividing GRT by the maximum number of passengers to provide a number that defines cubic space per passenger. Currently the *QM2* has one of the highest space-to-passenger ratios, at just over 57 (150,000 GRT divided by 2,620 passengers). At the other end of the scale, budget vessels might be as low as 28. Crew to passenger ratios tend to reflect a 2:1 ratio for premium lines and 1.5:1 for luxury vessels (see Table 1.4).

Table 1.4 *Spaces per passenger and ratios passengers to crew (to 2 decimal points)*

Ship	Brand	Year began operations	GRT	Passenger (pax)	Crew	Space per pax feet³	Ratio
Allure of the Seas	Royal Caribbean	2010	225,000	6296	2,165	35.74	2.91:1
Azura	P&O Cruises	2010	116,000	3100	1,200	37.42	2.58:1
Norwegian Epic	NCL	2010	153,000	4228	1,710	36.19	2.47:1
Seabourn Sojourn	Seabourn	2010	32,000	450	330	71.11	1.36:1
Silver Spirit	Silversea	2009	36,000	540	376	66.67	1.44:1
Celebrity Solstice	Celebrity	2008	122,000	2,850	1,500	42.81	1.90:1
Eurodam	Holland America	2008	86,000	2,104	929	40.87	2.26:1
Saga Ruby	Saga	2005	24,492	661	380	37.05	1.74:1
Queen Mary 2	Cunard	2004	150,000	3,056	1,253	49.08	2.44:1
Diamond Princess	Princess	2004	115,875	2,674	1,238	43.33	2.16:1
Titanic	White Star	1911	46,328	3,000	885	15.44	3.39:1

THE IMAGE OF CRUISING

The industry is diverse and it appears that this is indicative of the future direction for cruise developments. The following case studies present four contrasting cruise experiences. The cases are preceded by a table, which provides an easy comparison between basic features. The flag of registration is important because it refers to the legal status of the ship (see Chapter 3 for more information).

Table 1.5 *Comparison chart*

Vessel	Windstar	World of ResidenSea	Grand Princess	Queen Mary 2	Oasis of the Seas
Operating company	Windstar Cruises Ambassadors International Cruise Group	ResidenSea Ltd	Carnival	Carnival	Royal Caribbean
Built	1986	2002	1998	2003	2009
GRT	5,350	43,524	109,000	150,000	225,282
Draft	4.1 metres	6.7 metres	8 metres	10.09 metres	9.1 metres
Length	134 metres	196.35 metres	292 metres	348 metres	360 metres
Beam	15.8 metres	29.8 metres	36 metres	45.4 metres	64 metres
Speed	14 knots	18.5 knots	24 knots	26 knots	22.6 knots
Method of propulsion	Diesel electric (3) and sail (6)	Diesel electric	Diesel electric	Gas turbine Diesel electric	Diesel electric
Customer–space ratio	36 cubic feet per pax	66 cubic feet per pax	42 cubic foot per pax	56.25 cubic feet per pax	35.74 cubic feet per pax
Customer cabins	74	110 apartments & 88 studios	1,300	1,310	2,706
Number customers	148 (based on double occupancy)	656 (average is expected to be 320)	2,600	2,620	5,400 (double occupancy) 6,296 when full
Number crew	90	320	1,100	1,253	2,165
Marketing slogan	'180 degrees from ordinary'	'When you live to travel'	'Personal choice cruising'	'The grandest of them all'	'The nation of why not'
Flag – country of registration	Bahamas	Bahamas	Liberia	United Kingdom	Bahamas

CELEBRITY ECLIPSE

On the day that *Celebrity Eclipse* was meant to be celebrating her inauguration and naming ceremony in Southampton, the quayside was empty and there were no champagne bottles or streamers in sight. Instead the ship had made her way to Bilbao in northern Spain to collect 2,000 holidaymakers stranded by the eruption of an unpronounceable volcano (Eyjafjallajökull) and the resultant ash cloud that prevented aircraft from flying [31]. This public relations coup stands the company in good stead because, like many cruise brands, Celebrity has decided to target the UK and European market by positioning the *Eclipse* to sail out of Southampton for five months and from the Caribbean for the remainder of the year.

Celebrity is a cruise brand owned by the second largest cruise corporation in the world, Royal Caribbean Cruise Ltd (RCCL). The cruise brand originally emerged as an idea to capitalize on luxury cruising out of Bermuda. It was created by Greek shipping line Chandris in 1988 and merged with RCCL in 1997. The brand aims to 'exceed expectations' by focusing on high quality, superior design, spacious accommodations, grand style, attentive service and exceptional cuisine [32].

The brand's target market comprises discerning and wealthy 'baby boomers' (those who grew up in the 1960s and 1970s) who seek sophistication and first-class service [33] – 70% of Celebrity Cruises guests are experienced cruise travellers. While Celebrity Cruises was formerly known as a predominantly US-based brand, recent new builds have seen their ships being positioned in other markets; namely the UK, Europe and Latin America. *Celebrity Eclipse* is a Solstice class ship. Many ships are denoted by class after the first vessel designed to a pattern: in this case, the *Celebrity Solstice*. This pattern is important because, the cruise company can derive greater returns from investment in design and savings from constructing a common 'platform' [34]. The platform then can be made to replicate a successful formula, or used to make adjustments and try out new concepts with less financial risk.

Celebrity Eclipse carries 2,850 passengers [35]. The ship weighs in at 122,000 GRT. Among the attractions onboard are 13 bars and lounges, 10 choices of dining venues, a lawn club featuring real grass on the upper deck, an aqua spa and an internet café; 85% of the staterooms have verandas. The Corning Museum of Glass is an unusual departure from the norm, providing a glass-blowing show for guests to observe [36].

Figure 1.2 *Celebrity Eclipse*

The ship has an international crew and boasts a guest-to-crew ratio of 2:1. The brand states that their luxury staterooms and suites have the highest guest-to-space ratio in the industry and butler service is provided in all suites.

THE WORLD

The *World of ResidenSea* (40,000 GRT) is a novel concept [37]. This vessel was built by the Fosen Shipyard in Norway to continuously circumnavigate the world and to provide:

> The world's first ship to be designed as an ocean-going residence for full time occupancy . . . . the *World* provides spacious residences – fully furnished and equipped – and guest suites for family, friends, business associates or personal staff. [37]

This ambitious project has dual occupancy options. The ship has 110 private apartments, each with a fully equipped kitchen (galley) that can be either privately owned or rented. In addition, the *World* has 88 guest suites that can be booked by the general public. Guests are expected to be 40% from the US, 40% European and 20% from the rest of the world. The target market for ownership is homeowners with two or three residences, average age 55, who are wealthy, 'self made' entrepreneurs. A typical profile would describe such a person as active, with a love of the sea or sailing and a desire to guard her/his privacy [38].

The facilities include four distinctive restaurants, a nightclub, a casino, theatre, an art gallery, spa and fitness centre, two pools, a full-sized tennis court, a golf centre (including a real grass putting green) and a retractable marina. The ship also possesses three emergency hospital wards.

Figure 1.3 *The* World *in Torbay, UK (courtesy of Bob Harrison)*

The itinerary in a typical year includes 140 ports in 40 countries. The ship targets prestigious events, including sporting occasions such as the British Open, the Grand Prix in Monaco and the Cannes Film Festival. The staff onboard is international. The cost of purchasing an apartment begins at USD $2,255,000. Vacations can be booked for as long as an individual wants (minimum of three days).

The *World of ResidenSea*, as the first mixed-use resort ship continuously navigating the globe, set a new industry standard when it scored a perfect 100 points on its very first United States Public Health (USPH) inspection, and received an excellent rating on its Certificate of Compliance from the United States Coast Guard. These reports echo international acclaim from Bahamian authorities and *Det Norske Veritas* for the ship's health, safety, operational and construction standards, as well as the opinion that it is both well-maintained and operated in a very professional manner.

Contributing to the success of the *World*'s recent ratings is its unique Scandinavian wastewater cleaning system, whereby waste is filtered by a flotation system. Solid waste is dried and incinerated, and the ash is properly disposed of on land. The remaining liquid waste goes through an ultraviolet filtration process, and the resulting water is as pure as technical water. The *World* also burns marine diesel, a more environmentally acceptable alternative to the heavy fuels traditionally used in ships of its size, which enables this ship to enter more of the world's most fascinating ports [38].

GRAND PRINCESS

The *Grand Princess* is part of a modern fleet of ships operated by Princess Cruises. Princess Cruises entered the market in 1965 with a single ship cruising to Mexico. Today, its fleet carries more than 800,000 customers each year. Ships include *Ruby Princess* (2008), *Emerald Princess* (2007), *Crown Princess* (2006), *Caribbean Princess* (2004), *Grand Princess* (1998) *and Star Princess* (2002). Two additional new ships will join the Princess fleet by 2013 [39].

In 1977, the *Pacific Princess* was cast in a starring role on a new television show called *The Love Boat*. According to Princess Cruises, the weekly series, which introduced millions of viewers to the still-new concept of a seagoing vacation, was an instant hit and both the company name and its 'sea witch' logo (Figure 1.4) have remained synonymous with cruising ever since.

The *Grand Princess* was regarded in 2003 by Princess Cruises as the 'flagship of Personal Choice Cruising'. This concept seeks to empower

Figure 1.4 *Grand Princess*

customers to create their own selection of activities from a broad choice of facilities, amenities and services. In this way the vacation is then perceived as being potentially personally customized. The unique selling proposition centres on multiple dining options, flexible and varied entertainment selections, and a full complement of onboard activities ranging from shuffleboard to scuba certification. Furthermore, the experience is presented using marketing strap-lines such as 'affordable luxury' and 'big ship choice with small ship feel', to focus on the unique orientation of the vessel within the marketplace.

The ship is one of the largest in the world (although certainly not the largest). This enables the operator to include diversity and provide choice. There are 710 cabins (80% are outside staterooms) and have a balcony. Butler service is provided in suites and mini-suites. The ship's facilities include a chapel, a virtual reality centre, a casino, three dining rooms and three show lounges, five swimming pools (one is a swim-against-the-current lap pool), a children's centre and a teenager centre, 28 wheelchair-accessible cabins, a sports bar, an art gallery, a 9-

hole putting course and golf simulator, a sports court and jogging track, a wide variety of bars and lounges, including a wine and caviar bar, and the 'Skywalker's nightclub' and observation lounge, suspended 45 metres (150 ft) above the water (this design feature was changed in a refit in 2011). As Showker and Sehlinger [40] comment, size does matter for this type of ship, with its 2,600 customers and 1,100 crew.

The *Grand Princess* offers voyages on a range of cruises including circular routes around the Caribbean. Smaller resorts are accessed by ship's tenders (the small launches that are carried by cruise vessels for both practical and safety reasons). Princess Cruises has ownership of a Caribbean island 'Princess Cays', also accessed by tender. Princess Cruises is part of Carnival Corporation, one of the largest vacation companies in the world.

OASIS OF THE SEAS

The *Oasis of the Seas* captured the world media's attention when she was introduced late in 2009.

> *Oasis* is so huge it doesn't feel like a cruise ship, it barely seemed to move and it's possible with all that's going on onboard to rarely acknowledge the ocean. It's almost the anti-cruise. [41]

and

> Five times the tonnage of the *Titanic*, the *Oasis* is longer than any aircraft carrier in the US fleet. It is half as big again as the O2 centre. Stand it on its end and it would look down on Canary Wharf's towers. [42]

The above are typical reports focusing on the uniqueness and choice provided when a cruise ship is upscaled. The vessel is designed to meet the needs of international passengers and comes with a variety of amenities and options spread out over the 16 decks. It has four swimming pools (including a sloping deck beach pool), 10 whirlpools, miniature golf, zip line and a pair of 'Flow Rider' surfing simulators. There are RCCL 'signature' climbing walls, an ice-skating rink, a tree planted 'Central Park' area, 24 restaurants – including one that seats

2,000 people – and 2,706 staterooms of varying specifications, from the most basic though to duplex loft style suites. Most cabins have a balcony either facing out to sea or inwards towards the arcades.

The ship's social areas are subdivided into seven 'neighbourhoods': Central Park, Boardwalk, the Royal Promenade, the Pool and Sports Zone, Vitality at Sea Spa and Fitness Centre, Entertainment Place, and Youth Zone. In Central Park there is an original handcrafted carousel; the outside amphitheatre serves as a pool by day and a ocean-front theatre in the evenings.

The ship is 360 metres (1,187 ft) long, 64 metres (208 ft) wide, 65 metres (213 ft) high from the waterline, 9.1 metres (30 ft) draft and has a cruising speed of 22.6 knots powered by 4 bow thrusters with 7,500 horse power each. While official capacity is shown as being 5,400, the ship could conceivably carry 6,296 guests total if all upper berths were sold. In addition, the company predicts that as many as 2,394 crew (from over 71 countries) are likely to be employed onboard the ship at any one time.

Figure 1.5 Oasis of the Seas

QUEEN MARY 2

The *QM2* entered service as a Cunard liner in January 2003. She represented the epitome of scale and grandeur at sea, being the world's largest, longest, tallest, grandest ocean liner. The ship's voluminous public areas, grand ballroom, staircases and foyer areas and 360-degree promenade deck asdd credence to the claims for quality, luxury, image and space. In terms of accommodation, three-quarters of the ship's staterooms have balconies. There are several accommodation options – staterooms, suites, junior suites, royal suites, penthouses and duplexes. The two-storey duplexes even have their own private exercise equipment. Accommodation on the *QM2* is also linked to the type of dining experience offered. Guests who book a duplex, suite or similarly graded accommodation have permission to dine in the exclusive Queens or Princess Grills, while guests who reserve staterooms may dine in the Britannia restaurant. All the *QM2* restaurants reflect the Cunard attention to excellence and were rated five-star by the 2010 *Berlitz Complete Guide to Cruising & Cruise Ships*. [43]

Figure 1.6 *QM2*

The ship has 14 decks, containing sports facilities, shops, bars, lounges, 5 pools and 10 restaurants. There is a unique spa club, a casino, a planetarium, a bookstore and a college-at-sea. As befits a ship of this scale, the leisure options are numerous, with cultural and artistic diversions during the day and theatre productions, dancing, entertainment, a nightclub, casino and even karaoke by night. The ship was designed to take over from the *Queen Elizabeth 2* (*QE2*) to provide a luxury line voyage between New York and Southampton and to act as flagship for Cunard's fleet. Scale may well play a significant part for the *QM2* in terms of the grandeur and opulence inferred by the ship's size and awe-inspiring statistics but the other part of this equation concerns the ship's ability to access ports. According to Cruise Mates [44], around 50% of ports are likely to be 'boat ports', where the ship will operate tenders to transport passengers from ship to shore.

THE CRUISE MARKET

According to MSC Cruises Chief Executive Officer, Pierfrancesco Vago, the cruise industry in the twenty-first century is characterized by 'remarkable resilience and double-digit growth'.[45] Vago attributes this outcome to the way the industry has created a value-for-money yet consistently high-quality product with a very broad range of choice in relation to activities onboard. Moreover, the industry has developed markets by focusing on 'de-seasonalisation' and linking in to people's behaviours and vacation traits internationally so as to generate business all year round. The modern mega cruise ship continues to demonstrate innovation and mass-market appeal, but at a scale that would have been considered impossible only a decade ago. In many ways, the innovation has emerged not only to meet the ever-evolving needs of customers but also to differentiate cruise ships and cruise brands [12].

The implications of this analysis of the cruise market can appear contradictory. On one hand the numbers of traditional cruise customers appears to be both stable and increasing, yet there is clear evidence to suggest that real growth is likely to occur in emerging markets. In reality, cruise companies are continuing the trend that is presented in Table 1.5 – that is, companies adapt to emerging situations and seek new opportunities to take advantage of trading conditions.

Acquisitions and mergers

The last 25 years have been punctuated by a series of acquisitions and mergers [46] that appear to indicate a market subject to constant upheaval and change. This wave of activity slowed down in the period up to 2010 and has resulted in a picture

Table 1.6 *Segmentation in the Cruise Industry [46]*

Segment	Budget	Contemporary	Premium	Niche	Luxury
Share	5%	59%	30%	4%	2%
Cruise duration	Varies	3–7 days	7–14 days	7 days and upwards	7 days and upwards
Ships	Older, smaller	New, large and mega	New, medium and large	Small	Small and medium
Cruise lines	Thomson, Louis, Carnival, Royal Caribbean, NCL	Carnival, Royal Caribbean, NCL, Princess, Costa, Aida, Island Cruise, Star	Celebrity, Holland America, Cunard, Oceania, Regent	Swan Hellenic, Hurtigruten	Crystal, Silversea, Seabourn, Cunard, Windstar, Hapag Lloyd, Oceania, Regent
Itinerary	Caribbean, Mediterranean, Baltic	Caribbean, Mediterranean	Caribbean, Mediterranean, Alaska	Worldwide, Antartica, Greenland, Asia	Worldwide
Average cost per day (USD) per pax	80–125	100–200	150–500	400–1,200	600–3,000

Less Expensive ← ───────────────────────────── → More Expensive//

where three cruise companies dominate. Table 1.7 demonstrates some of the most significant examples.

In the aftermath of this volatile trading environment it would have been tempting to predict more of the same for the medium-term future but that would be to ignore salient nascent issues. Firstly, the largest companies – the Carnival Corporation, Royal Caribbean Cruise Ltd and Star Cruises/NCL – possess between them considerable purchasing power. Secondly, new ships create a wave effect, releasing older vessels into the market, which can then be utilized by emerging or newly formed cruise companies. Thirdly, cruise companies have learnt to be wary of market conditions and unforeseen events. Public opinion of globalization, the

Table 1.7 Examples of mergers and acquisitions adapted and developed from Bjornsen [46]

Consolidation by merger, acquisition or joint venture

Year	1996	1997	1998	1999	2000	2002	2006	2007	2008	2009
Carnival		Buys Costa (in part)	Buys Cunard	Buys Seabourne	Buys Costa (100%)	Merger P&O Princess		Sells Windstar Sells Swan Hellenic		
RCCL		Merger Celebrity					Buys Pullmantur			Joint venture with TUI
Apollo Management (Prestige Holdings)								Buys Oceania Cruises	Takes 50% control of NCL Buys Regent Cruises	
P&O Princess					Buys Aida	Merger with Carnival				
Kloster NCL/Star	Renamed NCL			Buys Orient line	Bought by Star Cruises				Sells 50% NCL to Apollo	

Cunard		Bought by Carnival
Chandris/Celebrity	Merger RCCI	
Costa	Bought by Carnival	
Epirotiki	Forms Royal Olympic with Sun cruises	Majority bought by Louis Cruises

incidence of terrorism and worldwide threats caused by health problems such as Severe Acute Respiratory Syndrome (SARS), which emerged in China in 2002, and swine flu, which was a key concern in 2009 and 2010, can influence customers' decision making. Recent industry commentaries demonstrate the resilience of the cruise industry in the face of the plethora of world events that have occurred.

The market in 2010 and 2011 shows Carnival dominating in the US and the UK (Table 1.8 below) but with an interestingly contrasting pattern in the rest of the world (see Table 1.9 below).

Cruise brands

Cruise brands, such as P&O Cruises, Royal Caribbean International, Costa Cruises, Celebrity Cruises, Princess Cruises, Saga Cruises and Norwegian Cruise Lines, guard their reputations with great care. As Moutinho [48] states, branding for tourism organizations is perceived to present significant strategic advantages.

Table 1.8 North American cruise market share [47]

North American cruise market share (predicted for 2011)	
Cruise line	% of market
Carnival Corporation	52.9
Royal Caribbean	27.6
Norwegian Cruise Line	9.8
Disney	3.3
MSC	1.6
Other	4.8

Table 1.9 The rest of world (other than North America) cruise market share [47]

Rest of world cruise market share (predicted for 2011)	
Cruise Line	% of market
Carnival Corporation	51.6
Royal Caribbean	25.6
Norwegian Cruise Line	7.7
Disney	1.9
MSC	5.1
Louis Cruises	1.7
Other	6.4

Thus, a brand name can hold connotations about a corporation or a company or a cruise ship. The brand may be more than a name in that a design or symbol can also be selected to represent the brand values: P&O Cruises formerly used a familiar nautical flag as their brand image, although that was replaced in 2006 with a rising sun motif. In addition, historical events add a recognition factor to some 'famous' names. Examples include the 'White Star' brand utilized by Cunard to identify their training provision onboard the 'White Star Academy' (see Chapter 11 for more information).

Cruise ships lend themselves very well to the process of branding. Passengers engage with the 'product' or the cruise in a series of complex ways that enhance the opportunity to develop brand loyalty. This is exemplified when reflecting on passenger routines from the point of booking and considering the glossy images in a cruise brochure, to the point of embarkation when faced with the scale and impressiveness of the ship in port, through to consideration of life onboard and then to the departure and disembarkation. This form of vacation creates a unique relationship between passenger and ship, passenger and cruise, and passenger and brand.

Branding is important in order to target new markets, engender repeat business, highlight brand recognition, define a firm's strategic approach to marketing and operations and, critically, to establish loyalty [48]. Laws [49] identifies the advantages that are accrued by the major corporations, in terms of resources and marketing strength, which mean they can afford to underpin brand development with impactful brand awareness campaigns, focusing in turn on the specific market segment that is deemed to be the target market for specific brand identities.

THE ECONOMICS OF CRUISING

The cruise business is represented by Chin [50] as being engaged in the 'production of pleasure for profits'. While the phrase is arguably an over-distillation of the machinations and drivers that explain the diverse corporate goals as held by business leaders in the cruise industry, it is a neat and somewhat elegant description. Of course many business types share this goal – to derive profits from people as they enjoy their leisure time – but it is a very modern affair that reflects on a world where increasing numbers of people are sharing in the wealth that is generated as a result of multinational or global free trade and enterprise.

In relation to Carnival Corporation and Royal Caribbean Cruise Ltd's contemporary mass-market brands, Vogel [51] describes a business model that has, over the years, become more dependent on revenue generated onboard, or more accurately, sales other than the cruise ticket itself. Typically, additional sales include: cancellation and travel insurance; shore excursions; bar and beverage sales; casino spend; shops onboard; hairdressing, spa and treatments; foreign exchange;

supplementary charges on dining; special services; and entertainment or leisure activity surcharges. Not all business models work this way – for example, Silversea Cruises [52] levy an all-inclusive charge that covers items such as alcoholic and non-alcoholic beverages, services of a butler, some shore excursions and all meals. Silversea vessels are much smaller than the industry giants, carrying between 132 and 540 guests with a customer-to-staff ratio that is almost 1:1. To achieve profitability Silversea position their business at the ultra-luxury end of the scale and charge accordingly. A seven-day voyage in the Mediterranean in 2011 is available at approximately £500 per night. In contrast, a similar seven-day voyage with Thompson Cruises is available at £100 per night.

The costs associated with cruising are: the vessel itself (requiring considerable capital investment); the crew (labour); fuel and consumables (mostly predictable); and administration (again mainly predictable) and, while these will each be examined further in subsequent chapters, it is worth noting that for a typical vessel most costs are known [51] and can be identified as fixed costs (those costs that, despite the number of people travelling on the ship, generally remain the same). Variable costs relate mainly to onboard revenues, which are entirely a matter for personal deliberation and individual choice. Ultimately, the lower the costs and the greater the revenue, the more profitable the company will be.

The cruise business is highly reliant on low customer-to-crew ratios – generally averaging around 2 or 3:1. Therefore, the costs of crewing a vessel are significant. If there are 1,000 crew onboard, each ship will also need an additional 500 crew to operate in a 12-month period to cover periods of leave and contracts. This additional crewing figure is referred to as the 'establishment' cost and, for most cruise operators, the figure is generally understood to be 1.5. The larger the ship, the more complex the task of securing sufficient skilled and semi-skilled workers at the right price to ensure the business remains profitable. This task is assisted by the ability of the cruise companies to operate internationally and to reduce operating costs accordingly. This will be further examined later in this book.

SUMMARY AND CONCLUSIONS

The cruise industry is both potent and portentous. In many ways the industry reflects strengths that have emerged as a result of the relentless growth connected with globalization. Powerful corporations exist and they have the resources to keep pace with the constant demands that are required when investing in new ships. Countries that benefit from globalization become wealthier and, as a result, large swathes of their populations have increased ability to purchase cruise vacations. Increasingly, sustained growth means greater levels of confidence and, in turn, increased innovation when developing cruise products. Demand coupled with positive publicity appears to create greater demand as the potential cruising population develops an increasing taste for this type of vacation. The industry also benefits from repeat customers, together with a high degree of loyalty.

This chapter has offered an introduction to the elements of cruising to highlight critical factors connected to its current status as a significant and growing part of the tourism and leisure field. The historical nature of developments has been reflected upon in order to examine how and why these changes have occurred over time. A number of cruise brands have been considered so as to outline the different types of cruises available and to contrast their services and styles. This will allow further discussion about the cruise brands themselves, which should encourage an understanding of the nature of this complex market.

REFERENCES

1. Mancini, M., *Cruising: A guide to the cruise line industry.* 2nd ed. 2003, Albany NY: Delmar.
2. Lück, M., P. Maher and E. Steward, *Cruise Tourism in Polar Regions: Promoting environmental and social sustainability?* 2010, London: Earthscan/James & James.
3. Gibson, P., 'Cruising in the 21st Century: Who works while others play?', *International Journal of Hospitality Management*, 2008. 27(1): p. 42–52.
4. Gibson, P., 'Credible Careers: Tomorrow's cruise hotel managers', *World Journal of Tourism, Leisure and Sport*, 2009. 3(1): p. 11–19.
5. CLIA. *Cruise Update*. 2010 [accessed October 2011]; Available from: http://www.cruising.org/pressroom-rescarch/2011-cruise-industry-mcdia-update
6. Wichakil, B., 'Thailand Sees Higher Foreign Tourists Despite Unrest'. 2010 [accessed January 2011]; Available from: http://in.reuters.com/article/idININdia-51329020100907
7. Squires, N., 'Venice Planning Entry Tax for Tourists'. 2010 [accessed January 2011]; Available from: http://www.telegraph.co.uk/travel/travelnews/8069480/Venice-planning-entry-tax-for-tourists.html.
8. Ward, D., 'Forty Years of Cruising: Key note presentation', *2nd International Cruise Conference*, Plymouth, UK. 2010: University of Plymouth, Devon, UK.
9. Bayley, M., 'Cruise Industry Futures', *Marine Hotel Association*. 2010: Barcelona.
10. Charlier, J.J. and R.J. McCalla, 'A Geographical Overview of the World Cruise Market and its Seasonal Complimentarities', *Cruise Ship Tourism*, R.K. Dowling, ed. 2006, CABI Publishing: Wallingford. p. 18–30.
11. United Nations World Tourist Organization. *International Tourism 2010* [accessed February 2011]; Available from: http://unwto.org.
12. Cruise Industry News, 'The Cruise Industry in 2010', *Cruise Industry News Quarterly Magazine*, 2010.
13. Ebersold, W.B., *Cruise Industry in Figures*. 2004, US Department of Transport: Washington. p. 1–5.
14. European Cruise Council, *Cruise Industry Report 2010/11*. 2010, ECC: London.
15. Weaver, A., A.G. Woodside and D. Martin, 'Complexity at Sea: Managing brands within the cruise industry', *Tourism Management: Analysis, behaviour and strategy*, 2008: p. 269–284.
16. Douglas, N. and N. Douglas, *The Cruise Experience: Global and regional issues in cruising*. 2004, Frenchs Forest, Australia: Pearson Education.

17. Lutgens, F., *Essentials of Geology*. 1992, New York: Macmillan. p. 269.
18. Day, C. and K. McRae, eds., *Cruise Guide to Europe and the Mediterranean*. Eyewitness Travel Guides. 2001, London: Dorling Kindersley.
19. Viator, 'World's Favourite Tourist Destinations'. 2010 [accessed February 2011]; Available from: http://travelblog.viator.com/top-50-travel-destinations/.
20. Cartwright, R. and C. Baird, *The Development and Growth of the Cruise Industry*. 1999, Oxford: Butterworth-Heinemann.
21. Gibson, P., 'Learning, Culture, Curriculum and College: A social anthropology', *Education*, 2003, Exeter: University of Exeter.
22. Ward, D., *Complete Guide to Cruising & Cruise Ships 2002*. 2001, London: Berlitz Publishing. p. 1.
23. Dickinson, R. and A. Vladimir, *Selling the Sea*. 1997, New York: Wiley.
24. Branch, A.E., *Elements of Shipping*. 7th ed. 1996, Cheltenham: Nelson Thornes.
25. Cruise Industry News, 'Hotel Operations: Staying ahead', *Cruise Industry News Quarterly Magazine*, 2010.
26. Dawson, P., *Cruise Ships: An evolution in design*. 2000, London: Conway Maritime Press.
27. Dingle, D. 'Cruising in the 21st Century – New developments', *Cruise and Ferry Conference 2003*. Earls Court, London: Informa Group.
28. Kontes, T.C., 'The Cruise Industry Revolution', *Cruise and Ferry Conference 2003*. Earls Court, London: Informa Group.
29. Michaelides, M. 'The Latest Developments in the Mediterranean Cruise Market: Challenges for the future', *Cruise and Ferry Conference 2003*. Earls Court, London: Informa Group.
30. Simpson, H., 'Abundance of Berths on Cruise Ships is Good News for Bargain Hunters'. 2011 [accessed October 2011]; Available from: http://www.miamiherald.com/2010/11/12/1921782/abundance-of-berths-on-cruise.html.
31. Palmer, J., 'On Celebrity Eclipse Cruise Ship for Bilbao Rescue'. 2010 [accessed October 2011]; Available from: http://news.bbc.co.uk/local/hampshire/hi/people_and_places/newsid_8632000/8632850.stm.
32. CelebrityCruises, 'CompanyProfile'. 2011 [accessed October 2011]; Available from: http://www.celebritycruises.com/aboutceleb/heroSingleTxt.do?pagename=company_profile.
33. Celebrity Cruises, 'Brand Guidelines'. 2011 [accessed October 2011]; Available from: http://media.celebritycruises.com/celebrity/content/celebrity_brand_guidelines/download-assets/CelebrityCruises_BrandInteractiveGuidelines_BrandOverview.pdf.
34. Gibson, P. and D.M. Turner, 'Catering on Cruise Ships', *Essential FM Reports*. 2009. p. 4–7.
35. Veness, S., 'Cruise Holidays: Celebrity lines up sophistication for British cruisers', *Travel Mail*, 2011.
36. Celebrity Cruises, 'Celebrity Eclipse'. 2010 [accessed October 2011]; Available from: http://www.celebritycruises.com/plancruise/ships/ship.do?shipCode=EC&cS=SIDENAV.
37. Synnove Bye, A., 'The Future of Cruise Ships: The experience from the World of ResidenSea', *Cruise and Ferry Conference 2003*. Earls Court, London: Informa Group. p. 3–5.
38. ResidenSea webpage. 2003 [accessed 2003]; Available from: http://aboardtheworld.com/
39. Princess Cruises webpage. 2010 [accessed October 2010]; Available from: http://www.princess.com/ships/ap/.

40. Showker, K. and R. Sehlinger, *The Unofficial Guide to Cruises 2003*. 2002, New York: Wiley.
41. Dunham Potter, A., 'Is Oasis of the Seas Worth the Price'. 2009 [accessed February 2010]; Available from: http://www.msnbc.msn.com/id/34276610/ns/travel-cruise_travel/t/oasis-seas-worth-price/
42. Adams, T., 'Oasis of the Seas'. 2009 [accessed 2009]; Available from: http://www.guardian.co.uk/travel/2009/nov/25/oasis-seas-biggest-cruise-liner.
43. Ward, D., *Complete Guide to Cruising & Cruise Ships 2009*. 2009, London: Berlitz.
44. Cruisemates, 'Queen Mary 2'. 2005 [accessed March 2005]; Available from: http://www.cruisemates.com/articles/reviews/cunard/qm2.cfm.
45. Vago, P., 'Reasons to be Cheerful'. 2010 [accessed 2010]; Available from: http://www.worldcruiseindustryreview.com/2010-2.html.
46. Bjornsen, P., 'The Growth of the Market and Global Competition in the Cruise Industry', *Cruise and Ferry Conference 2003*. Earls Court, London: Informa Group.
47. Cruise Market Watch, 'Market Share'. 2011 [accessed February 2011]; Available from: http://www.cruisemarketwatch.com/blog1/market-share-2/.
48. Moutinho, L., ed. *Strategic Management in Tourism*. 2000, Wallingford: CABI Publishing.
49. Laws, E., *Managing Packaged Tourism*. 1997, London: International Thomson Business Press.
50. Chin, C., *Cruising in the Global Economy: Profits, pleasure and work at sea*. 2008, Aldershot: Ashgate. p. 13.
51. Vogel, M., 'The Economics of US Cruise Companies' European Brand Strategies', *Tourism Economics*, 2009. 15(4): p. 735–751.
52. Silversea Cruises, corporate website. 2011 [accessed October 2011]; Available from: http://www.silversea.com/.

Selling cruises and cruise products

2

INTRODUCTION

Having considered issues relating to the way the industry has developed and the current make-up of cruise businesses, this chapter aims to investigate how the cruise companies take their product to the marketplace. This will be done by reflecting on marketing for the cruise industry, considering the formulation of a range of products and services, and analysing how cruise brands differentiate their products, develop service standards and create brand values.

THE MARKET

A market can be described as a 'system comprising two sides' ([1] p. 120), the 'sides' inferring demand and supply. The cruise market can be further defined, according to common interpretations, in three ways: product focused; need satisfaction; or relating to passenger identity [1]. 'Product focused' companies have advantages in terms of developing economies of scale although they may fail to take account of changes that occur within their target market incrementally over time. 'Need satisfaction' companies are good at understanding their customers but can have problems in making a strategic decision to identify specific focus. 'Passenger identity' companies can target specific groups of passengers. Evans *et al.* [1] note that most companies combine definitions in order to derive strengths from each of the three approaches.

Knowles, Diamantis and Bey El-Mourhabi [2] describe world events such as the terrorist attack on New York in 2001, the Gulf War and the prevailing economic conditions in the US and other major countries at that time, as vital in shaping the fortunes of tourism and leisure providers. Add to that the continuation of international unease in the face of potential acts of terrorism, the apparent switch to cruising undertaken by customers as a reaction to risk assessment and in line with cruise companies' strategic decisions to facilitate easy travel to port and the construction of safe itineraries [3] and a picture emerges of an industry acting to take advantage of market opportunities.

Cruise companies target specific markets and as a result they tailor their products and services to meet passenger needs [2]. Getting the marketing mix right is, for marketers in the cruise business, a case of building on the traditional four Ps: Price, Product, Place and Promotion, and including the three additional service-oriented components of People, Physical evidence and Process [4]. Throughout this book, evidence is provided to enable the reader to deconstruct the four Ps or the seven Ps so the traditional or extended marketing mix can be thoroughly examined. This chapter describes the type of input that is undertaken by the stakeholders in the selling of cruises and then considers the products of cruising when reflecting on the cruise market. The stakeholders that are examined are the cruise operators and travel agents.

CRUISE OPERATORS

As previously discussed, cruise operators or brands dominate the cruise market [5]. They either own or lease cruise ships and produce the planned itinerary and cruise product so as to target specific market segments. Cruise operators can be seen as wholesalers, while travel agents are retailers or brokers [6]. However, in common with many wholesale operations, better profit margins or more attractive, lower selling prices may be achieved if the product can be sold directly to the consumer. Therefore the majority of cruise operators also sell their products directly to the public, thus acting as both cruise wholesalers and retailers. While it is difficult to identify the percentage of direct sales, *Travel Weekly* [7] state that RCCL achieve approximately 10% and that other brands achieve between 6 and 20% of sales depending on the variables of types of customers, nationality, the cruise line and the cruise itself. Products are developed and packaged using market research, negotiation and sales and marketing.

All cruise companies exert considerable effort in establishing brand values and in constructing cruise products that are designed to meet and, ideally, to exceed passenger expectations. Market research collects data from existing and potential passengers using a variety of research techniques. This data can be used to interpret customer behaviour and predict buyer responses to new products. Increasingly, anthropologists are used to study target groups or individuals so as to better understand why people act as they do.

The products developed are an amalgam of services and facilities, some of which generate revenue while others are inclusive. This means that most cruises have fixed costs relating to such elements as transportation (fuel), food, labour, port administration and customs and variable costs relating to other elements, such as beverages or shore excursions. The cruise operator aims to reduce costs as much as possible without impacting negatively on quality. Negotiation is done to ensure the best price–quality ratio is achieved to take advantage of economies of scale and negotiating power. Negotiation is therefore undertaken for a diversity of consumables from engine or deck department stores through to hotel department stores and, in terms of buying power, considerable advantage is accrued by the largest corporations.

Traditionally, cruise companies have used travel agents as a primary distribution channel while concomitantly selling directly. Irrespective of the mode of distribution, and despite the growing importance of the Internet as both a distribution and marketing tool, cruise companies rely on the cruise brochure to sell cruises. Vellas and Becherel [8] describe how tourism operators design brochures with colour images, a carefully planned layout and promotions designed to attract early bookings. They note that the ratio of brochures to sales can be between 10–30 brochures for one sale. Pricing strategies are carefully considered to encourage early action by promising discounts for early bookings. Low-season pricing is adjusted to appear less costly than high-season pricing. Lead-in prices relate to basic cabin accommodation and supplements are payable for attractive alternatives such as outside cabins or sea-view cabins with balconies. Premium products such as suites with butler service come with premium pricing.

Brochures are produced well in advance of the cruise date and planning has to take into account fluctuating prices, rates of exchange for items purchased outside the country of the operator and changing market conditions [6]. It is reasonably common for cruise operators to update brochures so as to react to changing conditions. This can mean offering different prices in later editions and in some cases making amendments to the product if the change has come about for reasons outside the cruise operator's control.

The Internet is used predominantly as a complementary marketing tool. In this capacity it can be a point where information is presented to potential and actual customers to help them find out more about the cruise package in a way that brochures can never achieve [5]. For example, customers can visit the passenger feedback pages to see what passengers are saying about their vacations, or follow links to other important information, such as immigration or health matters overseas. The Internet can also be used to enable clients to book online and in this mode the customer assists the cruise operator in providing data in a format that it can be easily manipulated, thereby cutting out the costs associated with booking through a travel agent or sales assistant. The Internet can also be used to capture data for immigration purposes and for financial control, thus saving on potential administration costs.

Mancini notes the importance to the cruise industry of what is known as the wave season [9]. This period of time – normally between January and March – is when the market is more likely to book a vacation because the temperature is colder in

North America, the UK and Europe, and the potential of visiting warmer climates gains traction.

THE TRAVEL AGENT

Travel agents' core purpose is selling tourism products for commission. Most travel agents belong to professional associations that guarantee clients protection if the travel agent has serious financial problems. In the United States the American Society of Travel Agents (ASTA) and, in the United Kingdom, the Association of British Travel Agents (ABTA) are typical of such associations. Travel agents sell travel products such as airline tickets and tourist packages. They can also arrange insurance, car hire and hotel accommodation.

However, the high street travel agent is changing [10]. Faced with ever increasing competition from Internet intermediaries or online agencies, travel agents are finding themselves operating in a volatile market place. Airlines have cut commission rates. Travel firms have aggressively targeted their clients to sell directly and cut the travel agent out of the distribution system. Hatton notes that the travel agent's strength, in providing a highly personal and personalized service, also undermined their status and led to the travel companies' action in aiming to nurture brand loyalty by developing relationships with the client directly. In response, Hatton highlights the need for agents to accept the changing realities and to work closely with travel companies, to develop in-depth product knowledge and to retain customer loyalty by being efficient at what they do.

Examples can be seen in the context of cruise vacations. Some travel agents specialize in the cruise industry, forming alliances with cruise brands so as to focus on selling their product. In these circumstances, travel agents receive high levels of support from the cruise operators, who provide specialist sales events, training for the sales agents (including orientation cruises) and customized marketing materials. The Passenger Shipping Association (PSA) has established the PSA Retail Agents (PSARA) scheme in the UK, with the primary objective of increasing sales via accredited retail travel agents through customized product training and dissemination of information [11]. This, in turn, has led to the formulation of the Association of Cruise Experts (ACE) [12], an organization that supports training and development for those involved in cruise business.

MARKETING ACTIONS AND ALLIANCES

A market is the place where sellers and buyers meet to do business [1]. Marketing as a sophisticated process and discipline has emerged from this basic premise in order that cruise operators develop their product to meet customer expectations and then design a plan for marketing the product. The plan can include advertising, promotion, merchandising and public relations (PR). Advertising uses a number of communications media including: commercials on radio, television and the cinema; the Internet, newspaper and magazines; posters and billboards. PR can be gained from editorial or features in travel publications, newspapers and magazines. Merchandising reinforces the brand by using items such as pens, desk pads or mementos to remind the user about their vacation. Promotion can be associated with advertising or it can be incorporated in events such as sales promotions to visiting groups onboard cruise ships.

Cruise operators may form strategic marketing alliances with other service providers so as to create synergies and/or provide customers with incentives for remaining loyal. Crystal Cruises is a member of the Luxury Alliance, which includes Silversea Cruises, Orient-Express Trains and Cruises, Leading Hotels of the World, and Relais and Châteaux [13]. The 'World's Leading Cruise Lines' alliance includes Carnival Cruises, Holland America, Cunard Line, Seabourn, Costa Cruises, Princess Cruises and Windstar and provides incentives for loyalty within these brands [14].

LOYALTY

Loyalty is perceived as being important both in terms of the value of having a client who has a preferred predilection to act as an ambassador for the brand but also in terms of the value in retaining a customer. In effect this type of client works for the brand by spreading positive comments about the cruise to friends and acquaintances and, as a result, is an important part of the marketing equation. Companies such as Princess Cruises operate an incentive group called the 'Captain's Circle'. This club has three levels: Gold (2–5 cruises), Platinum (6–15 cruises) and Elite (16 cruises and more). The benefits include priority discounts, special events onboard, preferential services and benefits depending on the level of membership [15].

THE CRUISE PRODUCT

In common with other tourism products [8], the cruise has three economic features: heterogeneity (subject to a broad mix of variable components which render the experience uniquely individual for the tourist), inelasticity (products can't be stored; if they are not sold the sale is lost and therefore the cruise product is perishable) and complementarity (the cruise product is not one single service but a series of complementary services that when taken together form the cruise experience). Figure 2.1 (below) presents a typical pattern, showing how a cruise company interacts with the prospective customer in respect of the cruise experience.

The cruise is a defined package that may include travel to the port of embarkation, an itinerary spanning a defined period of time, an element of inclusive services and

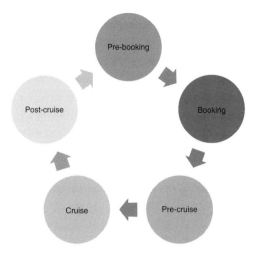

Figure 2.1 *The customer's interface with the cruise company*

facilities (such as meals, entertainment and leisure areas), accommodation to a specified standard, and various other services that are available at an extra charge. The
inclusive nature of the package will depend on the pricing strategy of the cruise operator. Some operators offer cruise-and-stay or cruise-and-tour packages that include
an additional element at the beginning or end of the cruise in the form of a defined
period of nights staying in a hotel in a resort or touring in the area. Ultimately the
complexity of the ever changing passenger experience means that cruise brands have
developed a sophisticated network to support operations (see Table 2.1 below).

The following elements that are described portray the products of cruising. Destinations and itinerary planning are commented on in a later chapter.

Table 2.1 *Meeting cruise passengers' needs – the cruise cycle*

Interface point	Departmental responsibility	Involving
Pre-booking	Reservations	Itineraries
		Marketing
		Commercial planning
		Cruise operations and planning
		Port logistics
Booking		Selling agents
		Direct sales
		Online sales
	Customer assistance	Loyalty club
		Passports and visas

Table 2.1 *Continued*

		Cancellations
		Dietary, mobility and medical
		Celebrations and special events
	Flights	Scheduled
		Charter
Pre-cruise		City stopover
	Documentation	Ticketing/labels
	Operations	Shore excursions and tours
		Port logistics
		Transfers
		Check-in
		Security and immigration
Cruise	Passenger services	Administration
		Accommodation
		Printer
		Laundry
		Cabin staff
		Florist
	Food and beverage	Chefs
		Galley
		Stores
		Wine and bars
		Restaurant
	Commercial	Shore excursion
		Shops
		Salon/spa

ACCOMMODATION

For many passengers, the choice of accommodation appears to be simply a matter of identifying the price that is acceptable in relation to the standard of accommodation available. However, a glance at the pricing structures operated by cruise companies quickly reveals that selecting accommodation is more complex than would first appear to be the case. Some cruise companies refer to the accommodation as cabins, but terms such as staterooms, mini-suites and suites are frequently used to replace or complement this nautical term. Some cruise companies sell penthouse suites onboard their vessels and these tend to be the largest, most luxurious and most expensive options [9].

Although cabin sizes can vary from just under 11 square metres (120ft²) to over 85 square metres (900ft²), the norm tends to be approximately 18–23 square metres (200–250ft²). Even a cabin of around 14 square metres (150ft²) is likely to have four beds configured as lower and upper berths. The upper berths can be folded back to create more space or to cater for two passengers rather than the maximum of four. Cabins may also permit the lower berths to be moved together to form a large queen- or king-sized bed. The largest cabins can be configured as suites with a lounge area. All cabins on modern cruise ships tend to be en-suite; that is, they have a shower room and toilet or a bath, shower and toilet [16].

In the main, cabins are compact versions of the equivalent hotel bedroom accommodation. The storage areas are carefully designed to maximize the use of space so as to create an impression of a facility with high specification. This exemplifies a common feature on most cruise ships – space is at a premium, so vessels are constructed to maximize the area that can generate revenue. In designing the passenger accommodation some cabins will inevitably have a good view or a restricted view, a location that is perceived by some passengers to be either more or less appealing because of proximity to certain facilities and, if located close to elevators or other sound-generating elements, some passengers may be unhappy about the resultant background noise. Ships are carefully designed to minimize noise incursion, yet on most vessels (as is the case in hotels ashore) there are some cabins that are recognized as being potentially problematic.

Customers learn how to make decisions from the brochure or cruise brand website. These information sources provide a range of data intended to assist the customer in making a selection. Floor plans provide a miniaturized cutaway view of the cabin (usually produced to reflect three dimensions: see Figure 2.2) that shows the relationship within the cabin of the furnishings, main features, the typical layout and en-suite facilities. Generally, photographs are used in conjunction with

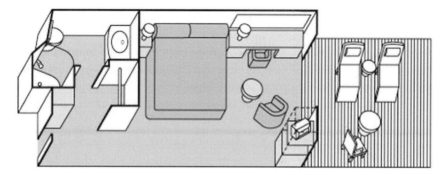

Figure 2.2 *Cutaway diagram of a stateroom*

the floor plans or, in the case of the website, a 360-degree scanning view can be shown. A description of the cabin contents usually accompanies these images.

The most common way of identifying cabin locations is by using deck plans. These are representational ship's plans that, when viewed in conjunction with a cross-section diagram of the ship, help customers to identify the precise location of a cabin or facility onboard. These plans are unique to each vessel, although similar vessels may well have many common features. The deck plans are produced in colour so that a code can be used to identify cabins by type and therefore by cost (see Figure 2.3). On some vessels, cabins that are on a lower deck are the least expensive, and cabins on higher decks are the most expensive. However, this pattern is not reliable for all ships. It is possible on a deck plan to identify the following:

- Inside cabins or staterooms: these cabins lack natural light although the use of ventilation, air conditioning, mirrors and artificial light frequently disguises this fact. Inside cabins tend to be the least expensive accommodation on offer.
- Outside cabins or staterooms: these will have a porthole or a window. Most modern cabins tend to have larger picture windows.
- Outside cabins or staterooms with veranda or balcony: as cruising develops, more accommodation is being produced to include private verandas or balconies with extra private space.
- Penthouse suites or suites: may be with or without a veranda or balcony. These tend to be the most expensive accommodation on offer.
- Cabins or staterooms with additional beds (berths).
- Cabins or staterooms with interconnecting doors.
- Cabins or staterooms or suites with facilities that are appropriate for people with disabilities.
- Cabins or staterooms with either shower or bath.
- The proximity to facilities, lifts and location compared to other decks and cabins.
- The proximity to safety equipment such as lifeboats, which may obscure the view from a picture window.

It is suggested that passengers expect more from cabin accommodation or staterooms than was previously the case. In many respects a cruise brand, carrying thousands of passengers and crew on large ships that offer a broad spectrum of leisure activities, can provide a balance for those seeking enhanced levels of privacy, by offering more spacious cabins that have attractive features such as balconies.

One obvious implication of producing this type of information is that customers can select the accommodation to a precise degree. This can benefit repeat passengers who have distinct preferences or satisfy passengers who have exacting requirements. A problem can occur because of what appears to be a commonly held misconception relating to the options for upgrading. Some travel agents are

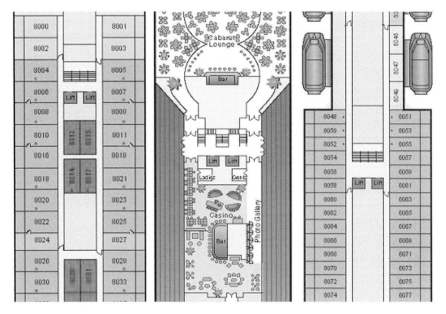

Figure 2.3 Deck plans

reported to advise passengers that when they get onboard that is the expected procedure to complain in order to get a higher category of accommodation without paying more. Sales and reservation teams operate a policy of aiming for 100% capacity and the flexibility onboard is severely constrained by the occupancies achieved. Spare cabins are scarce resources that are regarded as vital in order to deal with problems that may arise, such as plumbing faults or electrical failure, and, as a result, upgrades are in fact virtually impossible.

By producing deck plans, the cruise company can help prospective clients to identify the cabin location of their choice. Also, in a more practical sense, they also assist the passenger when she/he boards the vessel to be oriented or inducted more easily into shipboard life. Deck plans are reproduced in a fold-down version to act as an easy reference map for passengers onboard.

Cabin facilities vary depending on the cruise brand but a basic cabin or stateroom is likely to include:

- Two single beds that can convert to a queen- or king-sized bed
- Optionally an extra two upper berths that can recess into the internal wall and are reached by a store-away ladder
- Bedside tables
- A vanity unit and writing desk with built-in drawers, storage areas, mirrors and chair

- An additional small table and chair
- TV and radio with remote control: with a range of programming and films and onboard TV channel as relevant
- Tea and coffee making facilities
- Safe, hairdryer, refrigerator/minibar
- Direct dial telephone
- Bathroom with shower and WC
- Air conditioning

Some brands may also upgrade the facilities to provide:

- Internet points
- CD/DVD/VCR and/or hi-fi
- Balcony with furniture
- Separate living area or lounge with suitable furnishings
- Separate dressing area
- Jacuzzi
- Separate toilet

The décor in passenger cabins reflects the standards associated with the brand. Soft furnishings will be coordinated with carpeting and artwork so as to create the desired ambiance. Colour schemes are selected to fit the mood and to create an overall harmony in conjunction with décor and furnishing materials. Lighting is strategically located to provide the appropriate level of lighting for the purpose, whether reading, writing or personal care. Mirrors are used strategically to accentuate space and light.

Passenger cabins and staterooms are attended to by cabin stewards, who monitor the general condition of the accommodation and perform routine cleaning and servicing. The steward's daily tasks include making up beds, changing linen and towels as required, cleaning and vacuuming and ensuring that the cabin is prepared to a prescribed specification, e.g., the bathroom is laid out and the complimentary items are displayed. The steward also checks the room mini-bar and liaises with supervisors to deal with technical problems. Housekeeping supervisors and managers inspect cabins to ensure standards are maintained. Room service may be provided either by the room steward or separate personnel. Many large cruise ships have what is called a 'Bell-box', where a small team of chefs and room service stewards produce and serve requests for food and drink to passenger cabins as required. Some suites and penthouse suites are allocated a butler to provide a more personal service. The butler can facilitate the catering and service of parties and can act as facilitator to provide service and products that may be requested by the passenger.

DINING ONBOARD

The archetypal view of a cruise ship being a place to indulge in good food, good wine and good company is as true today as it was in the heyday of the traditional liners. Food is perceived to be a significant element of the cruise product. For most passengers the cost of eating onboard is included in the price of the holiday. There are exceptions, such as the provision of restaurants that carry a supplementary charge, but in the main the inclusive nature, and the high customer expectation, of the dining experience is a fundamental issue. Most cruise brands aim to differentiate what they do through the provision of food and dining options. They can create opportunities to define the product and to differentiate the brand, by constructing menus with a particular focus on style of cuisine and by designing restaurant and dining areas with a particular décor and atmosphere in mind. Therefore, on certain ships, the restaurant may have an Oriental theme with Japanese cuisine, and on others there may be an Italian theme. Cruise dining can be a highly calorific affair, yet corporate chefs take great care to meet specific dietary needs when they design menus.

Some brands have introduced greater options for personal choice in dining. By moving away from traditional dining arrangements that offered two sittings at dinner supplemented by open sitting at breakfast and lunch in large dining rooms, these companies were able to change the formula and attract clients who wanted more flexibility. Most large cruise ships operate at least two large 500-plus seater restaurants that sit to either side of a galley with a double-ended servery or hotplate. This facilitates the service of large numbers of people at dinner without the creation of lines at the door. Linking dinner service sittings with timings for shows and entertainment ensures that passengers are not left feeling disgruntled at having to go to one sitting or another. There is usually less of an issue with coordinating breakfast and lunch because passengers tend to have alternatives such as a buffet or room service breakfast and buffet lunch. Because a ship tends to visit ports during the day that also has a knock-on effect on the production and serving of breakfast and lunch.

The buffet

The buffet servery is a flexible option. It is often located on an upper deck and frequently it is designed to extend from one side of the ship to the other, with each side being a mirror image of the other. This enables large numbers of passengers to be processed without creating bottlenecks. At quiet times and when service changes from breakfast to lunch, lunch to dinner, dinner to supper and supper to breakfast, one side of the operation can be closed for cleaning and changing or replenishing the food items. This in turn creates a 24-hour facility that is both flexible and economical.

A small team of chefs under the supervision of a sous chef services the buffet. The galley team is supported by buffet assistants and supervisors, who help customers, clear tables and serve drinks as required. The buffet utilizes a combination of equipment that is designed to present food items at the correct temperature and in the most attractive way. Main food items such as soups, meat and fish dishes, cold dishes and desserts will be changed daily according to the duration of the cruise itinerary, although some standard items such as breads, salad ingredients, dressings and condiments will be on offer daily. Food items will be designed to complement the total theme on offer, with a culinary nod towards the next port on the itinerary.

The buffet requires fewer staff than the traditional restaurant and, because it can be operated with simple table layouts, standardized areas for beverages, fewer carpeted areas and large picture windows either overlooking the sea or the port, the servicing routines are more easily accomplished. The buffet takes the strain off the restaurant at breakfast and lunch, thus allowing staff to be deployed more effectively and for the galley to plan production more accurately. Very little waste is generated because food can be carefully produced in reaction to prior patterns of demand and prevailing consumption. Buffets are frequently organized with the galley and servery in the middle of the room and tables and chairs around the outside beside the windows.

Figure 2.4 *Buffet servery*

Buffets tend to be designed with a wash-up area beside the galley. Tables are cleared to a collection point (sometimes referred to as a DJ's box). Dirty plates and food residue is then taken by trolley to the wash-up. Food and stores are transported in the specially allocated lifts from the main galley to the buffet galley.

The main restaurant

Passengers can elect to eat as much or as little as they wish and nowhere is that more evident than in the main restaurants. While passengers may stack their plates full in the buffet, in the main restaurant, food is conveyed to the diner as frequently as the diner requests. There appears to be a certain psychology for some diners, who are concerned about what others might think if they are seen carrying a pile of food from the buffet. This concern becomes obscured if quantity is disguised within the routine of ordering courses from a menu. In the main restaurant(s) a menu is produced to reflect and differentiate the brand. The way it is configured might lean, perhaps, towards passengers used to eating out in the US or in Italy or in the UK. This can relate to the provision of distinct courses, the names of these courses, the food items included and the language used to describe them.

The main restaurants tend to reflect a style and standard that is somehow redolent of a more formal dining experience, with the use of uniforms to identify the maître d' (the abbreviated version of *Maître d'Hôtel,* meaning the overall restaurant manager), head waiters, waiters and assistant waiters or commis waiters and the presence of professionals such as sommeliers or wine waiters. The combination of white tablecloths, sparkling cutlery and glassware, careful selection of colours and hues, materials and furniture and subdued lighting add to the effect, as do the provision of music (sometimes live) and the theatricality of the environment. The setting plays an important part in developing interactivity between passengers and between passengers and staff. The food and wine are the reason for being in the restaurant but the experience is enhanced by the social factors.

Service styles vary depending on the brand and passenger expectation. Full silver service may be adopted by the luxury brands, semi silver or plated service by the contemporary and premium brands, while budget brands may have a combination of buffet and plated service. Each style of service is correlated to the skills of the server and the ratio of staff to passengers. Full silver service requires the greatest degree of skill in serving and presenting food and as a result there is a need for a higher ratio of staff to customers. Whichever service style is utilized, the common denominator for service staff is the need to develop the appropriate level of interpersonal skills. Table sizes cater for any number between two and eight people. Larger tables are more common on two sitting dining plans. Many cruise brands are introducing free dining situations where customers can pre-book tables depending on when they wish to eat and request either a private table or to join a group.

The formality of the dining area is not without reason. Formality and dress codes are features on many cruises. While there are new brands appearing that place an emphasis on casual informality, the norm for most cruise brands is still towards creating opportunities for passengers to dress to impress. This is likely to mean that passengers have the opportunity to dress formally once every four or five days.

Other dining options

While most meals tend to be regarded as a composite part of the cruise experience and inclusive with the cost of the vacation, increasingly, cruise brands identify that revenue can be generated by providing additional choice that brings added value to the overall dining experience. For example, on the *Star Princess*, passengers can elect to reserve a table in a variety of alternative restaurants, such as Sabatini's, an upscale Italian restaurant, or the Tex-Mex grill, both of which cost extra. On *Azura*, Sindhu is the name of the Select Dining restaurant from Michelin-starred chef Atul Kochhar and, once again, this attracts a supplement. *Al fresco* dining is on offer by some cruise brands, creating an opportunity for passengers to eat under the stars [15].

Other restaurants, such as pizzerias, burger and hot dog grills, tend to create alternative options that might be seen by groups of passengers, such as children, as

Figure 2.5 *Main restaurant, Queen Mary 2*

more appealing than the formal setting of the restaurants. Ice cream outlets may also be located on decks close to swimming pools and sunbathing or leisure areas. Afternoon tea and, in some cases, high tea (for young families) are served in restaurants and buffets. Finally, passengers tend to be able to make use of room service if the choice of dining options really doesn't meet their needs.

BARS

In the main, most bars begin to get busy after dinner. The routines of sailing are established relatively quickly as passengers find their way around and work out what they want to do and where they want to go. Bars generate revenue so although the busy times are from around 2200 onwards, there are numerous opportunities for passengers to purchase drinks:

Sailing day: drinks available on upper decks as the ship departs from port. Working from bars at key points, bar waiters mingle amongst the passengers selling cocktails and drinks to celebrate the departure. Live music is played to add to the atmosphere.

Dinner: a wine pre-ordering point is usually made available so that customers can ensure they order the wine that they want for dinner. During dinner, wine and beverages are available from a dispense bar, usually located within the galley. Wine lists, liqueur, cognac and fine whiskies lists, liqueur trolleys and merchandising displays all support the sales initiative. Sommeliers and wine waiters are on hand to help passengers.

Theatre: table service is available in all the entertainment venues. Cocktails of the day and special promotions are offered to highlight the range and options that are available.

Bars: various bars are targeted at groups of passengers such as sports bars with recorded or live sports displayed on TVs or screens and surrounded by sporting memorabilia, or traditional lounge bars using dark wood and comfortable settees and chairs to give a 'club' feel.

Champagne and caviar bars appeal to a certain clientele and exude quality and exclusivity. Piano bars combine relaxed intimacy and friendly ambiance.

Nightclub: with table service and a cocktail menu. Depending on the clientele onboard, different products are likely to be available. Cocktails are popular on cruise ships and many bars utilize pre-mixed blends that simply require combining with a spirit and ice before being shaken or blended and garnished.

During the day: drinks can be purchased from at least one bar inside the vessel and from pool bars on the sun decks throughout the day. Drinks are also available

Figure 2.6 *Bar on Aurora*

from mobile dispense points in the buffet and in the restaurant when meals are being served.

Lounges: passengers congregate in a variety of places for quiet moments or to play cards or read a book. While bar service is an option, tea and coffee are more likely to be consumed. Ships tend to develop a range of lounges according to the needs of passengers. These might include a library, a card or bridge room, writing room, observation lounge and general lounges. These areas can be used for quizzes and competitions, wine tastings and small group meetings.

The various bars can also be used for a range of activities including art auctions, competitions, karaoke, dance classes, fashion shows and entertainment shows. The bar staff work to a rota that covers the various areas within the ship and creates a fair and equitable pattern of work for everyone.

ENTERTAINMENT

The entertainments staff work for the Cruise Director who in turn reports to the Hotel Services or Passenger Services Director. This element of the cruise product does not generally create additional revenue although indirectly sales can be made that arise from entertainment activities.

Figure 2.7 *Theatre Ventura*

Theatres

The venues for the headline activities such as musical extravaganzas, comedy clubs, cabaret or magic shows. The theatres provide the largest areas for gathering passengers together so they can also be used for emergency drills and a meeting point for shore excursions. There are usually between two or three shows each evening. Shows and performances operate to a rotating schedule, which is designed to ensure that the programme appears fresh, interesting and new.

Daytime activity programme

Entertainment staff produce events during the day that are published in the ship's newspaper. These events can be very diverse to suit the types of passengers onboard. The team also includes port lecturers, dance instructors, and lecturers for cyber cafés or IT suites. The entertainment staff can manage fashion shows, arts and craft demonstrations, culinary demonstrations and wine tastings, often working with staff from other departments onboard.

Music and cinema

Musicians are employed to provide support for theatrical productions, show bars and bar areas, sailing days, deck parties and piano bars. A technical team provides cinema support, IT support for computers onboard, and stage support for lighting, sound and special effects. They also are available to help the musicians if they require technical support.

Leisure products

Leisure staff provide support for sport activities onboard, such as golf. Various water sports such as jet skis, water skiing, scuba and windsurfing may also be available from the aft section of some cruise ships. The vessel may rent bicycles to passengers to take ashore. Fitness classes such as aerobics, pilates and yoga are operated within fitness suites. A separate team will design activities for children, noting the specific needs that relate to specific ages. Princess Cruises operates the 'Pelican Club' for 3 to 7 year olds, the 'Pirateers' for children aged 8 to 12 and 'Off Limits' for teenagers 13 to 17 [15].

SHORE EXCURSIONS

Shore excursions are sold before and during the cruise. They are revenue generating but designed to add value to the cruise experience. Because of the constraint on time, shore excursions or tours ashore are configured to maximize the experience for passengers so they can get the most out of their time ashore. The range of options can be vast, depending on the port of call, and can include transferring to launches, travelling by coach, by bicycle, by horse-drawn buggy or taking a helicopter trip. Booking through the cruise company provides certain advantages – for example, in the event of a breakdown, the cruise company will take full responsibility for sorting the problem out and ensure that the passenger is not overly inconvenienced.

Shore excursions use third-party tour operators (although some cruise companies also own tour operations and can take advantage of this fact) to provide tours and develop a network of contacts to develop their shore excursion programme. The organization of tours for passengers is like a military operation, involving planning, crowd control, careful timing and efficient communication.

SPA, BEAUTY THERAPY AND HAIR CARE

This area is also revenue generating. Some cruise brands contract the service as a concession (an arrangement where the operator comes to a financial agreement

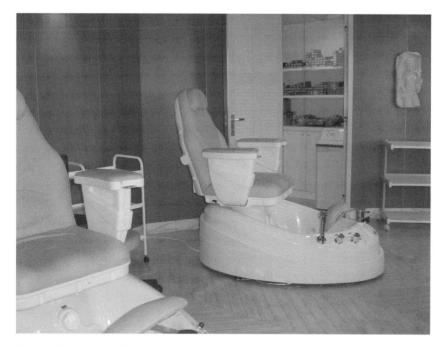

Figure 2.8 *Spa equipment*

with the cruise company to operate onboard) while others employ their own staff directly. There are a number of well-known beauty or hair stylist brands, such as Steiners, that operate on cruise ships and there are some brands, e.g. Lotus Spa, that are created to uniquely identify the style of operation that is run onboard specific cruise ships. Increasingly cruise ships recognize the growth in 'well-being' or 'spas' as contemporary lifestyle choices.

Treatments available include chakra stone therapy, thalassotherapy, foot massage, manicures and pedicures, hair styling, oxygenating facials, body wraps and health and nutrition lectures.

SHOPS

Shops onboard provide a welcome indulgence for passengers seeking to top up on their routine of retail therapy. Just because they are at sea doesn't mean they can't browse and pick up items of interest or, in some cases, necessity. Indeed, there is an added benefit to attract shoppers in that goods are sold duty free. Ships travelling in international waters do not generally pay duty. As for beauty therapy, shops onboard can be either concessionary or operated directly. If they are operated directly they tend to be line managed by the Staff Purser Administration or

Figure 2.9 *Shops onboard*

someone of similar rank. The range of shops tends to include a jeweller, fashion stores for women and men, a gift shop and a more general store that may also sell alcohol and cigarettes.

Shops onboard usually occupy a central area within the ship that mimics the shopping mall of a large city. The trend of constructing a large, impressive atrium on mega-cruisers suits this tendency and creates an additional advantage in allowing shops to develop temporary market stall areas by moving into the spaces opposite and adjacent to the main shop locations. This increases the overall trading area and helps to create a bustling market feel. Shops operating under concession are managed by companies such as Miami Cruiseline Holdings, Harding Brothers Duty Free, Nuance Global Ships and Flagship Retail Services Incorporated.

PHOTOGRAPHY

The ship's photographers are kept busy in the endless cycle of capturing magic moments. The opportunities to record important events occur from the point of embarkation right through to departure from the last port of call. This ensures that passengers can purchase posed, professional pictures in special presentation packs and have something special to remember. Contemporary cruise companies have

invested heavily in digital technology so as to customize photographs with digit-
ally composed and mastered backdrops as relevant to the port of call or event. For
example, passengers photographed disembarking in Venice may have their photograph framed within a montage of Venetian images. Photographers appear at the
gangway when passengers arrive onboard, are present during cocktail parties, gala
dinners and formal events. They accompany tours and attend passenger meetings.
Their job is to get the picture and then to sell the picture to the passenger.

Pictures are presented in corridor display areas so as to be easily viewed by passengers who may be en route from restaurant to show bar. It is difficult for passengers not to stop and look and the sale can be confirmed with the application of
carefully considered sales techniques. Some photographers are employed directly
by cruise brands and others are contracted by concessionary operators such as the
Cruise Ship Picture Company, Image Photo Services Inc., Ocean Images Ltd. and
Digital Seas Internet Cafes.

CASINO

Casinos onboard seem to meet the expectations of some passengers for that James
Bond moment. Casinos are described as a venue for 'action and excitement'

Figure 2.10 *Casino*

(NCL), while Carnival Cruises promise that 'You'll have the time of your life', and Royal Caribbean say 'There's nothing like the excitement of a winning hand at poker or a slot machine paying off'. Cruise ships aim to emulate the glitz and glamour of a Las Vegas casino. Gambling is a pastime for winners and the cruise vacation, as a result, becomes synonymous with success.

Cashless ships are becoming commonplace in the cruise industry. Passengers receive a card that allows them to purchase goods onboard and credit that to their account. Casinos also use this mode of purchase and sell tokens for slot machines or chips for gambling. Casinos are allowed to open on sailing although some ports permit the casino to trade even when the ship is in port. Casinos are generally operated to strict codes. For example the CLIA, a non-profit trade association consisting of the 17 largest passenger cruise lines that call on major ports in the United States and abroad, publish guidelines as can be seen in Table 2.2.

Casinos are open to players over the age of 18 (21 in Alaska and some other ports). Most have a dress code and are operated with minimum and maximum bets posted clearly at tables. Typical games on offer can include blackjack, craps, roulette, Caribbean stud poker, three-card poker, Baccarat and video poker.

Table 2.2 *Gambling guidelines*
Gambling Guidelines

All equipment purchased and installed on cruise vessels will meet the regulatory standards of the Nevada Gaming Control Board or other licensed jurisdiction for payback and internal software.
RULES OF PLAY
Each line will provide a gaming guide setting forth the rules of play for their casino. These rules of play shall generally follow those established for casinos in Nevada, New Jersey, or England. These house rules will also be made available in every casino. Each member line will post at every gaming table minimum and maximum betting limits for each game. Only adults are allowed to play the slots or the tables.
INTERNAL CONTROLS
All shipboard gambling operations will be inspected by each member line's internal audit department on a regular basis, not to exceed 12 months. All casinos will have detailed internal control procedures concerning the cash and coin counts, casino cage procedures and other processes, similar to licensed jurisdictions. Each line will employ some form of surveillance to assure operations are fair and equitable for all parties. Each line will separate the operation of the casino from the financial aspects of the casino as clearly as possible including specific duties for cashiers and table gaming staff.

Table 2.2 *Continued*

CUSTOMER SERVICE

The onboard casino operations will be the overall responsibility of the Hotel Manager or Director, who is charged with ensuring the highest standard of conduct for casino staff. In case of a gaming dispute, any passenger who feels he or she has an issue that cannot be resolved by the Casino Manager should bring it up to the Hotel Manager, and every effort will be made to resolve the problem. If the issue is not resolved on board the vessel, each ship will have at the casino cage a current list of contact information for their home office or casino operator where the passenger can pursue their dispute. The cruise vessel will have onboard comment cards for the inclusion of any comment, concern, or means to improve the gambling system on board the vessel. Gambling is strictly for the enjoyment of the passengers who choose to avail themselves of this form of entertainment.

WEBSITE

CLIA recommends to its member companies that these guidelines be posted on each company's website.

http://www2.cruising.org/industry/gambling_guidelines.cfm

WEDDINGS AND RENEWAL OF VOWS AND CELEBRATORY ITEMS

While onboard, passengers can elect to celebrate special occasions and on some vessels couples can get married. The facility to perform weddings is not offered on all ships because of the national laws that exist for the various ships and their flags or registration. However, where the law allows, the ship's captain can perform a marriage ceremony. This creates a unique opportunity for passengers and, in response, cruise companies have developed a selection of inclusive packages to cater for these events and to coordinate the entire event. The package can include champagne, photographs, a wedding reception, flowers, the ceremony, wedding cake and souvenir items.

Passengers may also purchase a package to renew their vows. Again the captain presides over the event and the package can be customized to include spa treatments, champagne and a formal renewal of vows ceremony. Honeymoons, anniversaries, birthdays or special celebrations can all be catered for as part of a package.

BRAND VALUES AND VESSEL CLASSIFICATION

The size of the ship will have a major impact on the kind of cruise experience passengers enjoy. Large mega-liners typically feature multiple swimming pools, casinos, spas, many dining options and lots of activities. Small ships forgo some of the amenities in favour of a focus on destination and a different cruise experience. Cruise observers may classify ships in a variety of ways – the number of passengers the ship holds, the quality of food, drink and accommodation, or an overall measurement of the cruise experience. While no single standard exists, there is value in analysing what is done to identify classification and measurement of standards. Many cruise lines operate ships in different classes so as to attract a targeted clientele. In this way a company can design specific itineraries that are commensurate with the size, the product range, the target market and in line with the selling price.

Classification of scale

According to Spartan Travel [18], the following figure illustrates descriptors of classification by either carrying capacity of ship or distinguishing characteristic.

Classifications by status and value

While Spartan Travel also identify three expense category ratings – budget, mid-range and luxury, other industry observers adopt more breadth in analysing this facet. For example, CLIA lists five categories: Luxury, Premium, Resort or Contemporary, Niche or Speciality, and Value or Traditional [19]. This scaling is also adopted by Bjornsen [20].

An analysis of this classification suggests that ships offering the ultimate in comfort, cuisine and attentive service are called luxury brands. This product tends to be the most expensive and whilst ships in this category are usually small, there are exceptions. The accommodation and public areas are always finely appointed and carry relatively few passengers in spacious staterooms, suites or duplexes, which tend to have balconies. Service options may include butler service. These ships tend to be the equivalent of what used to be called 'five star' quality. Some brands, such as Crystal Cruises, have adopted the rubric of 'six stars' to identify their unique level of quality.

Table 2.3 Defining vessel types

Definition	Description
Mega-liner	over 2,000 passengers
Superliner	between 1,000 and 2,000 passengers
Midsize	between 400 and 1,000 passengers
Small	less than 400 passengers
Boutique	special purpose, usually less than 300 passengers
Sailing vessel	a ship primarily powered by wind
River barge	a ship that primarily cruises on inland rivers

Next in rank are premium brands, which offer above-average food, service and amenities, including a high number of outside cabins with balconies. These lines aim to appeal to broad age groups, by providing a diversity of facilities for children, young adults and older adults, together with a wide range of entertainment. Premium brands, like luxury liners, have a high ratio of space to passenger aboard the ship.

Contemporary brands are the equivalent of floating resorts, with capacity spanning from the mid-sized vessel through to the most recent mega-liner or mega cruise ship. These vessels operate on the basis that they provide choice and value with a contemporary twist. Onboard amenities, such as ice rinks, golf ranges or climbing walls, are often impressive. Style may well be casual, although opportunities will exist for passengers to dress up on optional formal evenings.

Niche or speciality cruises focus on a specific aspect of the cruise, such as the destinations, in order to develop a uniqueness of product. These cruise companies are specialist in their fields. They pride themselves on having expertise in aspects such as cultural interpretation, soft adventure or enrichment activities. These companies target the more experienced traveller.

Budget or value brands usually use medium-sized, refurbished, older ships with fewer facilities than the new mega-ships. The product offer will take advantage of lower staffing ratios by using, for example, self-service options for main dining events. The ships are generally classically designed and while the products are economically oriented in terms of the selling price, the options of choice and travel make this form of vacation attractive to those who are relatively new to cruising.

CASE STUDY: CARNIVAL UK – GENERATING COMPETITIVE ADVANTAGE

Carnival UK is the Southampton-based arm of Carnival Corporation and the umbrella term used to signify operations relating to P&O Cruises and Cunard Line. The corporation's mission statement is 'to deliver exceptional vacation experiences through the world's best-known cruise brands that cater to a variety of different lifestyles and budgets, all at an outstanding value unrivalled on land or at sea.'

In a drive to ensure their UK brands achieve the best results, Carnival UK has put in place a series of initiatives to increase their competitive advantage. The UK based group has a 42% share of the UK market but are seeing more competition emerging from cruise brands such as RCCL and NCL. The UK has been the focus of a changing pattern of ship deployments to increase capacity and take advantage of increasing sales from a market where penetration is relatively low. The ships that are being deployed are at the newer end of the scale, so providing more choice, a higher calibre of facilities and frequently larger scale.

Cunard Line and P&O Cruises were once competitors but under the aegis of Carnival UK they are targeted at distinctive and specific markets. Both cruise brands boast 59% repeat trade and together they carry 750,000 passengers or guests per year (P&O Cruises carry passengers, while Cunard Line carries guests).

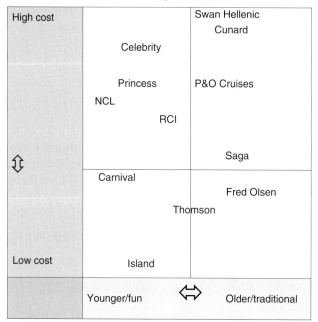

Figure 2.11 *Brand positioning*

Cunard's brand pillars are based on legacy and tradition, grandeur and elegance, being 'British' or more exactly 'properly British', the 'Cunarder' community, and built around legendary voyages. The brand pillars underpin the claim that their ships are the most famous ocean liners in the world.

In contrast, P&O Cruises' brand pillars underpin the promise to provide a world of extraordinary promises – premium quality, distinctly British, providing extraordinary choice, to be intuitively attentive and provide vacations that are about tailored individuality. Both brands aim to concentrate on TNT – tiny noticeable things. P&O Cruises loyalty club is known as Portunus and Cunard's is known as Cunard World Club.

On cruises each guest is asked to complete a Customer Service Question-naire (CSQ); 50% of all guests are said to do this, making the feedback both powerful and reliable in comparison to hotel service questionnaires, which have considerably lower completion rates. Managers are charged with achieving a minimum of 90% satisfaction for these CSQs and consid-erable attention is paid if a ship is underperforming or overperforming for any of the distinctive areas that make up the elements of each cruise.

The initiatives that are used by Carnival UK include: 'White Star Serv-ice' to establish service standards that are brand specific for Cunard; 'CRUISE', the service credo for P&O Cruises and 'Elev8', a brand burnisher intended to increase customer enjoyment by considering improvements in areas such as people, product and process. An exam-ple of how the brand has evolved can be seen in the way that staff have been empowered to deal with complaints. In the past complaints were referred to the office ashore but now managers have been provided with training to ensure any issues are dealt with fully onboard the ship. The resultant outcomes save money and create higher levels of satis-faction. Complaints recorded in the CSQs have reduced markedly.

Finally, Carnival Corporation has introduced an initiative they call 'Care'. This is intended to establish protocols and an action plan for support-ing their passengers or guests in the event of a mishap or emergency. Trained staff are 'on call' and prepared to fly out from the head office to a ship to provide critical support in the case of an 'event'. The staff are charged to be there for the cruise operator's customers when things do not go as planned.

SUMMARY AND CONCLUSIONS

This chapter identifies a number of inter-related issues connected to sales, market-ing and the cruise industry. In examining marketing and reflecting on the current infrastructure for selling cruises a contemporary picture emerges that presents a view of the dynamics in context. The cruise market is evolving. It is becoming multifaceted, with an emphasis on targeting and market segmentation and continu-ally identifying opportunities for growth and new developments. In relation to this the cruise product is also becoming more diverse as operators continue to seek new ways of meeting passenger needs and satisfying expectations. The cruise ship in the twenty-first century is still reliant on people for the critical part of the service product [1] and in many ways the human element will continue to make the differ-ence between achieving a successful quality outcome and being ordinary.

This chapter has examined marketing in general terms – selling from a wholesale and retail perspective, distribution options and the part the Internet and loyalty programmes play for cruise business. Cruise products have also been described to establish an overview of what is available and why it is provided. The list of products is not exhaustive, but aims to give a flavour of the type of services on offer.

REFERENCES

1. Evans, N., D. Campbell and G. Stonehouse, *Strategic Management for Travel and Tourism*. 2003, Oxford: Butterworth-Heinemann. p. 120.
2. Knowles, T., D. Diamantis and J. Bey El-Mourhabi, *The Globalisation of Tourism and Hospitality*. 2nd ed. 2004, London: Thomson Learning.
3. Barron, P. and A.B. Greenwood, 'Issues Determining the Development of Cruise Itineraries: A focus on the luxury market', *Tourism in Marine Environments*, 2006. 3(2): p. 89–99.
4. Aaker, D., *Strategic Market Management*. 6th ed. 2001, New York: Wiley.
5. Berger, A.A., *Ocean Travel and Cruising: A cultural analysis*. 2004, New York: Haworth Hospitality Press.
6. Dickinson, R. and A. Vladimir, *Selling the Sea*. 1997, New York: Wiley.
7. Travel Weekly, 'Cruise Lines Get Candid about Direct Sales'. 2011 [accessed February 2011]; Available from: http://www.travelweekly.com/Cruise-Travel/Cruise-lines-get-candid-about-direct-sales/#.
8. Vellas, F. and L. Becherel, *International Tourism*. 1995, Basingstoke: Macmillan Press.
9. Mancini, M., *Cruising: A guide to the cruise line industry*. 2nd ed. 2003, Albany NY: Delmar.
10. Hatton, M., 'Current Issues Paper: Redefining the relationships – The future of travel agencies and the global agency contract in a changing distribution system', *Journal of Vacation Marketing*, 2004. 10(2): p. 101–108.
11. PSARA, 'Benefits of PSARA Membership'. 2005 [accessed October 2011]; Available from: http://www.the-psa.co.uk/default.asp?PID=2&PPID=2.
12. ACE website [accessed October 2011]; Available from: http://www.cruiseexperts.org/.
13. Luxury Alliance, 'The World's Finest Travel Experience'. 2005 [accessed March 2005]; Available from: http://www.luxuryalliance.com/.
14. World's Leading Cruise Lines, 'Anywhere You Want to Go, Anyway You Want to Feel'. 2005 [accessed March 2005]; Available from: http://www.worldsleadingcruise-lines.com/intro.html.
15. Princess Cruises webpage. 2010 [accessed October 2011]; Available from: http://www.princess.com/ships/ap/.
16. Dervaes, C., *Selling Cruises*. 2nd ed. 2003, New York: Thomson.
17. CLIA, 'Gambling Guidelines'. 2011 [accessed October 2011]; Available from: http://www2.cruising.org/industry/gambling_guidelines.cfm.
18. Spartan Travel, 'Cruising Styles'. 2005 [accessed March 2005]; Available from: http://spartan.travwell.net/cruises/choosing/style/.
19. CLIA, *Profile of the US Cruise Industry*. 2010 [accessed February 2011]; Available from: http://www.cruising.org/news/press_releases/2010/01/state-cruise-industry-2010-confident-and-offering-new-ships-innovation.
20. Bjornsen, P., 'The Growth of the Market and Global Competition in the Cruise Industry', *Cruise and Ferry Conference 2003*. Earls Court, London: Informa Group.

Maritime issues and legislation

3

INTRODUCTION

In this chapter the cruise industry is placed in the context of the wider shipping industry. It is helpful when considering ships and shipping to reflect on the commercial nature of this global, multifaceted and complex industry. More importantly, international shipping complies with legislation that has serious implications for cruise ships and the companies that operate them. Finally, the chapter will conclude by identifying the role of international maritime organizations for cruise operations.

In Chapter 1 the development of the cruise industry was described from a historical perspective. This chapter seeks to take a more holistic view of the contemporary nature of shipping so as to develop a deeper understanding of the cruise industry in context. There are many constraints for operators in the international shipping arena that are in place to ensure certain safeguards exist, so the legal environment is also examined to highlight critical factors. Legal issues are paramount for a number of organizations that have vested interests in either developing the legal framework or in supporting operators to comply appropriately. For this reason, an overview is provided of a wide range of the major maritime organizations to illustrate the importance and involvement for the cruise industry and the maritime industry.

SHIPPING INDUSTRY

The cruise industry is a derivation of passenger travel that arose phoenix-like from what appeared to be the end of an era after World War II, when jet planes were introduced as mass transportation vehicles to replace the stately and seemingly invincible transatlantic liners [1]. Over the last three decades, the renaissance of cruising has been relentless and, for the large cruise corporations, it has also been highly lucrative, yet there remain a number of issues that have a broader impact from a shipping point of view in terms of operational effectiveness, fair trading, environmentalism and safety.

The shipping industry is, according to Farthing and Brownrigg [2], the most international of all industries. This reflects the nature of trade in transporting cargo or goods and people across seas and oceans internationally and the nature of the ships and their crew, which are frequently multinational. However, the shipping industry is actually better described as collection of industries [2], as is demonstrated in Table 3.1.

According to Equasis [3] the total number of vessels in the world fleet in 2009 stood at 74,991, or an estimated 853,276,000 GRT. This compares to 89,899 ships or 605,218,000 GRT in 2003 [4]. This presents an interesting development, where ships as individual units are decreasing in number but volumes or capacities are increasing. Clearly the interim period has been punctuated by ship's operators introducing larger ships and decommissioning older but smaller vessels. In 2004 Ward [5] stated there were 255 ships in the world cruising fleet and by 2009 that figure had reached 291 cruise ships [6]. The Institute of Shipping Economics and Logistics (ISL) commented that in 2003 around 75% of the world cruise fleet was owned by three major corporations: Carnival Corporation 41.7%; Royal Caribbean 22.9%; and Norwegian Cruise Lines/Star Cruises 8.9% [7]. This reality still exists, with the three largest cruise corporations still domi-

Table 3.1 *The components of shipping*

Wet bulk	Carry wet cargoes such as oil, chemicals, petroleum or anything in liquid form in tanks or specially designed holds (ships may be called tankers)
Dry bulk	Carry dry commodities such as iron ore, coal, grain, fertilizers, sugar, etc.
Cargo liners	Scheduled vessels that carry containers or space onboard to a specific timetable
Coastal and short sea	Sometimes called tramp ships, these vessels offer an alternative to road or rail as a means of transporting goods
Cruise ships or passenger liners	Cruise ships are more common than passenger liners, although some services such as Cunard still provide some liner services
Ferries	Tend to provide liner-like scheduled services with facilities to carry people, cars and other transportation
Offshore operations	This sector includes oil and gas rigs and supports exploration for mineral extraction at sea

nating. Between them they own 156 ships with a total of 327,300 lower berths (see Figures 3.1 and 3.2).

As the scale of cruise ships becomes ever larger, so too does the cost. A ship like the *Oasis of the Seas* cost US$1.4 billion to build [8]. Larger vessels bring greater revenues, provide more choice and variety for customers, and allow for

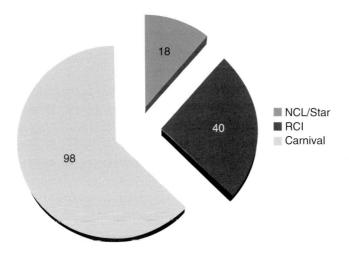

Figure 3.1 *Number of cruise ships owned by major cruise operators*

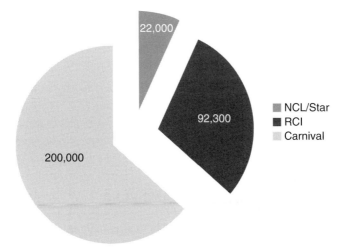

Figure 3.2 *Number of lower berths on ships owned by major cruise operators*

more economies of scale. On the other hand, smaller ships can be more exclusive and enable discriminating customers to select cruise products that meet particular needs while ensuring the itinerary is also unique and more accessible because of the ship's dimensions. Larger corporations have mixed portfolios of ships including different brands targeted at specific markets but for all there is a bias towards the larger-scale vessels. The impact of buying big, which has most recently been undertaken by the world's second largest cruise corporation, Royal Caribbean International, can be seen when comparing the number of lower berths on ships operated by the three largest cruise corporations (Figure 3.2) and comparing to Figure 3.1.

The spread of ownership may be consolidating but there is still evidence that a diverse range of ship management and ownership is practised outside this group of owner managers [9], including chartering, leasing and purchase of management services. Some companies, such as Louis Cruises, own a fleet of vessels, some of which are chartered to tour operators [10]. Others, like V.Ships, are involved in supplying crew and management services for cruise companies [11]. The *Hanseatic* is an example of a small vessel that is currently on long-term lease to German cruise operator Hapag Lloyd [12]. This complex pattern of ownership and management is fundamental for many operators involved in the contemporary cruise industry.

THE LEGAL ENVIRONMENT

According to Farthing and Brownrigg [2], the notion of freedom of the seas stems from principles that were set out in the United Nations Convention for the Law of the Sea (UNCLOS) in 1982, which came into force in November 1994. This convention created an umbrella approach for virtually all activities undertaken in, over and under the sea (including actions on and below the seabed). An important component for the legislation was the recognition that states possess an Exclusive Economic Zone (EEZ) that extends 200 nautical miles seawards. This convention allows freedom of navigation and/or rights of access or passage to shipping on the high seas with certain provisos concerning access to the EEZ. The regulation is an example of a collective international agreement that is established for the benefit of all signatories to the UN in order to allow for free enterprise, open competition and economic freedom [13].

SHIP NATIONALITY, REGISTRATION AND FLAG

The terms 'nationality, registration and flag' are sometimes used as if each was synonymous but that is not necessarily totally accurate and, indeed, a ship may be deemed to have the nationality of a state even if there is no evidence of documentation for that nationality and the ship is unregistered. When a ship is registered it is recorded officially and is indicative that the ship possesses a certain nationality. The registration sets in place the framework for the legal consequences attributed to the ship's owner, the ship's managers and the ship's crew. In public law, registration allocates the ship to a specific state together with the jurisdiction that applies from that state and protection from that state, including the right to fly that state's flag. In private law the registration creates protection for the title of the owner and those who may hold securities in the form of financial interests in the vessel. The flag is symbolic and flown at the ship's stern as a mark of identification but otherwise the term 'flag' is shorthand for the nationality of a vessel [2].

The implications of nationality for a ship and its owner present serious issues, apart from the aforementioned legal aspects, that can impact on operational costs. Some countries require that ships registered in that country be crewed either entirely by nationals or a given percentage of nationals. For example, the crewing, ship construction and ownership requirements to flag a vessel in the United States are said to be among the most restrictive of the maritime nations. Current manning regulations for US flag vessels engaged in coastwise trade mandate that all officers and pilots and 75% of other onboard personnel be US citizens or residents. In addition, US flag vessels engaged in coastwise trade, must be owned by US citizens and constructed in US shipyards. This construction requirement applies to the entire hull and superstructure of the ship and the majority of all materials outfitting the vessel.

A cruise ship has many options for registration with states or countries that may be other than the owner's nationality. The reasons and benefits for this are many, including:

- Creates neutrality in the event of conflict
- Reduces the tax liability
- Leads to reduced registration fees
- Reduces crewing costs

Panama, Liberia, Cyprus, the Bahamas and Malta were stated by Farthing and Brownrigg [2] to be five of the world's largest fleets, suggesting that, at this time, these states operated more liberal, economically attractive conditions and were seen to be effective and efficient in supporting the needs of ship operators. According to the ISL nearly half of the world cruise fleet is now attributable to the Bahamas and Panama. The Bahamas, Panama and Liberia had previously dominated the cruise shipping industry, but in 2003 there was a change of 19 vessels from Liberia to Panama because of the unstable political situation in the West African country [7].

According to the CLIA [14] predominant countries offering flags of registry for cruise vessels are the United Kingdom, Panama, Norway, the Netherlands, the

Bahamas and, despite the statement regarding regulations, the United States. All of these countries are member states of the International Maritime Organization (IMO), an organization that is centrally important for maritime developments relating to safety.

The CLIA identify a number of factors that must be met for a valid registry. One is that a flag state must be an IMO member nation, which has adopted all of the IMO's maritime safety resolutions and conventions. Secondly, a flag state should have an established maritime organization that is capable of enforcing all international and national regulations. Major flag registries are said to provide comprehensive maritime expertise and administrative services. In addition, they are required to conduct annual safety inspections prior to the issuance of a passenger vessel certificate and utilize recognized classification societies to monitor a vessel's compliance with all international and flag state standards.

MARINE POLLUTION

MARPOL (International Convention for the Prevention of Pollution from Ships) is an acronym that is formed by the first three letters of 'marine' and 'pollution' [15]. The MARPOL agreement has been ratified by approximately 90 nations, including the US and most other major maritime nations of the world. It encompasses six annexes that govern a broad range of maritime issues relating to potential marine pollution, including oil, chemicals, garbage and sewage and mandates proper disposal and/or discharge. Air pollution is the most recent addition to the agreement (Annex IV was added to MARPOL in May 2005). All ships operating in the US must also comply with US regulations, including the Clean Water Act and the Oil Pollution Control Act and likewise, ships operating in other countries must also pay due regard to additional regulations that may apply. In the US, the cruise industry works with the US Coast Guard, the federal Environmental Protection Agency and other federal and state regulators as well as maritime groups, such as the Center for Marine Conservation and Ocean Advocates, to find productive environmental solutions.

MARPOL is interpreted by the CLIA [16] for the purposes of operationalization of waste management by the cruise industry in a statement relating to practices and procedures. In respect of industry waste management standards, the cruise operators who are members of CLIA have agreed to incorporate the following standards for waste stream management into their Safety Management Systems.

'Graywater' and 'blackwater' are types of wastewater produced by ships carrying passengers or crew. Graywater is produced by showers, sinks or basins and in food preparation, while blackwater refers to sewage. On cruise ships, both are treated in accordance with industry regulatory requirements that are frequently more stringent and demanding than government regulations.

Table 3.2 *CLIA cruise industry waste management: practices and procedures*

The members of the Cruise Lines International Association (CLIA) are dedicated to preserving the marine environment and in particular the pristine condition of the oceans and other waters upon which our vessels sail. The environmental standards that apply to our industry are stringent and comprehensive. Through the International Maritime Organization, the United States and flag and port states, CLIA has developed consistent and uniform international standards that apply to all vessels engaged in international commerce. These standards are set forth in the International Convention for the Prevention of Pollution from Ships (MARPOL). The international standards of MARPOL have in turn been adopted by the United States and augmented by additional national legislation and regulation. The US has jurisdiction over both foreign and domestic vessels that operate in US waters where US laws, such as the Federal Water Pollution Control Act, the Act to Prevent Pollution from Ships, the Ports and Waterways Safety Act, and the Resource Conservation and Recovery Act – which applies to hazardous waste as it is landed ashore for disposal, apply. The US Coast Guard enforces both international conventions and domestic laws. The cruise industry commitment to protecting the environment is demonstrated by the comprehensive spectrum of waste management technologies and procedures employed on its vessels. CLIA members are committed to:

a. Designing, constructing and operating vessels, so as to minimize their impact on the environment;
b. Developing improved technologies to exceed current requirements for protection of the environment;
c. Implementing a policy goal of zero discharge of MARPOL, Annex V solid waste products (garbage) and equivalent US laws and regulations by use of more comprehensive waste minimization procedures to significantly reduce shipboard generated waste;
d. Expanding waste reduction strategies to include reuse and recycling to the maximum extent possible so as to land ashore even smaller quantities of waste products;
e. Improving processes and procedures for collection and transfer of hazardous waste; and
f. Strengthening comprehensive programs for monitoring and auditing of onboard environmental practices and procedures in accordance with the International Safety Management Code for the Safe Operation of Ships and for Pollution Prevention (ISM Code).

Table 3.3 *Waste management standards*

1. *Photo Processing, Including X-Ray Development Fluid Waste*: Member lines have agreed to minimize the discharge of silver into the marine environment through the use of best available technology that will reduce the silver content of the waste stream below levels specified by prevailing regulations.

2. *Dry-cleaning Waste Fluids and Contaminated Materials*: Member lines have agreed to prevent the discharge of chlorinated dry-cleaning fluids, sludge, contaminated filter materials and other dry-cleaning waste byproducts into the environment

3. *Print Shop Waste Fluids*: Member lines have agreed to prevent the discharge of hazardous wastes from printing materials (inks) and cleaning chemicals into the environment.

4. *Photo Copying and Laser Printer Cartridges*: Member lines have agreed to initiate procedures so as to maximize the return of photo copying and laser printer cartridges for recycling. In any event, these cartridges will be landed ashore.

5. *Unused And Outdated Pharmaceuticals*: Member lines have agreed to ensure that unused and/or outdated pharmaceuticals are effectively and safely disposed of in accordance with legal and environmental requirements.

6. *Fluorescent And Mercury Vapor Lamp Bulbs*: Member lines have agreed to prevent the release of mercury into the environment from spent fluorescent and mercury vapor lamps by assuring proper recycling or by using other acceptable means of disposal.

7. *Batteries*: Member lines have agreed to prevent the discharge of spent batteries into the marine environment.

8. *Bilge and Oily Water Residues*: Member lines have agreed to meet or exceed the international requirements for removing oil from bilge and wastewater prior to discharge.

9. *Glass, Cardboard, Aluminum and Steel Cans*: Member lines have agreed to eliminate, to the maximum extent possible, the disposal of MARPOL Annex V wastes into the marine environment. This will be achieved through improved reuse and recycling opportunities. They have further agreed that no waste will be discharged into the marine environment unless it has been properly processed and can be discharged in accordance with MARPOL and other prevailing requirements.

10. *Incinerator Ash*: Member lines have agreed to reduce the production of incinerator ash by minimizing the generation of waste and maximizing recycling opportunities.

11. *Graywater:* [For ships traveling regularly on itineraries beyond the territorial waters of coastal states], member lines have agreed that graywater will be discharged only while the ship is underway and proceeding at a speed of not less than 6 knots[1]; that graywater will not be discharged in port and will not be discharged within 4 nautical miles from shore or such other distance as agreed to with authorities having jurisdiction or provided for by local law except in an emergency, or where geographically limited. Member lines have further agreed that the discharge of graywater will comply with all applicable laws and regulations. For vessels whose itineraries are fully within US territorial waters, discharge shall comply fully with US and individual state legislation and regulations.

12. *Blackwater:* CLIA members have agreed that all blackwater will be processed through a Marine Sanitation Device (MSD), certified in accordance with US or international regulations, prior to discharge. For ships traveling regularly on itineraries beyond territorial coastal waters, discharge will take place only when the ship is more than 4 miles from shore and when the ship is traveling at a speed of not less than 6 knots[1]. For vessels whose itineraries are fully within US territorial waters, discharge shall comply fully with US and individual state legislation and regulations.

Across the world, the Coast Guard or similar agencies enforce MARPOL regulations 73/78 regarding ocean dumping from vessels. Under the international regulations it is illegal to dump plastic refuse and garbage mixed with plastic into any waters. In addition the regulations restrict dumping of non-plastic trash and other forms of garbage.

Most recently, much has been made of the need for cruise ships to carry low sulphur fuel in accordance with the requirements of special areas identified by governments in accordance with Annex IV of MARPOL. Cruise ships in designated Emission Control Areas (ECA) must use more expensive, special low-sulphur fuels or equivalent in order to generate lower levels of pollutants.

SAFETY OF LIFE AT SEA

According to Roemer [17], Safety of Life at Sea (SOLAS) was introduced in the form of an international treaty because of the sinking of the Titanic and resultant loss of life. The International Convention for SOLAS was first adopted in 1948. It is referred to as a 'living' document, that is, one that is continuously amended and updated. SOLAS is concerned with the establishment of international regulations that address maritime safety, including lifesaving, fire protection and ship stability. According to the US Coast Guard[18], cruise ships are regulated for safety by government agencies in the way outlined in Table 3.4.

While some vessels may well be registered in the US, current patterns suggest that most are not and for these vessels, the safety inspection is administered within the country of registration. The US Coast Guard requires any ship, irrespective of country of registration, to meet the SOLAS convention if they wish to take on vessels in US ports. US law expects that any cruise company advertising in the US will disclose the country of registration for their vessels. SOLAS is far reaching in its remit and requires compliance with stringent regulations regarding structural fire protection, fire fighting and lifesaving equipment, watercraft integrity and stability, vessel control, navigation safety, crewing and crew competency, safety management and environmental protection.

The Coast Guard, in respect of SOLAS requirements, examines all cruise ships when they first visit US ports. Thereafter, the vessels will be inspected, or checked for compliance, quarterly. Records relating to these inspections (called 'control verification examinations') are available for public scrutiny. Inspectors involved with these examinations board the ship to corroborate the structural fire safety that exists, to ensure lifesaving equipment is available and located as required in the appropriate condition, to witness fire and abandon ship drills as conducted by the ship's crew and to test key equipment such as steering systems, fire pumps and lifeboats. The Coast Guard has the authority to require correction of any deficiencies before allowing the ship to take on passengers at a US port.

In terms of crew-member competence, the US Coast Guard can suspend or revoke licences or merchant mariner's documents if a US-registered ship is found to be

Table 3.4 *Safety Oversight undertaken by the US Coast Guard*

Missions
Provide personnel and support to other Coast Guard units for Certificate of Compliance examinations.
Expand technical knowledge of cruise ship operations to continue as Coast Guard's experts in cruise ship operations, standards, examination, policy and doctrine.
Provide consultative services to other Coast Guard Commands on cruise ship issues.
Provide exportable training to Coast Guard units and supervise On-the-Job training to visiting Coast Guard personnel when directed and coordinate Coast Guard Industry Training pertaining to cruise ships.

operating below published standards for experience and training. On foreign flag ships, SOLAS requirements mean that ships must be efficiently and sufficiently manned and this is checked during control verification examinations. SOLAS is not designed to provide guarantees for health care and, as a result, for example, it is not a proviso that cruise ships carry a ship's doctor.

SOLAS requires that the ship's captain schedule and implement periodical fire and lifeboat drills. This is intended both to give the crew practice and to show passengers the critical action that may be required in the event of a serious incident or emergency onboard. For this reason SOLAS expects that all passengers participate in these drills. The drills are scheduled according to the duration of the cruise. In a one-week cruise the first drill would take place as soon all passengers were onboard and immediately prior to sailing. If the cruise lasts more than a week this is also the case but an additional drill would take place every week thereafter. For a cruise lasting less than a week, the drill takes place within 24 hours of departure from the home port.

Notices are to be posted in clear view in every passenger cabin or stateroom to provide easily understood information regarding safety issues. A notice will include:

- how to recognize the ship's emergency signals (alarm bells and whistle signals are normally supplemented by announcements made over the ship's public address system);
- the location of passengers' life preservers in that stateroom (special life preservers will be provided for children, if necessary, by the room steward);
- instructions and pictures explaining how to put on the life preserver; and the lifeboat to which passengers in that stateroom are assigned. Modern cruise ships carry a variety of survival craft. Passengers are invariably assigned to lifeboats or similar survival craft that can be utilized for emergency situations.

Crew members from the hotel department onboard play an important and potentially critical part in the safety routines and are generally responsible for assisting and directing passengers for emergency drills, although some may well have other safety duties. The regulations call for direction signs to be posted in passageways and stairways throughout the ship, showing the path to the lifeboats. The crew member in charge of each lifeboat will gather or muster the passengers assigned to that lifeboat, and give passengers any final instructions necessary in the proper method of donning and adjusting their life preservers. The crew should be prepared to help passengers and clarify the emergency procedures if necessary.

In 2010, SOLAS regulations came into force to dictate that cruise ships must no longer be constructed using combustible materials meaning that older vessels, and especially those build before 1980, must be upgraded or retired from service. Furthermore, SOLAS regulations were introduced in 2010 to ensure that cruise ships could return safely to port in the event of a critical incident. In effect the ship becomes its own lifeboat in this case [19].

SANITATION AND CLEANLINESS

In the US, the responsibility for maintaining an oversight of sanitary conditions on passenger vessels is undertaken by the Public Health Service (USPHS). The USPHS conducts both scheduled and unscheduled inspections of passenger vessels in US ports under its Vessel Sanitation Program (VSP), focusing on proper sanitation for drinking water, food storage, food preparation and handling, and general cleanliness. The USPHS will provide the public with results of inspections on individual vessels, and take reports of unsanitary conditions on individual vessels. In other countries similar inspections are undertaken by state bodies – e.g., the Australian Quarantine Inspection Service, the UK Port Health Authority and the Canadian Public Health Bureau appoint environmental health officers to implement similar inspections.

Cruise companies take these inspections very seriously; it is in the best interests of the company to be seen to comply, to be safe and to secure high scores. More details about this process can be found in Chapter 10.

MARINE SECURITY – MARSEC

MARSEC has been developed to establish regulations for crew competence that apply to training, certification and watch-keeping, so as to ensure safe practice and secure environments for passengers and crew. MARSEC was introduced specifically to respond to potential risks following the terrorist attacks on the World Trade Center in 2001. Prior to this, the International Maritime Organization monitored the International Safety Management code (ISM), which covered both mandatory safety and anti-pollution standards. MARSEC includes published Standards for Training, Certification and Watch-keeping (STCW). In July 2004 a code of practice was introduced internationally to address heightened tensions concerning the safety of shipping. The International Ship and Port Facility Security (ISPS) code is examined in Chapter 10 but the following information provides a summary of key elements.

MARSEC requires that ships will carry a designated vessel security officer and that this person will be responsible for the ship's security plan. It is expected that the security officer will be a senior deck officer who has a responsibility for standing watch. The responsibilities include: developing the ship's security plan; ensuring appropriate adequate training is provided for officers and crew; ensuring that the ship complies with the security plan; and maintaining knowledge relating to international laws, domestic regulations, current security threats and patterns relating to security issues.

The ship's security officer is to act as a liaison between the ship, relevant authorities and the company's security officer. Typically this individual would be involved with undertaking risk assessments, developing strategies and evaluating points of vulnerability. MARSEC operates three levels of security status:

Level 1 – minimum appropriate security measures required.
Level 2 – heightened risk of security incident.
Level 3 – probable or imminent security incident for a limited time.

Threat levels will be communicated by ports to ships in a timely fashion, so that a ship has sufficient time to consider best action. The ship's master may elect to elevate a threat level if the threat is considered above that stated by the port.

In the US, according to federal regulations, terminal operators and cruise lines share the primary responsibility for shoreside and shipboard security of passengers. The Coast Guard examines all security plans and can require improvements in security measures. Passengers embarking on international voyages may expect to have their baggage searched or passed through screening devices before boarding. The terminal operator and cruise line have strict procedures for passenger identification and visitor control. Passengers who wish to have friends visit the ship prior to sailing should check with the cruise line well in advance. All these security measures are designed to prevent the introduction of unauthorized weapons and persons on the cruise ship. More details on this subject are included in Chapter 10.

CRUISE SHIPS AND THE ENVIRONMENT

It is difficult for the casual observer to recognize the cruise industry as being environmentally friendly. The ships appear to consume copious quantities of fuel in order to ensure their guests are entertained continuously in comfortable air-conditioned settings. People on cruise ships appear to overeat, to over indulge and to generate waste. The ships travel to destinations where there are concerns about the sensitivity of the marine and land environments [20]. How in these circumstances can a cruise ship be carbon neutral or even attempt to be environmentally friendly?

According to the independent international shipping association known as BIMCO [21], ships that wish to include Alaska, the Pacific coast of North America and Scandinavia in their itineraries must use low-sulphur fuel. Cruise companies recognize that their passengers ask questions about the ethical stance the company

Figure 3.3 *Glass recycling machine*

takes on pollution and the environment so it makes logical business sense to adopt sound practices to ensure all that can be done in the name of environmentalism is being done. Large ships also include in their manifest a dedicated environmental officer aboard to make sure that regulations are being complied with and standards are maintained.

Several types of innovations have been introduced, including the reduction of exhaust emissions by using heat exchangers and exhaust scrubbers, as well as using shore-based power sources (known as cold ironing) in port so as to prevent harmful emissions being generated when the ship is tied up. In addition, MAR-POL regulations on dumping at sea means ship operators plan to recycle much of the waste that is produced and sewage systems aim to make sure pollution is prevented.

FINANCIAL RESPONSIBILITY

The US Federal Maritime Commission requires that operators of passenger vessels carrying 50 or more passengers from a US port must be financially secure and capable of reimbursing their customers if the cruise is cancelled. The Commission also requires proof of ability to pay claims arising out of passenger injuries or

Figure 3.4 *Can compactor*

death, for which the ship operator may bear some liability. The Commission does not have the legal authority to automatically secure these financial settlements for individual consumers.

If a cruise is cancelled, or there is an injury incurred during the cruise, the consumer will have to initiate action on his or her own behalf against the cruise line. Insurance for shipping is provided by many of the world's largest financial and insurance companies, such as Lloyd's of London, Lloyd's of America and the American Institute of Marine Underwriters.

MARITIME ORGANIZATIONS

It is important to be familiar with the plethora of organizations involved in the maritime and cruise industries. A number of these organizations – some of which have been previously mentioned – are listed and described below:

IMO (International Maritime Organization)

The International Maritime Organization (formerly known as the Inter-governmental Maritime Consultative Organization) was established in 1948 as an agency of the United Nations to set international maritime policy and regulate the shipping industry. In this capacity it provides a focus and central service developing a cross-governmental, consensual approach for safety and practices at sea. The IMO is the glue that binds together the treaties and conventions for international shipping, with responsibility for ensuring compliance for the implementation of regulations, although the principal responsibility for enforcing the regulations rests with the flag states or the country in which a ship is registered. 'Port state control' supplements flag state enforcement by allowing officials from any country that a ship may visit to inspect foreign flag ships in order to ensure that they comply with international requirements.

The IMO's slogan, 'Safe, secure and efficient shipping on clean oceans', encapsulates the agency's mission statement and yet, despite this seemingly mammoth task, the organization remains relatively lean in terms of scale because of the requirement for states or individual countries to undertake enforcement. The US Coast Guard represents the United States in this international agency. The IMO has been instrumental in the development and adoption of several important treaties or conventions, including the previously mentioned SOLAS (Safety of Life At Sea) agreement, the International Convention for the Prevention of Pollution from Ships (known as the MARPOL agreement) and the International Safety Management Code (ISM), which is part of SOLAS and the Standards for Training, Certification and Watch-keeping (STCW).

Classification societies

Classification societies are, in the main, organizations whose primary function is to inspect ships at regular intervals to ensure they are seaworthy and regularly maintained in keeping with classification societies' rules. Classification societies also inspect cruise ships for compliance with international safety regulations, including SOLAS, STCW and MARPOL. Major classification societies include the American Bureau of Shipping, based in the US; Lloyd's Register of Shipping, in the UK; Det Norske Veritas, in Norway; Bureau Veritas, in France; and the Registro Italiano Navale Group, in Italy.

Cruise Lines International Association (CLIA)
The CLIA is a marketing and promotion organization that represents 23 member cruise lines and approximately 19,000 North American travel agencies. The CLIA was formed in 1975 with the specific remit to promote the benefits of cruising. In undertaking this task the CLIA also undertakes training in line with its mission: 'To educate travel agents and to promote the value, desirability and affordability of the cruise vacation experience.' The CLIA joined with the International Council of Cruise Lines to establish the Cruise Line Coalition in 2001 to act as an information source for the industry.

Florida-Caribbean Cruise Association (FCCA)

This trade organization was inaugurated in 1972 to provide a forum for 13 cruise brands to meet and debate operational issues concerning its members. In this sense, the FCCA can highlight legislation, tourism development, port safety, security and other emerging issues so as to create solutions via cooperation and partnership. The FCCA also undertakes targeted training, such as customer service programmes for taxi drivers in ports as well as commissioning research that looks at the impacts of cruising. The association has also created a charitable foundation to help people in need.

North West Cruise Ship Association (NWCA)

The North West Cruise Ship Association is a non-profit body that represents nine cruise lines operating in Hawaii, Canada, Alaska and the Pacific Northwest. The association was established in 1986, initially to focus on security concerns, although it later developed a broader role, addressing government relations in respect of legal and regulatory issues. In addition, the association seeks to maintain positive links with the local communities in the respective cruising areas so as to tackle, for example, environmental protection, economic developments and other industry-connected concerns.

SUMMARY AND CONCLUSIONS

This chapter has examined a range of maritime issues that concern cruise ships and shipping in general. It has highlighted the importance of the IMO and commented on the range of regulations that are in place to help make shipping safe for crew and passengers. A range of representative groups supports the industry. Some, like the FCCA and the NWCA, have a geographical focus and represent cruise company interests in specific areas. Others, such as the CLIA, have a role in supporting with marketing. The CLIA also takes on a more political stance in working with governments and the IMO.

REFERENCES

1. Dickinson, R. and A. Vladimir, *Selling the Sea*. 1997, New York: Wiley.
2. Farthing, B. and M. Brownrigg, *International Shipping*. 3rd ed. 1997, London: LLP Ltd.
3. Equasis, 'World Merchant Fleet in 2009' [accessed December 2009]; Available from: http://www.equasis.org/EquasisWeb/public/HomePage
4. Lloyd's Register, *World Fleet Statistics 2003*. 2004, London: Lloyds.
5. Ward, D., *Complete Guide to Cruising & Cruise Ships 2004*. 2005, London: Berlitz. p. 1.
6. Cruise Industry News, 'The Cruise Industry in 2010', *Cruise Industry News Quarterly Magazine*, 2010.
7. ISL, *Executive Summary – SSMR market analysis* no.6. 2003 [22 March 2005]; Available from: http://www.isl.org/products_services/publications/samples/cruise.shtml.en.

8. O'Sullivan, O., 'Refits Versus New Builds', *World Cruise Network 2010* [accessed October 2011]; Available from: http://www.worldcruise-network.com/features/feature78403/.

9. Panaydes, P.M., *Professional Ship Management*. 2001, Aldershot: Ashgate.

10. Louis Cruises, 'Charters'. 2005 [accessed March 2005]; Available from: http://www.louiscruises.com/.

11. V.Ships, 'Leisure Management'. 2005 [accessed March 2005]; Available from: http://www.vships.com/.

12. Cruises, 'Hapag Lloyd Hanseatic Cruise Ship Overview'. 2005 [accessed March 2005]; Available from: http://cruises.about.com/od/cruiseshipprofiles/ss/hanseatic.htm.

13. Guilfoyle, D., *Shipping Interdiction and the Law of the Sea*. 2009, New York: Cambridge University Press.

14. CLIA, 'Background – Maritime Industry', 2011 [accessed March 2011]; Available from: http://www2.cruising.org/industry/maritime_industry.cfm.

15. IMO, MARPOL. 2011 [accessed April 2011]; Available from: http://www.imo.org/about/conventions/listofconventions/pages/international-convention-for-the-prevention-of-pollution-from-ships-%28marpol%29.aspx.

16. CLIA, 'Waste Management'. 2006 [accessed April 2011]; Available from: http://www2.cruising.org/industry/PDF/CLIAWasteManagementAttachment.pdf.

17. Roemer, M., *Cruising at Risk: Crises Management and Prevention in Cruise Industry*. 2008, GRIN Verlag.

18. US Coast Guard, 'Cruise Ship National Center of Expertise'. 2011 [accessed April 2011]; Available from: http://www.uscg.mil/hq/cg5/csncoe/.

19. World Cruise Network, 'Hidden Depths of SOLAS'. 2010 [accessed April 2011]; Available from: http://www.worldcruise-network.com/features/feature95151/.

20. Copeland, C. and L.o.C.C.R. Service, *Cruise Ship Pollution: Background, laws and regulations, and key issues*. 2007: Congressional Research Service, Library of Congress.

21. BIMCO, 'The Green Cruise Ship'. 2009 [accessed December 2009]; Available from: https://www.bimco.org.

4 Cruise geography

This chapter reflects on the part played by the destination in the cruise experience. In doing this the reader will consider geography from a cruise industry perspective, evaluate the primary and secondary cruise sectors, be able to identify major cruise ports in each sector and consider the attractions and features that are important in defining a cruise port and destination.

DESTINATIONS

In a practical sense, cruise companies regard the world as a series of sectors that meet various market needs. For the largest brands, this creates opportunities to configure operations to take account of:

- Seasonality, weather patterns and optimum conditions for cruising
- Sales and marketing
- Supply and servicing of ships

This chapter considers the influence and effect of geography on the cruise industry. To start with, it is impossible to consider the *locus* of cruising without reflecting on the conditions that arise from the prevailing climate. Passenger comfort and safety are directly impacted upon if a cruise ship sails in a particular part of an ocean or sea at a particular time of year. This also holds true for destinations visited and shore activities that may be offered.

As much as possible, cruise ships tend to avoid parts of the world where, because of geography, climate and seasonal variations, sea conditions occur that can create potential discomfort for customers [1]. There are many stories told of severe weather conditions in specific locations – for example, the Bay of Biscay, the Cape of Good Hope, the Bay of Bengal and the North Atlantic have reputations for providing extremes of weather for seafarers or navigators. Yet knowledge of

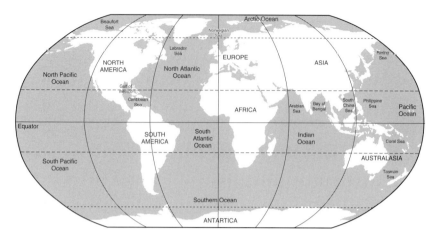

Figure 4.1 *The world: land masses and oceans*

weather patterns and records of tidal variations permit cruise operators to predict where ships can voyage with a high degree of safety to enable virtually all the world's oceans and seas to be traversed and all coastal ports to be visited.

Weather patterns are complex. They are influenced by many factors including: the Sun's rays, the Earth's rotational axis, which tilts 23.5 degrees from the perpendicular, thus creating seasonal variations (i.e. the four seasons), the land masses and oceans, currents and the moon's gravitational pull (creating tidal variations). The northern and southern hemispheres experience seasons at opposite times of the year, reflecting the position of the Earth as it orbits the Sun [2].

TROPICAL ZONES

The point where the Earth is closest to the Sun is known as the equator. The Tropics of Cancer and Capricorn are lines of latitude that run parallel to the equator at 25 degrees north and 25 degrees south respectively. This identifies the region that is known as the 'tropics'. Points above and below the equator can be affected by bad weather and storms although the equator can be calm. The weather effect when the wind and sea are calm is known as the 'doldrums'.

Tropical cyclones are triggered by latent heat, water condensation and cloud formations. These can be monitored and, to a degree, patterns can be predicted so that shipping is forewarned and can take appropriate measures. The majority of contemporary cruise ships, with the odd exception, are designed for cruising in relatively benign conditions and, therefore, itineraries are influenced in part by weather patterns. Cyclones can create winds in excess of 120 kilometres (75 miles) per hour. The specific names of tropical cyclones depend on the area [2]:

- Atlantic and East Pacific – hurricanes
- West Pacific – typhoons
- Philippines – baguios
- Australia – willy-willys
- Indian Ocean – cyclones.

TOURISTS AND CLIMATE

Cruise ships tend to focus on warm temperate climates and calm seas, although continuous growth in sectors such as Alaska, as well as growing interest in northerly sectors such as Iceland, Scandinavia and the Baltic ports and the emergence of Antarctica and the southernmost areas of South America, are testament to the diversity in choice that is now available for cruise tourists.

Invariably, tourists make judgements about visiting parts of the world by taking into account a broad spectrum of personal circumstances and by accessing new information or relying on prior learning about the place to be visited [3, 4]. These decisions are highly personalized and are likely to include: a desire to learn new things; a drive to satisfy personal motives; the need to address latent curiosity; the opportunity to relax and escape routines; and the requirement to experience a different climate to that which is the norm [4].

This need to identify an appropriate and desirable environment while on vacation raises questions about how tourists regard climate from a comfort perspective. According to Burton [1], it is possible to identify comfort zones for various tourist activities that take into account factors such as temperature, humidity, wind, rainfall, cloud and sunshine. Based on an analysis of world climates, Burton presents a five-stage model to describe tourists' clothing regimes in relation to climate type (see Table 4.1).

Table 4.1 Temperature and clothing zones

Latitude	Temperature zone and climatic type	Corresponding clothing zone
Equator	Hot – equatorial, tropical and desert	Minimum clothing and light protective clothing
	Warm temperate – Mediterranean and eastern margin climates	One layer clothing
	Cool temperate – marginal and continental types	Two layer clothing
	Cold climates	Three layer clothing
Poles	Arctic and polar climates	Maximum clothing

PRIMARY CRUISING REGIONS

The Caribbean

The Caribbean currently attracts more passengers than any other region in the world. According to Wild and Dearing [5], recent growth patterns in the Caribbean emerged because North American passengers were seeking cruises that offered certain characteristics and one of these was the need to remain close to home. The three years since 9/11 consolidated the Caribbean's position as the number one cruise region and while growth may have slowed since then, the position still reflects an upward trend.

Calculating passenger figures that impact on cruise destinations can be undertaken in a number of ways. For example: Potential Passenger Throughput (PPT) takes the number of cruises and multiplies it by the total number of passengers for each vessel to create a quick reference number; Passenger per Night (PN) calculates total numbers of nights spent in individual ports. As would be expected in terms of scale of operations, vessels operated by brands owned by Carnival Corporation, the world's largest cruise company, dominate in this region, with 54% of all passenger nights (PN) compared to Royal Caribbean (33%) [5]. According to the data produced by Wild and Dearing, the Western Caribbean was expected to attract larger numbers of passengers (estimated 2.75 million) during 2005 than the Eastern and Southern Caribbean (estimated 2.2 million).

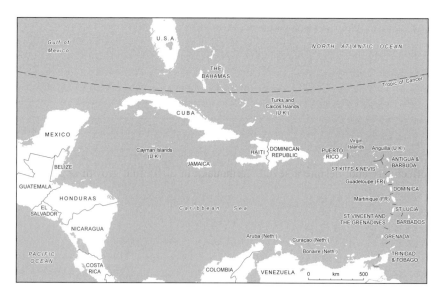

Figure 4.2 *The Caribbean*

Burton [1] describes the Caribbean as a '4000 km arc which sweeps eastward from Florida to the Venezuelan coast'. The islands are diverse in terms of physical character and climate, accessibility, historical background and political setting. According to industry sources, and despite the obvious attractions of warm crystal-blue seas and palm tree-ringed beaches for relaxation and swimming, another primary activity for many customers visiting some Caribbean islands is shopping. Ports such as Nassau have become known as duty free paradises.

The layout of the islands presents opportunities for cruise companies to create a variety of itineraries incorporating a number of contrasting islands. These can be scheduled to commence with embarkation at a port in Florida, such as Fort Lauderdale, Port Everglades, Port Canaveral or Miami. Alternatively, vessels can create an itinerary originating in the Caribbean, for example, from Puerto Rico or Barbados. In recent years, southern and eastern Caribbean islands have fared less well than western Caribbean islands, as itineraries are switched towards shorter four-day or seven-day excursions rather than two-week tours [1]. Competition for the tourist dollar has led to a situation where port fees for many Caribbean islands are relatively inexpensive – US$4–6 per customer. In this way, a vessel such as the *Diamond Princess*, with 2,500 customers, would pay around US$125,000 in port fees. In addition, cruise companies have ownership of islands (Royal Caribbean has ownership of Coco Cay, Holland America owns Half Moon Cay, Disney Cruises owns Castaway Cay, Norwegian Cruise Line owns Great Stirrup Cay, Princess Cruises has an island called Princess Cay) with concomitant benefits accrued in terms of both generating revenue from shore-based activities and controlling costs associated with ports of call. A cay (or key, as it is known in the US – as in Key West) is a low island or reef of sand or coral.

Some islands are less tranquil or accommodating to tourists than may be expected. Cuba, the largest of the Caribbean islands, located 145 kilometres south of Florida, has a history of being opposed to the politics of the USA and this has inhibited US tourist trade growth. Another recent example is political instability in Haiti [6], which had a detrimental effect on the island's economy and impacted negatively on cruise visits. However, in general, the situation on the majority of these 'island paradises' is calm and settled. Indeed, in Haiti, the cruise business was growing effectively and, despite a severe earthquake in 2010, that growth appears to be continuing [7].

Major island destinations

The Cruise Line Industry Association [8] describes three specific parts to the Caribbean – the Eastern Caribbean and the Bahamas, the Western Caribbean and the Southern Caribbean; selected destinations from these areas are described in this section. The Caribbean Tourism Organization [9] is a trade organization that represents many of the Caribbean islands: Anguilla, Antigua and Barbuda, Aruba, the Bahamas, Barbados, Belize, Bermuda, Bonaire, British Virgin Islands, Cayman Islands, Cuba, Curaçao, Dominica, Grenada, Guadeloupe/St Barts/St Martin, Guyana, Haiti, Jamaica, Martinique, Montserrat, Puerto Rico, St Eustatius, St Kitts and Nevis, St Lucia, St Maarten, St Vincent and the Grenadines, Suriname, Trinidad and Tobago, Turks and Caicos Islands, United States Virgin Islands. Some of these islands attract large numbers of cruise passengers. For example, Aruba, with a population of 107,000 [10], attracted 606,970 passengers in 2009 [11].

Eastern Caribbean/the Bahamas

The islands of the Bahamas are closely located to the Caribbean but are not part of this region [12]. However, the Bahamas' close proximity to both the South Florida Coast and the Eastern Caribbean, create a natural itinerary option for cruise planners, which means the islands are frequently considered an important element by association to the Caribbean. The combined Bahamas and Eastern Caribbean area is relatively accessible from US ports such as Miami, Port Everglades and Port Canaveral as well as San Juan in Puerto Rico, although because of the cumulative distance involved for this type of itinerary, the duration for some cruises is likely to be in excess of seven days. There is a diversity of ports in the region, including the aforementioned cays and islands that are privately owned by cruise companies [9]. A selection of ports is described below, followed by a table that presents information about population, language and currency. For this and subsequent tables relating to destinations covered in this chapter, populations are approximate and relate to the port or, in the case of an island, the island community.

The Bahamas
Nassau and Freeport on New Providence Island are the primary ports of call in the Bahamas with, for 2004, the former appearing as the sixth most visited port in the world and the latter the 16th [13]. The name Bahamas is a derivation of the Spanish *baha mar*, or 'shallow sea', and there are around 700 islands in this popular, self-styled, sun, sea and sand, paradise archipelago. The beaches are held in high regard but the islands offer a diversity of attractions to supplement the physical appeal of the miles of white or pink sand. These islands claim the world's third largest barrier reef, and a diversity of sea life, including whales and dolphins. The Bahamas have a population of 343,000 (70% reside on New Providence Island) and rely on tourism for 50% of employment and Gross Domestic Product (GDP), or the total amount of revenue generated from sales of products and services. The islands have historical ties with the UK – as evidenced today by the fact that cars still drive on the left, despite many of them being manufactured as left-hand drive [14]. Shopping, golf and gambling are all available for tourists to the islands [15]. The World Travel Awards are presented at an annual event, and are voted for by

travel agents from 200 different countries; the Bahamas were named the Caribbean's best cruise destination in 2004 and 2010 [16].

Puerto Rico
San Juan in Puerto Rico is both a port of call or destination and a base port. This dual role means the island is the seventh most visited destination in the world, according to Wild and Dearing [13]. Puerto Rico is described as an 'Island of Enchantment', with a broad range of multifaceted attractions that range from the archetypal tropical beach scene to the diversity of natural attractions while also encompassing a rich cultural heritage. Islanders reflect the scope of the island's mixed cultural origins, which has included African, Spanish, Indian and US influences. The population of Puerto Rico is just under 4 million. The currency is US dollars and both English and Spanish are spoken [17].

St Thomas, US Virgin Islands
St Thomas and the island's port, Charlotte Amalie, are feted as being popular for those who like shopping. Over the years, the island has become a leading tax-free haven and this, combined with the natural allure of the scenery and the island attractions, creates a powerful draw [18] – the island is the eighth most frequented port in the world [13]. Cruise visitors to the islands have easy access to a shopping mall next to the pier and can also enjoy water sports such as snorkelling and scuba diving expeditions as well as land-based activities [15]. (The word 'scuba' is an acronym of the phrase 'self-contained underwater breathing apparatus'.)

St Maarten
Philipsburg is St Maarten's port. With one half Dutch and the other French (referred to as St Martin) the island has two national identities and two personalities. The half of the island where most cruise ships call – at Philipsburg – is Dutch. The island ranks ninth in the world of most visited ports in Wild and Dearing's [13] survey. Visitors enjoy beach activities, water-based excursions and cultural experiences when visiting this island [12]

Antigua
This island is the 18th most visited in the world by cruise passengers [13]. Antigua is a verdant tropical island that boasts as an historical attraction, Nelson's Dockyard, the eighteenth-century base for the British naval fleet [12]. The island is popular for snorkelling and scuba diving and is said to be one of the sunniest of the East Caribbean islands [19]. English is the first language for the island.

Other Eastern Caribbean ports that are popular cruise destinations are Tortola, Dominica, St Lucia, Martinique and St Kitts.

Table 4.2 *East Caribbean destination facts*

Destination	Country	Region	Currency	Language	Population
Nassau	Bahamas	East Caribbean	Bahamian dollar	English	343,000
San Juan	Puerto Rico	East Caribbean	US dollar	English/ Spanish	3,749,000
St Thomas	US Virgin Islands	East Caribbean	US dollar	English	109,000
St Maarten or St Martin	Dutch/ French	East Caribbean	Euro	Dutch/English and French /English	73,000
Antigua	Antigua	East Caribbean	East Caribbean Dollar	English	89,000

Western Caribbean

The Western Caribbean is more convenient for cruises that depart from Florida or ports such as Houston, Galveston or New Orleans [12]. In addition, the itineraries for this region can be supplemented with Mexican destinations such as Cozumel (stated as being the third most visited port in the world [13]), Cancun, Veracruz and/or Tampico to add variety and distinctiveness to the cruise programme.

Key West

This is the southernmost point of land in the United States. Known as the Conch Republic, Key West is famous for being the favourite haunt of artists, celebrities, presidents and literary heroes such as Ernest Hemingway [20]. Yet the Florida Keys and Key West only became a fixture for visitors after an economic and social revival in the 1980s. The destination is cited as the tenth most visited port in the world [13]. The Keys' literary reference points, such as the homes of Ernest Hemingway and Tennessee Williams, and former president Harry Truman's Little White House, feature on the list of attractions to visit. Passengers may also partake in shopping or even go deep-sea fishing in the Gulf of Mexico.

Cayman Islands

George Town in Grand Cayman is the main port of call for this, the fifth most visited port in the world [13]. The islands are famous for the opportunity to swim with stingrays, although there are many other attractions and experiences available, including the spectacular diving available around the coral reefs, which are generously endowed with marine life. Grand Cayman Island is also home to the world's first sea turtle farm, the spectacular limestone and coral formations known as Hell, and the popular Seven Mile Beach [21].

Jamaica

This is the Caribbean's second largest island. Ocho Rios, Jamaica's port, comes 15th in Wild and Dearing's survey [13] and was voted best cruise port in the Caribbean by the World Tourism Awards in 2011 [16]. Jamaica has an array of natural wonders such Dunn's River Falls, and offers cruise passengers the opportunity to climb the waterfall, take an expedition to the Blue Mountains, an undersea tour or visits to caves [22]. The wide range of options reflects the natural and cultural diversity of this island. Music, epitomized by the late Bob Marley, plays a big part in Jamaican culture; reggae originated here, and it is still a focal point of the island's rich historical heritage.

Southern Caribbean

This part of the Caribbean tends to be seen as more exotic because the islands are located close to Venezuela in South America and the itinerary usually means utilizing a home port from within the area, such as Barbados and Aruba. Many cruises to the Southern Caribbean originate from San Juan in the Eastern Caribbean and include a mixed itinerary of ports from both the Eastern and Southern Caribbean. This region enjoys the Caribbean's sunniest climate.

Barbados

Bridgetown is the port for and the capital of Barbados, an island that lies at the eastern edge of the Southern Caribbean. This island has a softly rolling landscape in contrast to some of the other volcanic islands that have been considered so far. Barbados is a former British colony (it gained full independence in 1966) and maintains a strong British connection today [23]. Attractions include rum factory tours, tours of the island, as well as the many beautiful beaches and water sports.

Table 4.3 *West Caribbean destination facts*

Destination	Country	Region	Currency	Language	Population
Key West	US	Western Caribbean	US dollar	English	24,800
Cayman Islands	Cayman Islands	Western Caribbean	Caymanian dollar	English	56,000
Kingston	Jamaica	Western Caribbean	Jamaican dollar	English	2,749,900

Curaçao

Willemstad is this island's capital. Curaçao is the main island of the group of islands known as the Dutch Antilles. Curaçao has an unmistakable Dutch heritage, reflected in the style of architecture found in its capital [24]. The island has a host of activities for cruise passengers who may wish to visit its shops, underwater park and Seaquarium or ostrich farm.

There are many other islands in this area, including Bonaire, Trinidad and Tobago. Itineraries may also include Venezuelan ports such as La Guaira (for Caracas or Venezuela) and Cartagena.

Europe and the Mediterranean

While the Caribbean has benefitted from the changing pattern of cruising in the aftermath of 9/11, Europe and the Mediterranean are poised to develop exponentially as tensions concerning travel begin to ease [25]. Barcelona in Spain, Palma in Majorca and Venice in Italy lead the rankings list of most visited ports in Southern Europe, reflecting the trend for itineraries to be located more towards the west of the Mediterranean or the Adriatic [26]. Southampton in the UK has emerged as a leading port for the Northern region, being appropriately located to service a diversity of itineraries and, according to Wild and Dearing [26], the types of facilities to cater effectively for passenger and cruise ship needs.

Northern Europe

This cruise region benefits from a number of advantages. For US passengers it offers familiarity in terms of the types of culture, the geography of the countries and attractions offered by the major cities [12]. For European passengers it provides an easy departure from home ports. The countries and ports are, in the main, highly sophisticated [27] and able to cope with the complex demands that accompany the arrival of the largest of cruise ships. A number of cruise brands have traditional roots in this region: e.g. Cunard Line and P&O Cruises in Southampton. Indeed, historically the UK is the home of cruising.

Table 4.4 *Southern Caribbean destination facts*

Destination	Country	Region	Currency	Language	Population
Bridgetown	Barbados	Southern Caribbean	Barbadian dollar	English	273,000
Curaçao	Dutch Antilles/ Holland	Southern Caribbean	Netherlands Antillean guilder	Dutch/ English	192,000

Figure 4.3 *Western Caribbean destination facts*

The season for cruising in Northern Europe is relatively short but the ports are popular, meaning that traffic can be concentrated for this short season [26]. Wild and Dearing [26] note that the majority of passengers for this type of vacation are likely to be firstly, North American passengers, secondly UK passengers and thirdly German passengers. When marketing cruises in Northern Europe, cruise companies can focus on the British Isles, the Baltic, Iceland, the Arctic and the North Cape, the Norwegian fjords and Western Europe [25, p. 17]. The following represents key destinations from this area.

Southampton
Southampton is a city with a long maritime heritage. This heritage means that the city has experienced both growth and decline because of the historical develop-ment associated with shipping in general and the cruise industry in particular. It is currently experiencing growth. The port is well located for London and it has excellent transport links and the infrastructure to service cruise ships' needs. The port provides a launch pad for ships to travel to, or across, the Atlantic, to the

Mediterranean and/or the ports of Northern Europe and, because of this, is listed by Wild and Dearing [26] as the first ranked port in Northern Europe.

Helsinki

Helsinki is the capital of Finland. From a cruise perspective, the city is located in a strategically convenient part of the Baltic for itinerary planning. It is a bustling port with as many as 40 ferry departures to other ports daily in the height of season. The port is also attractive and close to the city centre [27]. Finland is different to other Scandinavian countries for two reasons. Firstly, it has a language that is closer to Russian and Estonian than to those of its Scandinavian neighbours. Secondly, it shares a border with Russia, which has led to a distinct history and culture. With two-thirds of the country covered by forest and 10% made up of inland lakes, the Finnish Tourist Board unsurprisingly emphasizes nature and the environment [28]. The port is a secondary base port as well as a port of call or destination.

Copenhagen

Copenhagen is the capital of Denmark, the smallest Scandinavian country, and, after Helsinki, the third most visited port in Northern Europe [26]. Copenhagen is a major cultural destination and, with its nightclubs and bars, has a reputation for being lively [28]. It is the home of the Carlsberg Brewery, which is both a tourist attraction and working production centre, and the world famous Tivoli Gardens – Europe's oldest amusement centre. Much is made of the figure of the Little Mermaid, a statue representing a character from Hans Christian Andersen's stories, which can be found in the harbour area. The city has been named Europe's leading cruise ship destination most years between 2004 and 2011 by the World Travel Awards [16].

St Petersburg

St Petersburg in Russia saw major growth in cruise passenger numbers in the first part of the twenty-first century, rising from 263 calls in 2003 to 1,500 in 2010. The city is often said to be the most beautiful in Russia [28]. The attractions it offers are both historical and cultural, including the Hermitage art gallery, a former Tsar's palace; the Mariinsky Theatre, home to the world-renowned Kirov Ballet; the former summer residences of the Tsars, located on the outskirts of the city; and St Isaac's Cathedral, the largest church in Russia [27].

Tallinn

Tallinn is a United Nations Educational, Scientific and Cultural Organization (UNESCO) heritage site. It is the capital of Estonia and boasts what is said to be one of the few examples of an old city that has been kept intact. Tallinn has a history as a port that can be traced back to the tenth century, although evidence suggests there was a settlement on the site some 3,500 years ago. The city offers a number of attractions, including parks, heritage buildings, palaces and museums [27]. Tallinn is the fifth most visited port in Northern Europe [26].

Stockholm
Stockhom is the sixth leading North European port [26]. It is the capital of Sweden, a country that has the largest unspoiled wilderness in Europe [28]. The city of Stockholm is located on a number of interconnected islands at one end of Lake Mälaren. It attracts visitors with its narrow pedestrian streets, good shopping and restaurants, as well as museums, royal palaces and heritage attractions.

The Northern European region may have a short season because of the inclement weather patterns that are endemic during late autumn through to early spring but the ports are popular and tourist-friendly. Whether a cruise is seeking the 'land of the midnight sun' while cruising past the fjords of Norway, or the Northern Lights of Aberdeen on the northeast coast of Scotland, passengers are left with many opportunities for memorable moments.

Southern Europe

In cruising terms this region encompasses the Eastern and Western Mediterranean and provides access to a range of countries from a large number of ports. The Mediterranean climate is conducive for vacations, with its long, dry, sunny summers [28]. The region offers great diversity, from historical attractions to sophisticated cities via beach playgrounds, and all within relatively accessible cruising parameters [12]. Distances between ports and attractions mean that cruise planners can schedule itineraries in this region to take advantage of best timing and economical fuel consumption, as well as high-calibre supply networks.

Table 4.5 *Northern Europe destination facts*

Destination	Country	Region	Currency	Language	Population
Southampton	United Kingdom	Northern Europe	Pound sterling	English	234,600
Helsinki	Finland	Northern Europe	Markka	Finish	1,320,220
Copenhagen	Denmark	Northern Europe	Danish kroner	Danish	1,167,569
St Petersburg	Russia	Northern Europe	Ruble	Russian	4,750,000
Tallinn	Estonia	Northern Europe	Krooni	Estonian	412,341
Stockholm	Sweden	Northern Europe	Swedish kroner	Swedish	2,000,000

The Mediterranean is popular with many cruise passengers. US passengers can take advantage of a pseudo 'grand tour' approach to visiting Europe, which facilitates border crossings, minimizes language problems and maintains a desired level of comfort. One drawback for US passengers can be the need to fly long distances to board the ship, although passengers are served by a multiplicity of arrival airports providing easy access to base ports. Another issue some passengers identify relates to political unrest in countries and regions close to the Mediterranean. Passenger concerns about destinations are easily remedied by changing itineraries – a factor that has helped to generate the growth in popularity for cruising.

UK and European passengers have relatively easy access to the Mediterranean. P&O Cruises, Cunard, Saga Cruises and other brands operate a variety of cruises that depart from the UK, while cruises that depart from the Mediterranean are usually just a one- or two-hour flight from local airports. The season in the Mediterranean is being reappraised to stretch the shoulder periods (the months between high and low seasons) so as to lengthen the duration.

Barcelona
Barcelona, in the West of the Mediterranean, is a Spanish city that has become the most visited port in the region [26]. Although this is primarily because of its status as a major base port, the city offers a broad range of attractions as a destination in its own right. The city is peppered with the characterful architecture of Antonio Gaudí, and many tours visit his unfinished cathedral, the Sagrada Família. The Ramblas provides an arterial walkway through the centre of the city past the Barrio Gótico, the medieval core of old Barcelona [28]. The port offers a contemporary setting for passengers to embark and disembark, with modern terminal facilities and a network of services for passengers and cruise ships [29].

Palma, Majorca
Palma is also a Spanish city in the Western Mediterranean. The island of Majorca is one of the Balearic Islands, located off the southern coast of Spain. The other principle Balearic Islands are Ibiza and Minorca and they are also ports of call for cruise ships. Majorca is well known as a holiday destination and in recent years the port has become a popular fly, cruise and stay product [29]. The island provides a diversity of resorts and accommodation for this type of package. Palma, its capital, is an attractive city that has a typical Spanish atmosphere, an impressive cathedral, a variety of shopping options, and is in close proximity to the beaches and attractions.

Venice
Venice is actually in the Adriatic Sea rather than the Mediterranean. This northern Italian city has had a long and turbulent history and seems to be continuously

struggling against the ravages of nature and time. Yet, in its unique island setting, with its canals and car-free environment, Venice is special. It is almost incongruous to stand in St Mark's Square beside antiquities such as the Doge's Palace and the Basilica and observe the vast scale of a Grand class cruise ship drift past. As a sea-based trading centre, Venice has a maritime culture and has always lived from and on the sea. Its excellent terminal facilities provide a point of arrival and departure and easy access to this attractive destination [29]. Recently, proposals have been made to construct a tidal barrier to counter flooding problems caused by a combination of the city sinking into the lagoon (2 centimetres in 100 years) and rising tides [30].

Naples

Naples is located just to the south of Rome in Italy. The city is overshadowed by the ominous presence of Vesuvius. This slumbering giant of a volcano provides a most impressive backdrop to Naples and has also led to the creation of some of the area's attractions – the excavated Roman ruins of Pompeii and Herculaneum. The port gives easy access to the vast city, which can appear both lively and chaotic. This is the Mediterranean's fourth most visited port after Barcelona, Palma and Venice [26].

Civitavecchia

This unfamiliar Italian port provides the gateway into Rome. The city of Rome is a 'must see' destination for travellers to Europe. The city boasts a veritable cornucopia of classical ruins and architectural gems, including the Forum, the Coliseum, the Vatican and St Peter's Square, all within a modern metropolitan setting. Getting from Civitavecchia to Rome usually means a taxi or coach journey on a tour, although the town also has a train station, which provides regular and easy connection. The port is a large sprawling area and ships can be located quite far from the port gate. This usually calls for either the provision of a coach link or shuttle service or taxi service to the town centre.

Savona

Savona in Liguria, Northern Italy is the seventh most visited port in the Mediterranean area [26]. Costa Cruises, one of Carnival Corporation's cruise brands, has leased the modern terminal building in the city and makes good use of the facility to support its operations. Savona is in the heart of the Italian Riviera – a region of pretty seaside towns, spectacular coastlines and a wide range of attractions.

Livorno

Livorno is a large, bustling port that services the surrounding region of Tuscany in Italy by providing a focal point for cargo, ferry and cruise traffic. The cruise terminal is around half a kilometre from the city centre but for many passengers that may be irrelevant. This is because a key attraction is the city of Florence, which is around 88 kilometres (55 miles) from the port. The port also provides access to the beaches of the area, the famous wine region (Tuscany is well known for wines, including the eponymous Chianti) and many other attractive towns such as Pisa, Lucca, San Gimignano, Volterra and Siena.

Piraeus

Piraeus is a Greek port that may be seen by some as the Civitavecchia of Athens. Yet Piraeus has long been the gateway to Athens and as a result it has a lively and bustling character. The harbour area is large and accommodates a diversity of shipping traffic, including ferries and hydrofoils that connect Athens and the mainland to the many off-lying Greek islands, cruise ships and cargo vessels. The 2004 Olympics led to considerable investment in the infrastructure for Athens and surrounding areas, and the city itself is another key destination for cruise passengers. Athens has many treasures to attract visitors, including the Acropolis, the Parthenon and the Agora, or marketplace [28]. The city can be reached from Piraeus by taxi, public bus, tour coach and underground.

Dubrovnik

Dubrovnik is a major Croatian city and port. Despite suffering from shell damage during the Bosnian War in 1991 and 1992, this famous old walled city has been completely restored to enable visitors to experience its atmospheric street scenery. Dubrovnik offers a set of contrasting experiences to visitors: the city holds much of interest, with its ancient walled ramparts and fortresses, pedestrianized narrow lanes and historical town buildings, while the surrounding countryside and coastline provides a rich mix of geography, culture and leisure.

Santorini

Santorini is a Greek island in the Cycladic island group in the Aegean Sea, some 200 kilometres (130 miles) from Piraeus. The island offers spectacular scenery from the highest point across the sweeping curvature of the crescent-shaped landmass out to sea. The island was originally a volcano but when part of the volcano collapsed into the sea the unique terrain was formed. Some claim that Santorini was the setting for the lost city of Atlantis.

Rhodes

Rhodes, named after the phrase 'The Island of Roses', is an attractive Greek island that embodies a place where ancient history combines with the contemporary beach and sunshine holiday. Rhodes is also the name of the capital city, which today presents itself as a medieval old town with strong historical connections to the Knights of St John.

Mykonos

Mykonos is another Greek island in the Aegean Sea. This small island, with a population of just 15,000, transforms during the summer when 800,000 tourists migrate inwards to inhabit the hotels, guesthouses and other tourist accommodation. Mykonos's charm is the appearance of the main town, with its winding back streets and white painted buildings, combined with the beauty of the island scenery.

The Mediterranean possesses many destinations and ports that are both special and worth a visit. The cultural and historical diversity of this region attracts a broad range of cruise tourists for a variety of reasons. There are those who may have ancestral links to the area, others who seek enlightenment or learning that the region can facilitate, some who are attracted to the beauty of the scenery and countryside, and those who simply enjoy the climate. Invariably, there are many who seek a combination of some or all of these.

North America

North America provides a focus for a number of embarkation points for US customers to join cruises and overseas customers to join as fly-cruise passengers. In some cases these ports are home ports for US vessels and cruise companies. In addition, cruise itineraries can be constructed from US and Canadian ports to meet passengers' needs for cultural, geographical and geological attractions. Irrespective of the cruise ship's flag or country of registration, there are critical implications from

Table 4.6 *Southern Europe destination facts*

Destination	Country	Region	Currency	Language	Population
Barcelona	Spain	Western Mediterranean	Euro	Spanish	1,621,000
Palma	Majorca	Western Mediterranean	Euro	Spanish	404,681
Venice	Italy	Adriatic	Euro	Italian	60,300 (central)
Naples	Italy	Western Mediterranean	Euro	Italian	1,000,000
Civitavecchia	Italy	Western Mediterranean	Euro	Italian	50,100
Savona	Italy	Western Mediterranean	Euro	Italian	62,04100
Livorno	Italy	Western Mediterranean	Euro	Italian	148,143
Dubrovnik	Croatia	Adriatic	Kuna	Croatian	42,641
Piraeus	Greece	Eastern Mediterranean	Euro	Greek	175,697
Santorini	Greece	Eastern Mediterranean	Euro	Greek	13,600
Rhodes	Greece	Eastern Mediterranean	Euro	Greek	110,000
Mykonos	Greece	Eastern Mediterranean	Euro	Greek	9,000

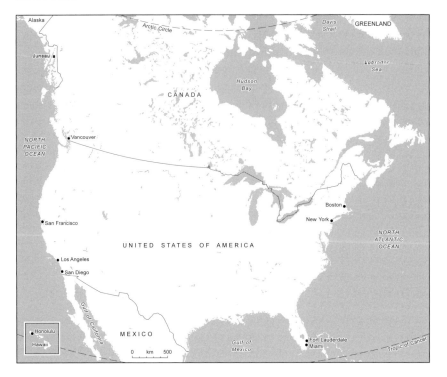

Figure 4.4 *United States of America*

a port health point of view for ships visiting US ports (this is examined in depth elsewhere) because of the actions of US port health officials.

North America is the largest cruise market and, as a result of concerns relating to security when on vacation abroad, the growth of numbers of cruise passengers joining from US ports has been considerable. This is emphasized by the fact that, of the top five cruise destinations in the world [13], Miami and Port Everglades appear as numbers one and two and Port Canaveral appears as number four. All three ports are in Florida. Cruise companies have benefitted in consolidating their operational support from within the US and creating economies of scale from supply networks for merged brands. In addition, cruise companies have developed what is known as horizontal and vertical integration from their operations. Horizontal integration is attained within the cruise industry from addressing a diversity of market segments by using different brands strategically. Vertical integration is achieved by creating opportunities to derive synergies and generate revenue from ownership of parallel operations such as shore excursions, travel agents, terminal operations and so on. The following list provides a brief outline of features relating to major North American ports.

Miami

The port of Miami on Dodge Island is the busiest home port in the US. As such it provides a home base to Carnival Cruise Lines, Norwegian Cruise Line, Royal Caribbean International, Oceania Cruises and Windjammer Barefoot Cruises. The port has state-of-the-art facilities and has eight terminals with designated berths that can be used flexibly depending on the type of shipping. In addition to hosting passengers who are embarking on cruises, the port also provides facilities for cruise passengers arriving at Miami as a destination port, with many options for excursions visitors, or for those arriving in the city a day or so before departure [31]. While cruises can depart to many places, the main target is the Caribbean.

Port Everglades

Port Everglades is located close to Fort Lauderdale Airport, making for a relatively easy transfer for fly-cruise passengers who are primarily cruising to the Caribbean. Port Everglades, the number two port in the world, hosts many cruise brands, including Carnival, Celebrity, Costa, Crystal, Cunard, Holland America Line, Mediterranean Shipping, Princess, Radisson Seven Seas, Royal Caribbean International, Seabourn and Silversea Cruises. The port provides a breadth of pre- and post-cruise tours in the area [32].

Port Canaveral

Port Canaveral has six cruise terminals, with another two in construction. The port is home to Carnival Cruise Lines, Disney Cruise Line, Royal Caribbean International, Holland America Line and Norwegian Cruise Line. The port is in what is known as Florida's Space Coast and visitors can take the opportunity to include tours to the Kennedy Space Centre or indulge in a range of other activities [33].

Juneau

The port of Juneau provides access to the seasonal (May to September) attractions of Alaska. Juneau was a former gold-rush town that became the region's state capital. As a cruise destination, the city provides opportunities for exploring the area's mining heritage, participating in outdoor pursuits, visiting glaciers, whale watching and even dog sledding. Trips to the glacier are available by helicopter. However, the city is somewhat more than a departure point for environmental pleasures, boasting an air of sophistication with its many art galleries and quality restaurants. Most of the major cruise brands that are marketed to US passengers sail to Juneau.

Ketchikan

Ketchikan is Alaska's southernmost city. Despite a high average rainfall there are many outdoor pursuits available, including kayaking, trekking and visits to national parks, lakes and forests. The city is a centre for native culture, with an array of museums and attractions available to visit.

Los Angeles

Los Angeles was the original home for the television series *The Love Boat*, which ran between 1977 and 1986. LA is famous for its many attractions, including Hollywood, Disneyland and Universal Studios. The World Cruise Centre at LA can manage a visit by the largest cruise ships [34].

Long Beach

Long Beach is fast approaching the scale of operation undertaken at neighbouring port Los Angeles [13]. Carnival Corporation has a terminal at this port and many cruise brands use Long Beach as a departure and home port. Itineraries from this port can include Baja California, the Mexican Riviera and Alaska.

Tampa

Tampa in Florida handles around a quarter of the number of passengers of Miami [13]. However, Tampa is expanding rapidly and attracts many of the leading cruise brands, including Carnival Cruise Lines, Holland America Line, Royal Caribbean International and Celebrity Cruises. The port has a well-developed 'tourist friendly' downtown waterfront area and many excursions are available to augment passenger experiences.

There are a host of additional ports that can be investigated within this large area, such as Vancouver, New Orleans, Galveston, Skagway, New York, New Jersey, Boston, San Francisco, Galveston, Philadelphia and Seattle. Competition is fierce and growth combined with recent trends means many ports are experiencing 'boom' conditions [35].

Table 4.7 North America destination facts

Destination	Country	Region	Currency	Language	Population
Miami, Florida	US	North America	US dollar	English	2,376,000
Port Everglades, Florida	US	North America	US dollar	English	10,688
Port Canaveral, Florida	US	North America	US dollar	English	9,038
Juneau	US	Alaska	US dollar	English	31,275
Ketchikan	US	Alaska	US dollar	English	14,500
Los Angeles, California	US	North America	US dollar	English	3,800,000
Long Beach, California	US	North America	US dollar	English	465,000
Tampa, Florida	US	North America	US dollar	English	337,000

Oceania and South Pacific

Oceania, including Australasia (Australia, New Zealand and Asia), and the Pacific represent a major expanse of sea and land. This cruise region offers the culturally vibrant and exotic ports of Asia, such as Indonesia, Malaysia, the Philippines, Singapore, Thailand, India, Vietnam, China, Hong Kong, Japan, Sri Lanka and the Maldives, to the tropical islands of the Pacific, such as Tahiti, Fiji, Papua New Guinea, New Caledonia, Vanuatu, Samoa, Tonga and the Cook Islands. Australia offers the attractions of her cities, such as Sydney, Melbourne and Freemantle, and the uniqueness of the coast, the coastal resorts and the countryside [36]. New Zealand is still basking in the post *Lord of the Rings* effect – publicity from these films has created heightened interest in the country, and this has been reflected in the increased number of ships visiting the ports of Auckland and Wellington.

This region is located in the southern hemisphere and as a result the seasons are a reversal of the pattern recognized in the northern hemisphere. So the summer cruising season for Australia and the South Pacific extends from November to April [12]. This vast geographical area is likely to experience continuous growth, with emerging economies such as China and India fuelling opportunities for new consumer markets and new, relatively accessible, itineraries.

Sydney
Sydney is probably the best-known city in Australia, although it is not the capital (Canberra). The city has a highly picturesque setting, with its harbour side scene, the Sydney Opera House and the Sydney Harbour Bridge, which were all blatantly and successfully exposed during the Millennium and New Year's celebrations to the world's media. It has two cruise terminals in the Overseas Passenger Terminal at Circular Quay and Wharf 8 Darling Harbour Passenger Terminal that are in close proximity to the city's attractions [37].

Auckland
Auckland, on New Zealand's North Island, is the country's largest city although, again, not its capital (Wellington). It has an idyllic setting, surrounded by islands and beautiful scenery. The city is both cosmopolitan and close to nature, with tours to volcanic regions, rainforests and beaches within easy reach. The city is heavily influenced by Polynesian and Maori culture and this is reflected in the people, the place names, the history and heritage of the area.

Fiji
Fiji is a group of 300 islands in the South Pacific with a population of approximately 893,000. The largest two, Viti Levu and Vanua Levu, hold 80% of the country's population. The islands represent many peoples' vision of what tropi-

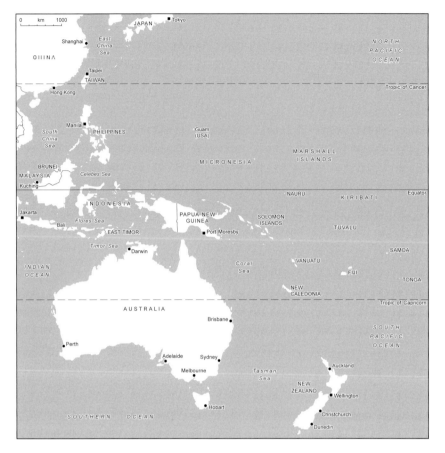

Figure 4.5 *Oceania and the South Pacific*

cal islands should be like. There are white beaches, coral reefs, clear seas with a myriad variety of fish and sea life, alongside rainforests and pseudo-native villages. Contemporary Fiji also offers attractive shopping facilities in the capital Suva, as well as modern hotels and a range of restaurants and nightlife to suit all types of tourists.

New Caledonia

French New Caledonia consists of one major island and several smaller ones, lying halfway between Australia and Fiji. The main island, with its capital Noumea, is the third largest in the Pacific after New Zealand and Papua New Guinea. The French cultural influence, coupled with that of the local Melanesian one (Melanesia is the name given to the island group that New Caledonia belongs to), creates an interesting backdrop for this island. A large lagoon surrounds the territory, and the landscape is a mix of mountains and rainforests alongside attractive sandy beaches.

Hong Kong

Hong Kong was formerly a British protectorate until it was returned to China in 1997. It retains a mix of eastern and western influences and the dynamism of a city on the cutting edge of a changing world. Hong Kong promotes itself as a shopper's paradise but in reality there is more to this energetic self-styled 'cruise capital' of Asia. To the Western tourist a visit to Hong Kong by cruise ship is a special opportunity to savour the unique blend of sights and sounds [38].

Singapore

The Republic of Singapore is one main island surrounded by 63 smaller islets. It is an economically successful country, which is proud of its contemporary feel, its diverse culture and its friendliness. Visitors can experience gardens, skyscrapers, the famous Raffles Hotel (home of the Singapore Sling), a strong sense of fashion and a technologically advanced community.

OTHER CRUISE DESTINATIONS

The cruise regions mentioned so far only scrape the surface when it comes to cruise itinerary options. Further research will undoubtedly reveal a plethora of destinations that are not mentioned here but which hold vital importance for cruise products as part of an itinerary, and links are provided at the end of this chapter to help the reader carry out such research.

Table 4.8 *Oceania and South Pacific destination facts*

Destination	Country	Region	Currency	Language	Population
Sydney	Australia	Australasia	Australian dollar	English	4,500,000
Auckland	New Zealand	Australasia	New Zealand dollar	English	458,336
Fiji	Fiji	South Pacific	Fijian dollar	English	837,000
New Caledonia	New Caledonia	South Pacific	Comptoirs Francais du Pacifique franc (XPF)	French	256,000
Hong Kong	China	SE Asia	Hong Kong dollar	Cantonese and English	7,000,000
Singapore	Singapore	SE Asia	Singapore dollar	Mandarin, English, Malay, Hokkien, Cantonese	5,183,700

Some additional destinations are worth highlighting and have until now been omitted for reasons of their geography. For instance, nothing has been said about most of Africa and the islands off that continent, such as the Canaries, Mauritius and the Seychelles. South America has also gone unmentioned, despite its obvious appeal and wealth of interest. A few ports from these areas are now highlighted to draw attention to the potential of these destinations.

Atlantic Islands

A number of primarily volcanic islands form part of cruise itineraries in the northern hemisphere. These are the Canary Islands, Madeira and the Azores. The Canary Islands of Tenerife, Lanzarote, Gran Canaria and Fuerteventura are governed by Spain, although they fall outside the jurisdiction of the European Union (EU), which means cruise ships with an EU registration can create an opportunity to sell duty-free alcohol. An EU-registered ship that has an itinerary made up of destinations or ports that are all EU member states would not be able to make such sales. Madeira and the Azores are Portuguese islands. The Canaries are relatively close to the coastline of North Africa and benefit from a temperate climate all year round. Madeira has a similar climate and is a popular cruise destination for passengers who enjoy the verdant scenery and charm of Funchal, the island's capital. The Azores offer a different type of destination. These islands have a quietness about them that reflects their remote setting. They were once a convenient stopping point for transatlantic crossings, but are now less frequented because the need for such a logistically convenient stopover is much reduced [28].

Rio de Janeiro

This major Brazilian city conjures up images of Sugarloaf Mountain, with its world famous statue of Christ, arms open, facing out over Rio's population. Copacabana beach and Ipanema beach are also well known as playgrounds for the locals and tourists alike. In the main the city is representative of Brazilian exuberance, as is experienced in the ever-present music, dancing and festivals.

Buenos Aires

Buenos Aires is the capital of Argentina. It is an optimistic and proud city with a much publicized past. The architecture is European, with influences from Britain, France, Italy and Spain representing the city's heritage. There are museums, theatres and art galleries demonstrating the cultural proclivities of the locals. Much is made of the links between the nation and the tango – a dance that reflects passion and drama [28].

The Galapagos Islands

The Galapagos Islands are Ecuadorian islands in the Pacific. Despite being almost barren, these small islands are popular cruise destinations because they present an ecosystem that is quite unique. The water is cold yet the islands lie on the equator, so the mix of land and sea creatures is diverse. Due to a lack of natural predators, the indigenous animals – including giant tortoises, marine iguanas, penguins and sea lions – have not developed a fear of humans. The area is extremely sensitive and cruise ships and passengers are managed with great care [28] to minimize environmental impacts.

Cape Town
Cape Town is the capital of South Africa. The city is located is another place where cold and warm collide. This time it is sea currents from the Atlantic and the Southern Ocean. Cape Town is a natural harbour that makes an excellent destination for cruise tourists, with the attractions of the city, the friendly locals, the dramatic geological scenery of Table Mountain, the famous regional vineyards and the beaches.

Seychelles
The idyllic Seychelles in the Indian Ocean can be described as truly beautiful islands. The clean sandy beaches, clear seas, palm trees and granite outcrops peppering the shores offer a relaxing port of call for cruise itineraries. The flora and fauna are unique on these islands because of the distance from the nearest landmass. Cruise tourists are most likely to visit Mahé, the main island.

Panama Canal
The Panama Canal is not really a destination in its own right, but it is vital as a link between the Atlantic and the Pacific and a fascinating experience for cruise passengers. Ships first used the canal in 1914 and from then it was operated by the US until 1999, when it was returned to the Panamanian government. It has three sets of locks to accomodate the different sea and water levels, and it takes, on average, around eight to ten hours for vessels to get from one side to the other. Ships' dimensions must not exceed 32.3 metres in beam, 12 metres draft and 294.1 metres length (depending on the type of ship).

Suez Canal
The Suez Canal started operations in 1869 to provide a link between the Mediterranean and the Indian Ocean. This shortcut meant ships could avoid lengthy and potentially dangerous sailing around the Cape of Good Hope. Since that time, with occasional closures due to war, the canal has become one of the world's most important trading routes [28]. The canal can allow vessels up to 150,000 GRT with a 15-metre draft to traverse it, although plans were underway to increase this to a 20-metre draft by 2010.

Table 4.9 *Other destination facts (population figures are approximate)*

Destination	Country	Region	Currency	Language	Population
Canary Islands	Spain	Atlantic	Euro	Spanish	2,125,000
Madeira	Portugal	Atlantic	Euro	Portuguese	245,000
Azores	Portugal	Atlantic	Euro	Portuguese	238,000
Rio de Janeiro	Brazil	South America	Real	Portuguese	6,100,000
Buenos Aires	Argentina	South America	Argentine peso	Spanish	12,998,000
Galapagos	Ecuador	Pacific	US dollar	Spanish	20,000
Capetown	South Africa	Africa	Rand	IsiZulu, IsiXhosa, Afrikaans, Sepedi, English	3,500,000
Seychelles	Seychelles	Indian Ocean	Seychelles rupee	Creole and English	81,100
Panama Canal	Panama	South America	The balboa or US dollar	Spanish and English	3,405,000
Suez Canal	Egypt	Africa	Egyptian pound	Arabic	488,125

SUMMARY AND CONCLUSIONS

This chapter provides a description of the major cruising sectors, together with a brief taste of a number of destinations. Considerably more can be said about all the destinations that are included, and certainly about those that are not. However, this is not possible in such a broad-based textbook and it is recommended that readers undertake further research to examine key issues related to destinations and cruise sectors. There are many sources that can be used to undertake such research, including web-based tourism sites, geography textbooks and tourism guides.

The cruise industry generates considerable business for destinations but for some there is a cost. That cost may be in terms of the increase in people visiting particular destinations, the demands placed on the local population to 'package' and thus hybridize the cultural experience, and the possibility of pollution or ecological impact. These issues can also be examined further so as to reflect on the balance of positive and negative impacts for destinations.

The following three case studies are included to stimulate discussion and widen understanding of destinations. The first considers the case of 'Destination South

West', a regional initiative that was introduced to increase cruise business to the southwest of England. In the second, the action taken by some cruise companies to purchase and operate private islands is examined. The final case study considers Barbados as a cruise home port and a cruise destination. Questions are included at the end of each case study.

CASE STUDY 1: SELLING THE SOUTHWEST OF ENGLAND

Resorts seeking to capitalize on the burgeoning cruise industry phenomenon could learn by examining the case of 'Destination South West'. This initiative originally represented an alliance between 8 ports throughout the southwest of England but later became a representative group for 12 ports – Ilfracombe, Torbay, Dartmouth, Plymouth, Fowey, Falmouth, Penzance, Lyme Regis, Portland, Poole, Mounts Bay and the Isles of Scilly. It was supported using a combination of European Regional Development Social Funds and match-funding from county and local councils, tourist bodies, attractions such as the Eden Project, the National Maritime Museum in Cornwall, the National Trust, Britannia Royal Naval College and the ports (21 public and private partners). The funds identified helped support a new partnership that aimed to develop and extend the number of cruise ship visits to ports within the region. At the time of writing the partnership still exists, albeit with over 30 partners and considerably less support funding in place.

Bob Harrison, an experienced professional with 30 years of industry experience, coordinated Destination South West at sea and ashore. He was appointed as Director of Cruise Operations. Harrison used his knowledge and contacts to gain access to senior managers involved with itinerary planning and his insights into the experience of cruise passengers and their requirements have been invaluable. He also recognizes the difficulties that cruise executives are faced with when planning itineraries and can orient his strategy accordingly. Although Harrison left his post in 2010 he still advises the body and acts on their behalf occasionally.

The £230,000 three-year project was launched in February 2002. Destination South West started by putting in place an informative website (www.destinationsouthwest.co.uk). The website allows visitors to click on a port name and get access to a lot of information, including: a cruise calendar to identify which ships are calling and when, marine charts, town maps, suggested shore excursions, video clips of some attractions, 360-degree shots of the port area where passengers land, and distance and times between ports and attractions. This information, which helps the itinerary planner make decisions, was also replicated on a DVD, to provide an easy-to-use reference pack in support of direct selling and to use as a give-away at exhibitions. Websites and DVDs were produced in German and English so as to appropriately target the German and US cruise markets.

There were a few problems. For example, events such as the terrorist attack on New York (9/11), the outbreak of foot and mouth in the UK in 2003 and the emergence of SARS, all potentially impacted upon or informed cruise passengers making purchasing decisions. In many cases people were ill informed about the implications of these critical incidents; passengers to a port in Cornwall were overheard asking if purchasing a woolly pullover might create a risk of catching foot and mouth.

Cruise companies such as Holland America, Princess, Cunard and Seabourne all commented that they liked the uniform packaged approach. The results of the project showed a picture starting in 2001, with 10 vessels calling into ports in the area, through to 2004, when there were 106 cruise ships calls. This figure stayed generally constant up to 2010, although reduced funding remains a constant source of concern. Some ports in this region offer berths where the ship can go alongside. Indeed the busiest port, Falmouth has such facilities. Harrison believes that in the main passengers prefer as few tender operations as possible (where launches transport passengers from ship to shore). This despite the fact that many cruise brands include a tender operation as an element of the total cruise experience. In his opinion, more than two tender operations in a cruise is too many, because passengers begin to object to the time delay, the potential discomfort if sea conditions are not calm and queues, which can form at either end of the operation because of security and logistical factors. The business generated by Destination South West includes 21 turnarounds where passengers embark and/or disembark at the beginning and/or end of a cruise. Dartmouth is reported to operate one turnaround while Falmouth has 20.

Harrison describes recent research on passenger spending, which focused on Cork in the Republic of Ireland. He quotes this Irish research because he believes there are parallels between Cork and the type of destinations in the Southwest and similarities between the types of passengers. This research identified that each passenger spends £197 and that the crew spend is marginally less. There is, however, some disagreement about levels of spend and some sources suggest that at times the crew can actually spend more than some passengers. This is explained because in port manning means that minimum levels of crew must remain onboard when the ship is in port to ensure that safety is maintained. As a result crew members cannot go ashore in every port but when they do go ashore they are more likely to spend greater amounts of money. Based on estimations, Harrison believes the cruise passengers spend in the southwest of England is £16.7 million, with a crew spend of £1.7 million. That is a total of £18.4 million from a project with a £285,000 budget and could equate to 438 jobs for the local community. When a cruise ship comes to Falmouth, the local department store, Marks and Spencer, takes on extra staff. The project has attracted high-profile vessels to the ports in the partnership and it is reasonable to highlight the benefit this creates for the port itself as part of the image and vision on display. When the *World* was visiting Falmouth as part of her itinerary, there were 2,000 people standing on the headland to see the ship as she sailed out of the harbour.

Figure 4.6 *Holland America Line (HAL) Prinsendam in Falmouth*

How was this level of success achieved? The website was seen to be important. The quality of information and the ease of use are fundamental. Destination South West possessed a tacit understanding of the cruise industry and their requirements. The project used business to business (B2B) marketing. Personal contacts were also important, developing relationships and encouraging visits to the area by the decision makers all helped to confirm action. Attendance at trade and travel conventions was of importance because it gave Destination South West a presence. Douglas Ward, the author of the Berlitz *Complete Guide to Cruising & Cruise Ships*, was appointed honorary president and this link was also thought to be useful because of opportunities to enhance networking and raise the project's profile. The initiative has helped to develop the level of support, quality of welcome and overall focus. In Torbay, for example, shop-mobility trolleys were made available and the mayor attended personally to welcome the passengers. In other ports, such as Plymouth and Falmouth, portable tourist information display units were available for passengers to consult.

Local problems that result in negative business impacts include conflicting schedules from ferry operators competing for berths, and under-keel clearance in port areas that inhibit ships' mobility and access because of tides and times. The project has helped to lengthen the tourist season, bringing a lot of people from the US, Europe and elsewhere in the UK to the region and this potential for cruising expands continually. The Passenger Shipping Association states that there was a 37% increase in visits to the UK between 2003 and 2004 and it is, in itself, identified as the fastest growing market in the world. The potential for the southwest of England is high. Even the weather, often regarded by some as a turn-off, is seen by many US passengers as an attractive experience. In 2005, the local government office was impressed with the project and aimed to extend it for a further two years. Levels of investment have always been low, however, and there is a constant struggle to persuade members to contribute. There are major benefits in acting in concert. Ports that don't act in competition can derive benefits through cooperation. Harrison believes that cruising is for everyone and the challenge is to inform those who don't recognize the fact that it has changed and how. As Destination South West enters its ninth year, the future seems to be less certain because of funding issues, yet the members are determined to ensure the good work developed over the years continues.

This case study presents a narrative account of how a particular region in one country created the impetus to develop and sustain cruise tourism growth.

Question 1
Consider the key actions and identify the critical elements that led to the outcome of this initiative.

Question 2
What are the risks for this project and how can they be countered in terms of the following?

- Internal competition between neighbouring ports
- Ensuring the ports remain attractive as cruise destinations
- Securing finance to ensure that the project develops.

CASE STUDY 2: PRIVATE BEACHES AS PORTS OF CALL

Private beaches, such as those owned or leased by cruise brands in the Caribbean or the Bahamas, are seen as a useful alternative to neighbouring popular ports of call. Often the beaches are on cays (keys). Cays are small, low-lying islands consisting mainly of coral and sand. Cruise lines such as Disney, Princess Cruises, Norwegian Cruise Line, Holland America Line, Costa Cruises, Royal Caribbean International (which has two islands) and Radisson Seven Seas Cruises are all involved in this type of investment.

But what are the advantages and are there any disadvantages in having a private beach port? Most of the islands are constrained by their location and facilities, thus requiring that ships anchor off the coast, with passengers then ferried to the island jetty by tender. This transfer can add an exciting dimension to a cruise, although those with small children or with a disability may be inconvenienced. The notion of a private cay or beach can be an attractive idea for passengers because of the romanticism implied or because the idea may signify to some a prestigious and unique benefit.

The visit to the cay is often scheduled to include a morning arrival and late afternoon departure. This optimizes usage of the cay and allows the company to build in additional services such as barbeques, water sports and organized games and activities. This in turn creates opportunities to generate revenue from the activities and facilities. Kayaking, sailing, snorkelling and scuba diving may be offered and a range of children's activities can be scheduled. In addition, some companies may offer special activities such as massages in private cabanas (Disney and Holland America) and 'surf and turf' Olympics (Costa Cruises). Royal Caribbean has built a replica of a Spanish galleon and sunk a small airplane in the waters off its Bahamian island, 140-acre Coco Cay, for snorkelling tours and scuba divers.

Services may be provided by the cruise company or subcontracted to local employees or contract providers. The services are under the quality assurance and control of cruise management with, in some cases, shipboard staff being used ashore to create a seamless service. In addition to this approach to developing their 'products', cruise companies are also introducing 'beach clubs' in popular destinations, which are managed and operated directly or as part of a contract by the cruise companies.

However, some observers are critical of this approach [39], noting that issues relating to the environment and the amount of waste generated by tourists both on the ship and when visiting these fragile islands are important and in need of further examination. In addition, points are raised about the ethical position of cruise companies in relation to the playgrounds of the Caribbean and the Bahamas. Cruise companies generate large amounts of revenue from their islands when selling products and services but, it is claimed, in doing this the direct contribution to locals trading in the Caribbean is being eroded [39].

Question 1
What are the significant issues in terms of advantages and disadvantages for the various stakeholders: the cruise company, the locals, the passengers and the relevant authorities?

Question 2
In some ways this approach to developing a resort is criticized as being an example of 'enclave tourism', where tourists are sheltered from a local environment by barriers intended to protect the tourists and manage their experience [28, p. 453]. Why is this and what are the implications?

CASE STUDY 3: BARBADOS – AN ISLAND PARADISE?

Barbados is located in the Southern Caribbean [40]. It is considered to be the most easterly of the Caribbean islands, being some 100 kilometres from its nearest neighbour – a factor that may contribute to the comparatively decreased impact of hurricanes. It lies to the northeast of Venezuela (South America). The island is 'seed'-shaped, 34 kilometres long and 23 kilometres wide. It has a population of 273,000 people [10] with a literacy rate of 99.7% [41]. The temperature averages between 24 and 30 degrees Celsius.

Figure 4.7 *The port at Bridgetown*

The island has a number of geographical advantages: firstly it is fortunate to have easy access to clean water, which is collected in caves deep within the countryside; secondly it has excellent beaches and a diversity of seascapes because of the relative calm on the west coast and the rugged Atlantic-facing west coast; and thirdly, the people are very friendly. Crime is not unknown; indeed, over recent years, a small number of incidents have been publicized reflecting concern about the changing face of Caribbean societies [42]. Yet for many the image of an idyllic beach resort, a warm climate, excellent facilities and a welcoming population predominate.

Table 4.10 Tourists and cruise visitors (in thousands)

	1990	1995	2000	2001	2002	2003	2004	2005	2006	2007	2008	2009
Tourist arrivals	432	442	544	507	4 97	531	551	547	562	573	568	519
Cruise visitors	363	485	533	528	523	559	721	563	539	616	598	636

Tourism matters to Barbados, being worth approximately $172 mil-lion. Cruise business contributes around $78 million to that figure [43]. Table 4.10 above shows the relationship between tourist arrivals and cruise visitors. According to the Barbados Port Authority [44], cruise passengers were due to rise by 14% in 2010 while the number of ships was set to increase by 8% (see Table 4.11).

Figure 4.8 *Typical west-coast beach*

The port of Barbados is located to the south of the capital Bridgetown. When it is at full capacity there can be seven ships in port of varying dimensions. The port works hard to ensure the deep-water facility is capable of welcoming the largest of vessels. The port facility includes duty-free shopping and passenger facilities alongside the usual security and port authority provision. A new taxi rank has been constructed at the terminal and excursions depart from outside the building along the frequently overused roads around the island. It appears to most visitors that there is a disproportionate number of vehicles travelling the high-ways and that, coupled with the large number of roadside shacks sell-ing beer or rum, impacts upon journey times and wear and tear on the tarmac.

Table 4.11 *Visits of cruise ships to Barbados 2009 and 2010*

CRUISE SHIPS IN BARBADOS			
MONTH	**2009**	**2010**	**% CHANGE**
JANUARY	83	67	–19%
FEBRUARY	69	56	–19%
MARCH	65	71	9%
APRIL	44	41	–7%
MAY	15	14	–7%
JUNE	11	11	0%
JULY	13	7	–46%
AUGUST	10	7	–30%
SEPTEMBER	12	7	–42%
OCTOBER	14	17	21%
NOVEMBER	49	46	–6%
DECEMBER	76	70	–8%
TOTAL	**385**	**414**	**8%**

Passengers arriving in Barbados have a number of options in relation to activities. Many jump in a taxi outside the terminal building and head for a beach such as Paynes Bay or Cranes Bay. Beaches are open to everyone, so even the grandest hotel can't claim ownership of the stretch of sand outside their property. The beaches on the relatively calm west coast are typically soft sand made up of ground coral and bordered by azure seas. Coral reefs can be found close to the beaches and most beaches host an array of restaurants, beach bars, water sport facilities and vendors. The crew often head for the Boatyard, which has the benefit of being a short distance from the port, with excellent facilities, and is usually passenger free. Over the years rising sea levels have begun to reduce the size of many beaches, particularly along the popular west coast. Some conservationists also suggest that ships constantly moving in and out of the port have an impact on beach erosion and coral reef damage [45].

Alternatively, passengers can book an excursion such as a visit to Harrison's Cave, a trip on an underwater submarine, a catamaran cruise or even a day at the wildlife park. At certain points around the island turtles can be seen, drawn in by the attraction of easy food and growing

Figure 4.9 *Submarine excursion*

to large dimensions in the relatively safe waters. Off Paynes Bay snorkelling is organized from flotillas of excursion vessels to view the turtles that seem to cruise effortlessly in the crystal-clear sea like benign water-based spacecraft. The island also possesses a colony of monkeys. These green monkeys are generally quite timid but can be seen at feeding time in the wildlife park. The underwater submarine accesses reefs off the west coast and allows excursionists the opportunity to view the wealth of sea life that can be seen just off the island.

The future for cruise tourism on the island is apparently strong. Yet local newspapers are full of articles decrying the problems that exist, which include: the uncertainty of the business; the impact of large numbers of passengers on the infrastructure of the island; competition from new destinations in other parts of the world such as Dubai; and the price of fuel, which means some cruise operators select destinations closer to US mainline home ports. Yet the island has also been able to attract cruise operators who use the location as a convenient home port for fly cruises. The government and tourist authorities welcome this business because of income generated both before and after the cruise. Passengers are often put straight onboard coaches to by-pass immigration controls and the lengthy queues that incoming passengers are met with at the airport, thus enjoying a seamless journey from aircraft to ship and *vice versa*.

Figure 4.10 *Harrison's Cave*

Ultimately, cruise business plays an important part for this island's economy. Most Caribbean islands fit the description of being a third-world country and, despite the glamour of the hotels, the lure of the beaches, the high-calibre, upmarket restaurants and the show of wealth from the immigrant European and US locals, Barbados has problems balancing its budget [41]. Cruise business creates jobs and generates income but cruise companies are commercial entities with a clear mandate to create profits. If a Caribbean island wishes to increase port fees the cruise company can remove that island from its itinerary. CARICOM was created to create a single Caribbean market and to aim to ensure that the partners benefit from a common political approach when negotiating with trading partners. Barbados is a member of CARICOM and therefore can benefit from the unilateralism that should emerge from within this entity [46].

Question 1
What are the positive and negative issues that arise for Barbados as a direct result of attracting cruise business?

Question 2
Consider who the stakeholders are for cruise tourism in Barbados and discuss how they might perceive opportunities for the future.

REFERENCES

1. Burton, R., *Travel Geography*. 2nd ed. 1995, London: Pitman.
2. Rees, R., *Mitchell Beazley's Family Encyclopedia of Nature*. 1992, London: Mitchell Beazley.
3. Gibson, P., 'Life and Learning in Further Education: Constructing the circumstantial curriculum', *Journal of Further and Higher Education*, 2004. 28: p. 333–346.
4. Bansal, H. and H.A. Eiselt, 'Exploratory Research of Tourist Motivations and Planning', *Tourism Management*, 2004. 25(3): p. 387–396.
5. Wild, P. and J. Dearing, 'High Achievers', *Lloyd's Cruise International*. 2005. p. 19–28.
6. BBC News, 'Crisis in Haiti'. 2004 [accessed March 2004]; Available from: http://news.bbc.co.uk/1/hi/world/americas/3378671.stm.
7. Booth, R., 'Cruise Ships Still Find a Haitian Berth'. 2010 [accessed October 2011]; Available from: http://www.guardian.co.uk/world/2010/jan/17/cruise-ships-haiti-earthquake.
8. CLIA, 'Bahamas and the Caribbean'. 2011 [accessed April 2011]; Available from: http://www.cruising.org/vacation/destinations/bahamas-caribbean
9. Caribbean Tourism Organization, 'Caribbean'. 2011 [accessed April 2011]; Available from: http://www.onecaribbean.org/.
10. United Nations. *Population Statistics 2010*. 2011; Available from: http://esa.un.org/unpd/wpp/Excel-Data/population.htm.
11. Aruba Cruise Tourism. *Aruba Cruise Passengers*. 2010 [accessed August 2011]; Available from: http://www.aruba.com/news/general-news/arubas-cruise-tourism-and-newsletter/.
12. Mancini, M., *Cruising: A guide to the cruise line industry*. 2nd ed. 2003, Albany NY: Delmar.
13. Wild, P. and J. Dearing, 'Caribbean Stronghold', *Lloyd's Cruise International*, 2004(69): p. 27–38.
14. Bahamas Tourism Office, 'Experience the Bahamas'. 2005 [accessed April 2011]; Available from: http://www.bahamas.com/bahamas/.
15. Dervaes, C., *Selling Cruises*. 2nd ed. 2003, New York: Thomson.
16. World Travel Awards, 2010 [accessed April 2011]; Available from: *www.worldtravel-awards.com*.
17. Puerto Rico Tourist Office, 'Go to Puerto Rico'. 2010 [accessed April 2011]; Available from: http://www.topuertorico.org/tinfo.shtml
18. US Virgin Islands Tourism Authority, 'St Thomas'. 2010 [accessed April 2011]; Available from: *www.visitusvi.com/*
19. Antigua Barbuda Tourist Information, 'Antigua and Barbuda'. 2010 [accessed April 2011]; Available from: http://www.antigua-barbuda.org/.
20. Florida Keys and Key West Tourism Association, 'Florida Keys and Key West'. 2010 [accessed April 2011]; Available from: http://www.fla-keys.com/.
21. Cayman Islands Department of Tourism, 'Cayman Islands Tourist Information'. 2010 [accessed April 2011]; Available from: http://www.caymanislands.ky/.
22. Visit Jamaica, 'Explore Jamaica'. 2010 [accessed April 2011]; Available from: *www.visitjamaica.com*.
23. Barbados Tourism Authority, 'Barbados'. 2010 [accessed April 2011]; Available from: http://www.barbados.org/.
24. Curaçao Tourist Board, 'Curacao'. 2010 [accessed April 2011]; Available from: http://www.curacao-visitor.com/.
25. Wild, P. and J. Dearing, 'Growth Culture', *Lloyd's Cruise International*, 2004. p. 17–24.

26. Wild, P. and J. Dearing, 'Rising Stars', *Lloyd's Cruise International*, 2004.
27. Cruise Europe, webpage. 2010 [accessed April 2011]; Available from: http://www.cruiseeurope.com/.
28. Boniface, B. and C. Cooper, *Worldwide Destinations*. 4th ed. 2005, Oxford: Butterworth-Heinemann.
29. Medcruise, 'Cruising in the Mediterranean'. 2010 [accessed April 2011]; Available from: http://www.medcruise.com.
30. BBC News, 'Venice Launches Antiflood Project'. 2003 [accessed August 2005]; Available from: http://news.bbc.co.uk/2/hi/europe/3026275.stm.
31. Port of Miami, 'Cruise'. 2009 [accessed April 2010]; Available from: http://www.miamidade.gov/portofmiami/cruise.asp.
32. Port Everglades, 'For Travel Professionals'. 2010 [accessed April 2011]; Available from: http://www.sunny.org/travelagents/index.cfm.
33. Port Canaveral, 'Cruising from Port Canaveral'. 2010 [accessed April 2011]; Available from: http://www.portcanaveral.org/.
34. Cruise the West, 'Cruise Partnership'. 2005 [accessed April 2005]; Available from: http://www.cruisethewest.com.
35. Mott, D., 'Home Comforts', *Lloyd's Cruise International*, 2004. p. 17–19.
36. Cruise Down Under, 'News'. 2010 [accessed April 2011]; Available from: http://www.cruisedownunder.com.
37. Sydney Ports, 'Sydney Ports: First port, future port'. 2010 [accessed April 2011]; Available from: http://www.sydneyports.com.au/home.asp.
38. Hong Kong Tourism, 'All About Hong Kong'. 2010 [accessed April 2011]; Available from: http://www.discoverhongkong.com/eng/mustknow/index.jhtml.
39. Robertson, G., 'Cruise Ship Tourism'. 2004 [accessed April 2005]; Available from: http://www.lighthouse-foundation.org/.
40. Barbados Tourist Office, 'Key Facts about Barbados'. 2011 [accessed April 2011]; Available from: http://www.barbados.org/keyfacts.htm.
41. Barbados Integrated Government, 'Key Facts'. 2011 [accessed April 2011]; Available from: http://www.gov.bb/bigportal/big/.
42. Jessop, D., 'Crime in the Caribbean'. 2010 [accessed April 2011]; Available from: http://www.bbc.co.uk/caribbean/news/story/2010/06/100614_jessop.shtml.
43. CARICOM, 'Number of Tourist Arrivals into Barbados'. 2011 [accessed April 2011]; Available from: http://www.caricomstats.org/Files/Databases/Tourism/BBTO.pdf.
44. Barbados Port Inc., 'Barbados in Cruise Control'. 2011 [accessed April 2011]; Available from: http://www.barbadosport.com.
45. Burke, L. and J. Maidens, *Reefs at Risk in the Caribbean*. 2004, Washington: World Resources Institute.
46. Nation News, 'Our Caribbean: A season of new pressures for CARICOM'. 2011 [accessed April 2011]; Available from: http://www.nationnews.com/articles/view/our-caribbean-a-season-of-new-pressures-for-caricom/.

5 Planning the itinerary

By the end of this chapter the reader should be able to define the cruise destination, identify critical factors relating to the designing of a cruise itinerary, examine different methods for analysing and evaluating destinations, understand the reasons why ports and destinations are successful for cruises, and consider operations and planning for shore excursions or tours. Previous chapters have reflected on travel geography [1] coupled seasonality and optimum conditions for cruising, as well as sales and marketing and the supply and servicing of ships, as important factors in the planning of an itinerary. This chapter will examine options for analysing destinations themselves.

WHAT IS A CRUISE DESTINATION?

This is a relatively complex question to answer. Davidson and Maitland [2] describe a model that denotes an interplay between a 'generating region', the place that the tourist will come from, and 'destination regions', the place tourists will go to, linked by a 'transit region', the place where the tourist spends time before arriving at the destination. In this version of a tourist system, potential tourists within a generating region are subject to a variety of 'push' factors, such as disposable income, leisure time, motivation and ambition and the presence of demographic change. Information is channelled back to the generating region from the destination region, developing 'local' perceptions and stimulating further visits.

For the cruise industry, noting the significant changes in recent years in terms of the construction of larger vessels with enhanced facilities, the key destination can be interpreted as being the ship itself. Indeed, the ship has a significant place in the cruise tourism system, as can be seen in the following modified model.

This reworked version of the tourism system suggests that the ship plays a pivotal role in the relationship between generating region and the ultimate tour destination

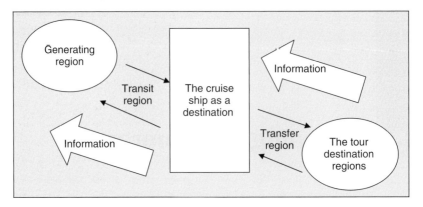

Figure 5.1 *The cruise tourism system (after Davidson and Maitland, 1997)*

regions. In a sense, over the duration of a cruise, it becomes a centre for interpretation; a safe and familiar zone from which it is possible to choose whether to select, sample and engage with situated experiences. Some passengers prefer to stay onboard during a port day, rejecting the attractions on offer ashore in preference for the shipboard experiences. Information travels from the destination region to the ship and then from the ship to the generating region. Of course this can be further developed when considering that some cruise companies have experimented with selling cruises to nowhere.

As different forms of cruising evolve, so too does the part played by the destination in the cruise holiday menu. The largest of cruise ships are virtually self-contained resorts, with options for all types of people available throughout the cruise at all times of day or night. For cruisers on this type of vessel, the destination competes with the onboard activities. For smaller luxury vessels, the ship accesses unique destinations that are out of reach to larger vessels.

WHAT MAKES A GOOD PORT OF CALL?

Ports of call or destinations invariably offer a mix of elements which, when viewed together, have potency. Cruise ships are businesses that rely on customer satisfaction. The main feedback from cruise tourists is obtained using a survey document that is generally distributed, completed and returned at the end of the cruise.

Passengers' feedback suggests ports should offer interest, be culturally stimulating (different to the normal), safe or non-threatening, friendly, accessible and user friendly. It is difficult to find an ideal port that ticks all these boxes, so in reality compromises are made and the difference between expectation and perception of actual experiences tends to stimulate positive reflection.

Ports of call derive considerable income from cruise ships and popular destinations sell themselves aggressively in order to attract cruise tourism. An analysis of port advertisements in *Cruise International* [3] reveals the following range of attractors (see Table 5.1).

A variety of marketing communications (trade magazines, direct selling) and forums (trade shows and conferences) are utilized by marketers to sell the benefit of destination ports. Increasingly, the Internet has become a powerful tool as a communications medium and examples can be seen below and in previous chapters as to how individual ports and consortia approach the task of using the Internet as an aid to sales.

www.cruisejamaica.com

www.arubabycruise.com

http://www.cruisedownunder.com

www.marmariscruiseport.com

An analysis and comparison of the above will provide interesting lessons relating to the use of the Internet as a marketing tool for the cruise industry.

Table 5.1 *Analysis of attractors*

Unique experiences	Heart of the city location
Average 10.75 metres (35 ft) water at low tide	Shopping
Deep draft sheltered berths	Capacity for mega cruise ships
Gateway port with easy access to destinations	ADA-accessible passenger loading bridge and mobile gangway
Port an attraction in itself	Comfortable, efficient and secure
Duty free	Dual-ship terminal
Suitable as homeport, port of call or repositioning cruise port	Warehousing space (storage, stores and baggage handling)
Professional service	Panoramic views
Island port with diversity of attractions	International airport nearby
Cruise terminal with state-of-the-art facilities	Perfect weather year round/warm weather destination
Sightseeing tours/shore excursions	Cultural and historical treasures
Exciting nightlife	Water sports and land sports

ANALYSIS AND EVALUATION

There are many analytical tools that can be used to measure the potential value of a port. Invariably, the decision is complex and takes into account many practical factors. For an established cruise brand, there is much to be gained from building on experience and planning itineraries based on what is known because of the reliability factor. For the cruise ship, experience of visiting a port creates a knowledge bank about the destination, which helps to ensure that planning is effective and that quality assurance is less of an unknown quantity. For the port of call, experience enables agents, port officials, contractors, tourist organizations and the local population to form and develop a relationship with the visiting ship and its community.

According to Lloyd's [4], a company such as Silversea involves a broad group of stakeholders when composing an itinerary. This group includes captains, sales teams and passengers. Passenger questionnaire responses inform the process, as do world events. The company adopts an eclectic approach to itinerary planning to reflect the developing and ever-changing needs and wants of clients. Therefore, plans are incorporated to ensure that those with a phobia of flying are accommodated, new ports are included to ensure the itineraries are not seen as staid or lacking adventure, land-based activities including cruise and stay programmes are constructed and details relating to passenger expectation are incorporated throughout. For Silversea this means focusing on the luxury end of the market with 'one-off' unique or prestige events included in itineraries to create special moments in keeping with customer expectations, e.g. a dinner in a St Petersburg museum, or a private opera in the Sydney Opera House. Silversea are also reported to have reduced the duration of the average cruise from between 14–16 days to 9–12 days in response to passenger wishes.

Problems related to itineraries can be concerned with practical matters such as tendering – the ferrying of passengers by ship to shore using ships' tenders. Tendering is said to be unpopular with many passengers because of a combination of factors. For some it increases travel to land time and reduces time ashore; for others it is an unwelcome form of transport that can raise concerns. On a more positive note, the experience can add to the total experience package by providing a frisson of excitement. Passengers who transfer from the grand scale of the cruise ship to the more human-scaled tender have an opportunity to enjoy a different mode of transport with a unique view of both the port (outbound) and the ship (inbound). Some ports of call have reputations related to how they deal with visiting cruise ships. According to some captains there are ports where the authorities increase port costs without prior notice, where an expensive landing tax is levied and where a charge is made for compulsory but unnecessary tugs.

In respect of a ship's itinerary, the purpose of destination analysis is most likely to be strategic – that is, related to long-term corporate objectives and connected to creating sustainable competitive advantage. This focus invariably blends analysis that utilizes strategic logic, or a reflection of the appropriateness for the target market, and research data in deciding what makes a useful itinerary or component of an itinerary. Analysis can also inform tactical decision making, feeding in to the overall strategy with a more medium-term concern, such as changing an itinerary because of emerging problems or heightened risk.

Analysis can be oriented from different perspectives – for example, a destination can be examined by a tourist agency, by a tour operator or by a cruise company. In this sense the analysis can be defined as being either internal or external, or both. Internal analysis reflects on issues such as strengths and weaknesses, including core competence (those unique characteristics that say what a company does best), the tangible and intangible resources (the former are the physical entities such as buildings or stock while the latter include skills and brand names) and financial aspects. External analysis considers the view outside, but of importance to, the study area and considers opportunities and threats [5].

Analysis of destinations in general terms can consider approaches that are driven by business considerations with a view to maximizing financial returns or a reflection of sociological perspectives to create a depth of understanding about the destination [6, 7]. The implications in this consideration suggest that the former approach is possibly more focused on opportunities and threats for a business venture in a pragmatic manner whereas the latter may be intended to unearth social and cultural meanings that can be vital but also, in their own way, almost esoteric (providing information that is only useful to a specific group with specific knowledge).

The following list provides a range of analytical tools that can be applied in the task of itinerary planning. These tools can be used to look at the macro environment (the far influences that can be said to affect the whole industry) or the micro environment (the near influences that immediately surround a business) [5]. They can consider the destination as an attraction or tourists in terms of their needs and wants. In the first instance, a range of analytical approaches is suggested that are generic by nature – that is, they can be applied to a number of types of settings. Thereafter, various analytical approaches are suggested that have more direct relevance to tourism and destinations.

SWOT

The SWOT analysis (sometimes referred to as TOWS or TWOS) is the archetypal approach to undertaking then summarizing a strategic evaluation. It embodies an internal analysis, in terms of strengths and weaknesses and an external analysis, by reflecting on opportunities and threats [5]. In relation to a port of call it is possible to apply this analysis as an overview of strengths, weaknesses, opportunities and threats to understand the port or destination's perspective when considering inherent factors, or it can form an important analytical tool from a cruise operator's perspective when examining a port or destination in the context of an itinerary. The SWOT analysis is frequently applied when considering historical factors that have had a major impact in the past, current and nascent factors that are likely to impact on future performance, and factors that render the organization distinct from the competition. The best SWOT analysis is one that is supported by logic, argument and evidence.

PESTLE analysis

This is a very common analysis that is used by organizations to study the external macro environment. The acronym (using initials to shorten the phrase) or mnemonic (creating a word from the acronym to aid memory) stands for: Political, Economic, Social, Technological, Legal and Environmental.

Variants of this analytical tool include PEST, SPECLE, STEP, PEST, STEEP, SPECLE, SCEPTICAL: the initials of these acronyms can generally be identified through a process of logic and elimination when examining the next sentence. The final example, Social, Cultural, Economic, Physical, Technical, International, Communication and Infrastructure, Administrative and Institutional, Legal and Political, was constructed by Peattie and Moutinho [8] with specific regard to travel and tourism. This type of analysis has four stages: scanning to identify signs of risk or environmental changes, monitoring to recognize patterns and trends, forecasting to calculate future environmental changes, and assessing existing and expected trends to predict impact.

Critics suggest that although the tool is an effective way of identifying issues relating to key elements in a macro environment, limitations exist because the results can be undermined by a fast pace of change and if the analysis fails to identify complex inter-related factors [5].

Porter's five forces framework

Michael Porter [9] developed a model that considered competitive forces that can be used for destination planning. His analysis led to the construction of a framework that he proposed could assist a business in developing a competitive strategy by reflecting on five competitive forces, namely:

- Threat of new entrants
- Threat of substitute products

- Power of buyers or customers
- Power of suppliers
- Rivalry among businesses.

This micro-environmental approach provides an interesting mode of analysis, which cruise operators can consider when planning itineraries in a competitive environment.

Porter's Diamond analysis and associated work

Developed in the 1980s, the Diamond analysis has, in some respects, a more direct application to studying ports or destinations because it was originally intended to be a study of regional or national competitiveness [10]. This model identifies four factors that help to define a destination's competitiveness:

- Factor conditions – physical resources, human resources, capital resources, infrastructure and knowledge resources
- Market structures, organizations and strategy
- Demand conditions
- Related and supporting industries

Wahab and Cooper [11] comment on developments to this work undertaken by Smeral [12] to create a set of guidelines. These guidelines reframe Porter's original four factors to incorporate factor conditions within those aspects that are considered most relevant for tourism, namely:

Market structures, organizations and strategies – dealing with image and market position, product development and promotion, desire for growth.

Demand conditions – availability and development of quality facilities and services, seasonal influences, focus on tourist spending power, aiming to attract repeat visits, presence of an integrated policy for tourism.

Government – research and awareness of tourism market trends, focused training made available, minimal bureaucracy, inclusively environmentally aware and open to proactive management of change.

Successful application of these analytical tools relies on the quality and reliability of contemporary data as well as a careful consideration of the inter-related nature of the stated factors.

Boston Consultancy Group (BCG) matrix

This method of analysis was designed to consider a product portfolio and to make logical calculations about development [13].

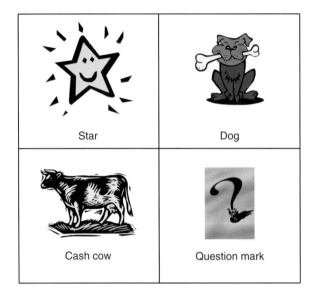

Figure 5.2 *BCG matrix*

From a strategic perspective this approach can be applied to a cruise destination to consider growth rate, growth potential, passenger popularity, barriers for development and sophistication of facilities.

TALC – Tourist Area Life Cycle

This theory [14] is predicated on the premise that resorts are products, which have a series of evolutionary stages in relation to consumer demand [13]. These stages are:

- Exploration: visited by a small number of tourists, access may be difficult.
- Involvement: tourist numbers grow with the result that basic services evolve and interaction increases with the local community.
- Development: resort is promoted, external forces take an interest in gaining control of the resort, growth in visitor numbers accelerates to create an imbalance of locals to tourists at peak times, facilities improved.
- Consolidation: tourism a major contributor to local economy, growth has levelled off, resort has achieved an international reputation.
- Stagnation: losing fashion status, over-reliance on repeat trade, various social and environmental problems.

There are two alternative directions that can emerge as the next evolutionary stage:

- Rejuvenation: major impetus undertaken to reposition the resort through marketing and investment in facilities through a partnership of public and private sectors.
- Decline: dependency on day rather than staying visitors, change of use for visitor accommodation.

This theory presents interesting ideas for analysing a resort but there is also another dimension to be examined in terms of the part cruise tourism plays in impacting upon the life cycle of a resort or destination.

Doxey's irridex

The term 'irridex' is a derivation of the word 'irritation', thus explaining that this model considers Doxey's [15] work in examining potential decline in the patience and support as proffered by a local population when faced with certain patterns of incoming tourism. Shaw and Williams [16] suggest that this model provides a useful focus when considering the impacts on a host community by reflecting on the community's reaction to tourism as an evolving industry.

In many respects Doxey's irridex shares Butler's (1980) overview of life-cycle stages. The irridex charts progression from euphoria to apathy, then irritation through to, eventually, antagonism, while Butler's model describes exploration, involvement, development, consolidation, stagnation and decline or rejuvenation.

Components of the destination amalgam

Cooper, Fletcher, Gilbert and Wanhill [17] identified four 'As' that present a view of what the authors describe as being the components of a destination. In this model, each 'A' represents the following:

Attractions – These are described as being man-made (such as the Sydney Opera House or the Pyramids of Giza) or natural features (for example, the Grand Canyon or the glaciers of Alaska) or events (the Open golf tournaments or the Olympic Games). It is feasible for certain attractions to incorporate some or all of these options.

Access – This component includes an analysis of transport links that will consider roads, rail, airports, shipping access in the port or harbour and the logical integration of these options to serve the visitor. Cooper *et al.* [17] believe that the way a destination deals with supporting and providing 'innovative provision' is important. This can include establishing walker's trails, cycling routes, horse and coach options and helicopter rides.

Amenities – There is a line to be drawn between a support facility and an attraction that can be difficult to locate. Cooper *et al.* [17] note that the attraction does what it says – it attracts – while the amenity is there to support the attraction. Therefore, restaurants, shops, bars and hotels are generally considered to be amenities. For the cruise passenger this can be a moot point, as it is conceivable for shopping complexes, high-profile hotels such as Raffles in Singapore, or a prestigious restaurant run by a famous chef to be attractions in their own right. That may well be the case but this component also includes availability of important localized provision of a broad swathe of services, for example, toilets, swimming pools, entertainment, hairdressing, exchange offices, security services and casinos.

Ancillary services – This alludes to the presence and function of agencies or bodies that act to coordinate, develop and market the destination, such as tourist offices, city tourist departments or travel and convention centres. These services help establish the destination as an entity with a recognizable profile and image. The body or agency can provide leadership or facilitate cohesion for the various stakeholders in the destination and provide information, services and advice to tourists or tour groups.

VICE

This is an acronym that is associated with environmental and sustainable practices for tourism [18]. The acronym identifies: Visitor satisfaction, Industry profitability, Community acceptance and Environmental protection as key guiding principles. This approach has developed potency in the recent past as tourist authorities have sought to establish and action strategies for sustainable development. As such it can be a useful measure for a cruise operator to identify when considering a destination and reflecting on the policy and practice that it adopts for sustainable development.

In this respect it is also possible to consider other analytical approaches that can be undertaken for the destination that tie in to sustainability such as heritage analysis, which addresses the notions of preservation, conservation and exploitation [19] and analysis that examines possible relationships between tourism and cultural heritage assets [20, p. 16]. It is possible to reflect on the various forms of analysis that are represented above and to construct through research a series of discrete tourist resources that typify a destination's attributes – for example, natural attractions, man-made attractions, shopping experience, hospitality resources, restaurants, non-polluted environment, airport, weather, security, taxi and local transport, friendliness, etc. – and then to rate these in order to create a cumulative and comparative score. In most cases this approach is taken by cruise companies when they survey passengers. However, as Lockyer [21] identifies, this method of analysis can result in flawed understanding. While this approach is manageable and relatively easy to undertake, the bluntness of responses hide the subtlety of reality. This reality suggests that consumers make judgements based on a complexity of factors that can be highly subjective because of individual circumstances. In this sense it appears logical to reflect on the consumers or passengers before making interpretations about the destination.

This final section, relating to analysis of a destination, reflects on ways the tourist can be studied to seek ideas about motivation and drive that can help planners to understand the characteristics that make a destination attractive or not. Abraham Harold Maslow is a central theorist when considering motivation [22]. His five-level 'hierarchy of needs' model suggests that human beings are motivated by unsatisfied needs, and that certain lower needs need to be satisfied before higher needs can be addressed. His model commences with basic physiological needs (food and drink), followed by safety and security, then by love or friendship, esteem and, finally, self-actualization.

TOURIST MOTIVATIONS

In terms of the tourist, Cohen [23] established a tourist classification that identified the following typologies:

- Organized mass tourist (package orientated – little contact with local culture)
- Individual mass tourist (as above but with personal choice)
- Explorer (comfort combined with independence – unique experience with a safety net)
- Drifter (immerses with local culture – no itinerary)
- Institutionalized tourism (high on familiarity)

Cohen's typology was developed by Plog [24], who was instrumental in creating a psychographic classification for tourists that is regarded by many as a seminal study. In his study, Plog theorized that tourists were positioned on a continuum with Psychocentrics, who are 'self-inhibited, nervous and lacking desire for adventure', at one end, with characteristics such as fear of flying, territorially boundedness and general anxieties. Midcentrics occupy the central point, while Allocentrics ('outgoing and independent, keen to explore') are found at the other extreme. Plog believed that the majority of the population could be found in the central area.

On the subject of desire and ambition for travel, Dann [25] described seven elements of motivation. He stated that key characteristics to note are:

- Travel is a response to what is lacking yet desired
- Destination pull exists in response to motivational push
- Motivation can exist as fantasy
- Motivation can be described as a classified purpose
- Motivational typologies can be described such as sunlust, wanderlust, etc.

- Motivation is impacted upon by tourist experiences
- Motivation as auto-definition and meaning

This work can be compared to McIntosh and Goeldner's [26] four categories of motivation, which identify:

- Physical motivators – related to body and mind, reduces tension
- Cultural motivators – the desire to see and know more about other cultures
- Interpersonal motivators – the need to meet new people
- Status and prestige motivators – recognition and attention, personal development, ego

Framke [7] believes that decision making for tourists takes place at home; the push factors are more powerful than the pull factors. Framke asserts that in this sense the benefit of studying destinations and creating tourism research is to help to construct marketing plans that can, in turn, attract the tourist to the destination. In cruising terms, however, there are more complex matters at work.

LOGISTICS, POSITIONING AND PLANNING

Deciding upon an itinerary is a matter of identifying ports of call that meet customer needs, as described earlier in this chapter: safe or non-threatening, accessible, interesting, culturally stimulating (different to the normal), friendly and user friendly. From the perspective of the cruise operator, an itinerary aims to comply with a range of practical and logistical goals to ensure that the quality of the cruise experience is maintained when the cruise customer ventures ashore.

There are many examples of cruises that break the mould in terms of designing and planning an itinerary, yet the majority of companies fit the following pattern:

- Itineraries commence from a port of embarkation and conclude at a port of disembarkation, which may or may not be the same place.
- Many cruises are scheduled for 7, 10 or 14 days to correspond with customer availability and to meet customer expectation for duration.
- Some cruise operators schedule cruises to be cyclical (continually repeating an itinerary for a set period of time) or bi-cyclical (alternating between two co-located schedules over a period of time).
- Despite their size, many of the larger vessels are designed to hold only sufficient stores to comply with these standard cruising patterns.
- Many itineraries are aimed to create an arrival time at port in the morning and a departure time in the mid- to late afternoon.
- Itineraries may make use of ports where ships can receive fuel (bunkers) supplies and stores (including food, drink and drinking water – referred to

as 'potable' water), offload waste (compactors and rubbish collection) and access specialist support services (technical).

- Most itineraries maximize the number of days at port and minimize the number of days at sea.
- Cruise companies examine port costs carefully when selecting ports of call to ensure the cost–benefit ratio is acceptable.
- Arrival and departure ports are selected with due regard for infrastructure in terms of onward travel, security and terminal facilities and procedures.

In addition, a number of cruise companies adopt a process of selection to take advantage of their distinctiveness in scheduling. Factors to be noted for these companies can include the following:

- Schedules to include world cruising (circumnavigates the globe), unique cruising (a different itinerary every cruise), short break or taster cruises, a cruise without a destination (to enjoy the ship as a destination), fly cruising (attracting customers to fly to the embarkation port), sector cruising (a cruise that may be constructed from within a world cruise or lengthier voyage).
- Selecting exotic ports, less frequented ports, ports with more complex arrival and departure issues.
- Ports that provide connection and location for cruise and tour vacations.

In all these cases, there are critical issues to consider that arise from the itinerary planning process to be borne in mind by the operator. Among the most complex of these issues is the matter of border and passport control, immigration and documentation. This will be considered in more depth later in this chapter. Passenger and crew health needs are also serious matters for consideration. In some countries travellers are more susceptible to adverse health caused by bacterial agents, mosquitoes or other insects, contaminated food caused by poor food hygiene and potential hazards caused by the local water supply. Preparation can help in some of these cases – for example, immunization can help by protecting the traveller from an attack – but there is also a need to inform customers and crew about risks so they can take appropriate action. Cruise companies take care to forewarn their passengers about potential risk and advise them to contact their doctor or seek appropriate advice if they need further information. In general, where it is deemed unsafe to drink water ashore, passengers should be advised to buy bottled water, to avoid food items that may have been washed before consumption, and to avoid ice cubes if the water source for the ice is not guaranteed or verifiable.

When the draft of the ship (depth below water) means the ship cannot safely tie up alongside the quay or jetty because of shallow water, the general condition of the approaches to the port in question or the tidal variations, the itinerary may declare that the port is a 'boat port'. In these cases passengers will land by way of the ships launches or tenders while the vessel anchors safely offshore. Invariably, boat ports reduce the amount of time that can be utilized ashore because of the travel to shore time and the potential problems that may arise in meeting passengers' requests to disembark immediately. Boat ports require cruise personnel to establish and marshal a control point at the arrival point onshore to manage the process of arrival and return.

For vessels that return to ports on a regular or relatively frequent basis, much can be gained from the familiarity of key personnel in dealing with port officials, agents and contractors. Continued experience with immigration helps the pursers' department to smooth the progress of the process of arrival, disembarkation, passengers in transit (departing the vessel with the aim of travelling to another country), re-embarkation and departure. The cruise company will make use of a port agent to act on the cruise ship's behalf: to be the shore-based facilitator and deal with a range of matters, including official and immigration requirements, supply, onward travel, shore excursions, technical support and specialized services.

Familiarity and knowledge of the port will also be important when advising passengers about local conditions and what to expect when they proceed ashore, and can be used by cruise staff to ensure passengers have an enjoyable and safe visit. In some ports the point of arrival is a considerable distance from the centre of the town, or distant from the main point of interest, and the cruise company may need to contract a shuttle bus service to transport passengers promptly and safely to the optimum location where they can be left to their own devices to walk or find private transfers to a desired location. Usually, shore excursion coaches will be at the ship's side or close to the passenger arrival point.

Planning the cruise is, as has been seen earlier, a matter of ensuring that the itinerary is appropriate to meet the needs of the target market coupled with a broad range of other internal and external factors. The next section considers these internal and external factors so as to develop an understanding of planning issues.

THE ELEMENTS OF PLANNING

As Moutinho [27] states, planning for tourism should be 'integral', that is, it should take a multidimensional and systematic approach so as to be viable in the long term. Operating an international cruise corporation does not provide carte blanche in terms of avoiding social responsibility and, indeed, it would be counterproductive, in these days of rapid communication, for any business to be seen to be taking an ethically unsound approach to operations.

The global picture is complex in this respect because a cruise operator must understand from a planning perspective the implications of visiting certain countries from a political, environmental, social, technological, legal and economic standpoint. Each country is likely to possess a policy for tourism that will impact on incoming tour operators, including cruise companies [28]. This policy, Goeldner and Brent Ritchie suggest, should emerge from planning that takes a balanced view concerning economic value and social well-being.

Good tourism planning can provide long-term benefits to the local population in terms of the resultant provision of infrastructure for tourism (developing essential services, establishing effective transport, creating communication networks and commercial facilities). The superstructure for tourism [28], such as hotels, restaurants, car rentals and attractions, while emerging in relation to tourists' needs, can also provide benefits for the indigenous population.

Integrated planning linked with policy formulation ensures that destination management is strategically considered to maximize the benefits of tourism while mitigating the disadvantages that can emerge from it. Laws [29], affirms that the 'packaging' of tourism has resulted in four major outcomes: resorts emerge in response to demand as a type of homogenized replication of a standard model; environment and ecology are put under pressure by developments; the destination is presented selectively and in an over-simplified format, which in turn can modify the way locals behave; and while economically, employment and commercial opportunities grow, there is a consequential penalty on the demand for infrastructure.

Cruise companies operate within this milieu. The potential to impact on destinations by disgorging an additional 3,000–5,000 passengers from each mega cruise ship is great and tourism planners must consider these factors in order to manage the sustainable nature of their destination. Equally, each cruise operator should aim to understand the destination in order to comply with regulations and local laws and to make sure the quality of the passenger experience is maximized.

REGULATIONS

Tourism policy can affect cruise operators in a number of ways. In the first instance, there is a complexity of regulations to be considered. These regulations may relate to a broad range of factors, including: the mobility of people, goods and capital; health and safety laws; environmental protection; consumer protection; shipping; ownership of key facilities; and security.

In terms of the mobility of people, goods and capital [16], cruise companies can be faced with the prospect of dealing with border controls. This can create issues relating to passport and visa controls, customs, financial exchange and the passage of people, as they travel on a cruise ship, to arrive at and depart from destinations.

A ship arriving in a foreign port must be cleared for arrival before passengers can disembark. This routine differs depending on the regulations that apply and the nationality of the ship by registration. The clearance is likely to involve the port authority receiving a declaration about the passengers, crew and goods onboard and information relating to the ship's itinerary. Goods and passengers joining or leaving the vessel while in port are also noted as part of this routine. In some countries, port health officials inspect the vessel to measure the levels of sanitation and hygiene onboard. Increasingly, declarations are sought that confirm there are no health problems onboard or that the ship presents no security risks [30].

Recent problems regarding health exemplified by SARS, the Norovirus and terrorist threats have changed the way that cruise ships and tourists travelling internationally are managed by port authorities. Heightened states of alert result in raised levels of security. Security regimes for cruise ships in US ports include the following security measures:

- 100% screening of all passenger baggage, carry-on luggage
- Intensified screening of passenger lists and passenger identification
- Restricted access to any sensitive vessel or terminal areas
- Stringent measures to deter unauthorized entry and illegal activity
- Notice given to U.S. Coast Guard 96 hours before entering U.S. ports, and passenger and crew identification information submitted to federal agencies
- Coast Guard-established security zone around cruise ships [Cruise Line International Association (CLIA)] [31]

In Europe, an agreement between 15 of the member states called the 'Schengen treaty' was introduced in 1985 to facilitate the free passage of people between member states or treaty members [32]. The impact on cruise ships will depend on the passengers' nationalities because, in theory, passengers from European countries that are part of the 'Schengen treaty' do not need to be processed through a border control. Complications can arise because of visa requirements, which may be different for non-Schengen and Schengen countries if, for example, a non-EU crew member has to be repatriated at short notice.

According to Europa [32], the name 'Schengen' originates from a small town in Luxembourg. In June 1985, seven European Union countries signed a treaty to end internal border checkpoints and controls. As time has passed, more countries have joined the treaty and currently there are 25 Schengen countries, all of which are in Europe. They are Austria, Belgium, the Czech Republic, Denmark, Estonia, Finland, France, Germany, Greece, Hungary, Iceland, Italy, Latvia, Lithuania, Luxembourg, Malta, the Netherlands, Norway, Poland, Portugal, Slovakia, Slovenia, Spain, Sweden and Switzerland.

Regulations concerning port health can, as was stated earlier, result in a visit from health officials who will inspect any part of the ship to ensure that the vessel is operating safely and hygienically. The galley is often a primary focus because of the risks that can exist when storing and preparing foods for consumption. Most

Figure 5.3 *Passports ready for port authority inspection (courtesy of Tom Hunter)*

large vessels employ an environmental safety officer, who is responsible for ensuring that the ship complies with regulations and meets minimum standards.

MARKETING AND DEMAND

The previous section identifies a feature that is stressed by the cruise industry – that it is the safest way to travel [31]. According to Goeldner and Brent Ritchie [28], this gets to the heart of an individual's psychology or motivation: 'a person is thus possessed of two very strong drives – safety and exploration – and he or she needs to reduce this conflict'. The CLIA recognize this conflict, but in high-lighting the industry's safety record and describing the ship as, 'comparable to a secure building with a 24-hour security guard' [31], they aim to show how the regulatory framework actually enhances the passenger's potential enjoyment of their vacation.

More and more, cruise companies are adopting what is referred to as a 'psycho-graphic' approach to market segmentation [28]. Market segmentation is under-taken in order to divide a defined population so as to reflect characteristics and thus to maximize the potential success of a marketing campaign. Traditionally segmentation considered geographic factors (where individuals lived), demo-graphic factors (their age, gender, family circumstances), socio-economic factors (occupation, social class and income), but psychographic factors consider values, motivations and personal issues. Thus a cruise vacation can be sold as a 'lifestyle' choice. From a planning point of view, the implications are as follows: do the destinations meet the psychographic needs in terms of travel preference of the pas-sengers and do the products and services onboard meet the psychographic needs in terms of travel preference of the passengers?

LOGISTICS

Logistical planning can take a number of guises. For example, this type of plan-ning can focus on: supplies and services (fuel, provisions or consumables); sched-ule planning (coupled with fuel consumption); or capacity management (maximiz-ing efficiency when dealing with large numbers of people). Cruise ships can travel at speeds of up to 25 knots but to do so is counterproductive economically. At this speed, the ship consumes fuel at a greater rate, although greater distances can be travelled. Cruise itineraries are planned so that the ship can travel comfortably between ports to ensure:

- fuel consumption is at an economically optimized rate
- the arrival time and departure time is as per the schedule
- that the mix of destinations is appropriately balanced to meet customer needs
- that regulations are complied with.

Cruise companies tend to include 4–5 ports of call for a 7-day itinerary and 8–10 ports of call for a 14-day itinerary [29]. Increasingly, as the industry expands, there is a need to locate embarkation ports to ensure new markets are accessed [28]. Fly cruising presents similar questions about safety, customer resistance, opportunity and, increasingly, the tyranny of airport check-ins [33].

SHORE EXCURSIONS

Cruise companies offer shore excursions or tours for a variety of reasons. Obviously, these activities are revenue generating and provide a vital contribution to a cruise company's bottom-line profitability but the provision of tours adds to the complete package that is the cruise vacation. For many passengers, the tour continues to develop the pattern seen onboard relating to the provision of a secure and a hassle-free quality vacation, by providing a relatively safe, easily organized and managed 'foray' into a different culture or, alternatively, an opportunity to sample an activity. This tourism experience, involving an element of being chaperoned or mentored, cossets the individual.

Invariably, shore excursions are entirely optional and, therefore, sales and marketing are important aspects in the process of managing this element of revenue generation. Sales are encouraged and undertaken before the passenger joins the ship. In most cases, passengers or potential passengers are introduced to shore excursions in the cruise brochure, where summaries of key tours are included as a form of appetizer. Tours provide a link in the chain that is described in the brochure, with the cruise ship as a destination together with the options for spending time onboard and the ports of call as secondary attractions, with the tours identifying the best options for spending time ashore. The choice faced by passengers is whether to be independent on arrival at the port or to leave the organization and subsequent implementation of the shore experience to the cruise company.

It is in the best financial interest of the cruise company to sell tours and yet, as is the case with everything regarding marketing in general for cruise passengers, considerable care is required to ensure that sales are made with sensitivity to the setting. High-pressure sales techniques are counterproductive in this type of community setting where passengers are socially attuned with each other and experiences are shared. Shore excursion sales are more likely to be successful using a subtle selling approach.

Promoting sales

While the brochure is the initial marketing communication used to introduce the notion of shore excursions, it is interesting to examine just how that is done. Emphasis is placed in the itinerary on key features and activities that can be experienced ashore and, often, these component parts are highlighted within specific tours. Some cruise brochures send a message to the cautious traveller that tours are the best way to take the stress out of visiting ports of call. Shore excursions receive prime billing in relation to describing options ashore, complete with clear guidance as to how to book before joining the ship. Usually, the message contains a compelling prompt that to avoid disappointment the tour should be booked as early as possible.

When the tickets are sent to the passenger, the pack of information that accompanies the ticket includes a shore excursions brochure. This is the primary vehicle for promoting sales before departure and to prompt sales onboard after departure. This reference material uses language most carefully in order to maintain an intellectual bond with the reader, taking care to develop the appropriate style of copywriting, to be truthful and to avoid contravening legislation related to mis-selling.

Virtually all companies use their websites to present their products to all who visit the worldwide web. This is done in general as a marketing initiative and as a form of distribution. Prospective and existing clients can visit the website in order to find out more, to make comparisons, to make bookings and to communicate with the cruise company and (in some cases) with other passengers. Providing the market has access to it, the cruise company website is an excellent vehicle for promoting shore excursions.

The itinerary and operational aspects, such as deadlines for closing sales in order to confirm arrangements, can affect sales onboard. Adverts in the ship's newspaper and, if available, on the ship's television channel, promotions near the tours office, direct sales, and connections made by port lecturers all form part of the marketing plan. Equally, a successful first port of call can generate additional sales via word-of-mouth communication.

It is also interesting to consider the issue of time in relation to tours. Depending on the itinerary and port of call, ships may arrive at a port at 0800 and depart at 1700. This creates an opportunity to sell half-day and whole-day tours. Many passengers realize that the tour presents the best, most time-efficient way to visit and experience the port of call. The added security factor is that most prestigious cruise companies guarantee to look after their passengers if a tour is delayed by delaying sailing or, if that is not an option, by ensuring they meet the ship at the next possible port of call.

Drivers for sales:

- Scarcity value
- Security aspect
- Best choice promotion
- Natural choice option

Table 5.2 Sales options

Cruise brochure	Website	Promotions	Word of mouth
Tour brochure	Ship's TV	Direct sales	Port lecturer

What makes a good shore excursion?

This depends on the passenger and the cruise company. As is portrayed in the cruise brochure, ports of call or destinations are selected for a variety of reasons. Most importantly, though, cruise companies will want to identify which facets are most attractive to their passengers and capitalize on these. Here passenger demography plays a part: tours are considered according to the type of passenger. In this way, families, older passengers, active couples, young singles and all other identifiable market sectors can be satisfied.

The cruise company seeks a product that strikes a chord in terms of the image and content when considered in relation to the cruise and the cruise brand. The tour must provide an itinerary that fits the ship's timetable. The logistics surrounding the tour as supported by the tour operator at the port must be in synergy with the requirements of the ship and passengers. At the same time, the tour operator must also assure health, safety and security.

A cruise company's expertise or experience is likely to have an impact. Prior experiences are important in building relations with tour operators, in understanding what to expect on the quayside when dispatching tours, and in recognizing the tours that are popular and achieve the best scores in passenger surveys.

Designing the tour

The quality of communication between the cruise company, their agent and the tour operator in the port of call is paramount. The port agent acts as a facilitator, although for many companies the communication between cruise company and tour operator can be direct and continuous. Initially, the cruise company constructs an itinerary, taking into account logistical factors such as fuel and travel time, and creating a balanced cruise programme that will sell. The travel operator liaises with the shore excursions department to agree the shore excursions programme and to construct tour brochures and plans resources.

The extent and diversity of the programme will take into account the number and type of passengers onboard the ship as well as the time in port and the availability and quality of transport, such as coaches, sea or river craft, trains, helicopters or light aircraft. The availability of trained guides is also important. In many ports the expansion of cruising as a vacation has created the potential for increased traffic. As a result, several ships may visit ports on the same day, thus diluting the availability of shore excursion resources and increasing crowding. Arrival time at a port may be critical in gaining access to resources in such a way as to avoid overcrowding. However, cruise companies are less likely to include a port in an itinerary if overcrowding and quality control are concerns.

Figure 5.4 *Tour bus returning to the ship*

Most tour brochures tend to include reliable half-day or full-day favourites. These include the 'banker' sites – the primary reason for an attraction being an attraction. It is hard to imagine passengers not visiting the pyramids in Cairo if their ship calls at Port Said or Alexandria. Full-day tours tend to include a lunch. Morning tours are generally more popular than afternoon tours since passengers tend to feel their time is better spent independently in the afternoon. Some cruise companies provide cars or minibuses to cater for individuals, couples or smaller groups who prefer to remain apart from other cruise passengers. 'Party' tours, including music, dancing, drinks and food, are popular with a younger demography on island destinations. Cultural tours are popular with passengers from cruise ships where the emphasis is on discovery and learning. It also follows that cruises with themes generate interest in specific types of tours: for example, a vineyard visit in New Zealand may suit an individual attracted to a gastronomy-themed cruise, and a tour to the opera in Italy might meet the needs of a music lover.

Before arrival

Tours are made available with minimum and maximum numbers. On leaving port the shore excursions office will be aware of the actual numbers sold and availability. This team will be briefed to note the content of tours, those that are likely to be over-subscribed, best alternatives, tours that might suit specific types of passengers (e.g. those with walking difficulties) and any other special features. Many passengers like to talk to a member of the shore excursion team to get a feel for the tour, and for that reason it is helpful for the team to experience as many tours as they can so as to build up their knowledge.

As mentioned previously, the port lecturer is an important part of the sales equation. Many port lecturers liaise with shore excursion teams to help inform the passengers about the content of tours and to help them make the best choice in order to optimize enjoyment of their time ashore. Port lecturers also accompany tours as escorts and provide an additional point of quality control, feeding back perceptions and impressions to the shore excursions manager from both their own and the passenger's point of view.

Approximately one day prior to arrival, the shore excursions manager will contact the tour operator with final numbers. The tour operator will already have been appraised as to numbers before the ship sailed and will have an outline idea relating to resource needs. The tour operator can advise the ship if an extra allowance of numbers is possible to increase last-minute sales. The shore excursions manager can decide whether a tour, which is close to minimum numbers, should run or be cancelled and compensate the tour operator accordingly. This decision is often a matter of applying a cost benefit analysis, i.e., does the benefit of operating the tour, losing some revenue while satisfying customers, outweigh the cost of cancelling it and creating dissatisfaction? In some cases, a shore excursion that goes ahead despite not achieving minimum numbers may even avoid making a loss because it receives last-minute sales.

Sales onshore and on the ship generate a ticket and receipt for the passenger as proof of purchase and entitlement to join a tour. In some cases, tickets will identify the passenger by name, providing extra security in case the ticket is mislaid. Advice regarding special conditions – the need to wear walking shoes, to dress sensitively for certain religious buildings, dietary requirements and so on – is clearly communicated at the time of sale.

On arrival

The imminent arrival of a ship to port triggers a series of actions to clear the ship formally for arrival by satisfying the port authorities that due process has been followed and that all requested administrative tasks have been completed. When cleared for arrival by the port authority, the ship can then tie up alongside the quay or lie at anchor off the port, as directed.

It is customary for shore excursions officers to be among the first people to go ashore – to meet the tour operator and check that arrangements are in order and that passengers can join the respective tours. The process of disembarkation requires careful planning in order to ensure that the correct passenger gets to the joining point for the correct tour at the correct time.

Passengers are usually asked to meet at a gathering point close to where they will disembark to receive an adhesive colour-coded badge. Ship's staff are in communication by radio and they coordinate disembarkation and guide passengers to the relevant tour point. Many cruise companies encourage ship's staff to accompany tours as escorts. This enables the ship to have a representative with the passengers who can, if necessary, act for the company and also provide comment about the quality of the tour upon return. Escorts are generally fully briefed by the shore excursions team and provided with a checklist to complete. Tours are marked simply and visibly with codes that equate to the badges worn by passengers.

A shore excursions officer is responsible for meeting returning tours and registering passengers. The tour operator and the shore excursions manager agree the numbers of passengers who have undertaken tours so that the cruise company can make payment to the tour operator.

Figure 5.5 *Joining the tour*

Other duties

In addition to selling tours, the shore excursions office is a tourist information office and a travel agency. In its capacity as a tour information point, staff are frequently asked to supply facts and information about the port of call. This can include basic information, such as the distance from ship to town or city centre, or more complex, for example, relating to custom and practice. Most shore excursions offices hold data files to help staff answer these questions, but they also rely heavily on staff developing their own knowledge with experience.

As a travel agency, staff may be called upon to arrange hotels or onward travel arrangements, such as booking flight and train tickets or organizing taxis and ferries. This side of the business also generates revenue through commission on sales. Some cruise companies operate a separate travel company ashore that can deal with these passenger needs on demand. On the larger ships, a separate post can be created within the hotel department to manage flights.

Tour guides

Good tours rely on good tour guides. The interaction between a tour guide and passengers is essential to the success of a shore excursion or tour [34]. This individual entertains, informs and organizes to varying degrees depending on the needs of the passenger. As the scale of the cruise industry continues to expand, the need for high-quality tours and guides follows suit.

In general, this type of person has an in-depth knowledge of their field and is highly skilled as a communicator. This can include fluency in languages, a well-tuned but carefully practised sense of humour and an ability to empathize with a broad range of people. Frequently a guide will also have the ability to undertake first aid and be able to assert her or himself whenever necessary.

Many tourist organizations operate an accreditation scheme for tour guides to ensure they are appropriately qualified for the task. Frequently, it appears, guides are over-qualified for the task, possessing higher-level degrees in their subject and being regarded almost as experts in their subjects. Depending on the type of passenger, mature guides may find that they are at an advantage, with a breadth of life experiences that can lend themselves to this type of job. All guides must be physically fit because of the rigours of the job.

Attractions, tour operators, coach companies and other tourist venues can employ guides. Some are freelance or self-employed. Guides are utilized: on walking tours; coach tours; within notable buildings or sites such as art galleries, cathedrals or castles; as trail guides; as sports guides; or as interpreters (cultural or site interpretation rather than linguistic interpretation). For many cruises there may be

Figure 5.6 *Tour groups in Kusadasi*

some tours that are particularly popular and the guide will have to plan with the tour manager how best to orchestrate visits and timings to maximize passenger enjoyment.

Tour guides may work with tour managers, who coordinate the shore excursion provision, and coach drivers. In addition they tend to develop good working relations with those employed by the attractions that they are visiting and/or key locations that form part of the tour. The guide may also need to identify any tour escort (normally an employee of the cruise company). See Table 5.3.

Table 5.3 *Points for good practice: the tour guide*

A good practice guide

1. Ensure you have all contact details and emergency numbers (just in case).
2. Establish a good rapport with the coach driver, go over the itinerary for the tour and identify potential problems that may not have been foreseen (e.g. roadworks).
3. Make sure you know the details relating to the itinerary, including method of payments for access to sites, etc.
4. Test the microphone – ensure it is in good working order and can be heard in all parts of the coach.
5. Practise using the microphone – many people hold the microphone loosely against the chin because it is consistently at the correct distance from your mouth in this position.
6. Make sure you get a courier's seat or front seat; check the seat belt.
7. Inspect the inside and outside of the coach for cleanliness and general condition. This is the responsibility of the coach driver but you should reassure yourself that the coach is in appropriate condition (no cracked windows, tyres in good condition, clean, no damaged panels, lights and air conditioning working, etc).
8. Greet clients – smile!
9. Before departure, do a head count.
10. Before the engine starts, introduce yourself and point out safety aspects as directed.
11. Sit before commencing commentary.
12. Check that your clients are OK and are listening – glance back.
13. Don't talk too much and adopt an appropriate pace and intonation of speech.
14. Start by saying what the tour is going to be, with an outline of stops, comfort breaks and meal breaks.
15. Be precise about return to coach times; repeat these messages to stress timings and help passengers to identify the coach by appearance, number and location.
16. Be particularly clear if the coach might have to relocate after stopping and passengers debus.
17. At meals it is best to sit with the driver unless an alternative arrangement has been made.
18. Passengers are likely to expect toilet stops and souvenir stops.
19. When directing, say things like, 'On the right you will see'. Always make sure you don't talk over a particularly interesting sight.

Table 5.3 *Continued*

20. Don't forget camera or photographic moments.
21. Be identifiable – umbrella, your clothes, a hat – something that is easily remembered and easily seen.
22. Be vigilant about hazards. Uneven pavements, low ceilings, etc.
23. Know your passengers: find out a bit about them and use that in your talk (if appropriate, that is).
24. Keep language simple and be willing to answer questions. Remember the people at the back may not hear the question, so repeat it to them before giving the answer.
25. Include all age groups by aiming to provide a commentary for everyone that might be on the tour.
26. Explain local rules and customs so that people know why things are as they are.
27. Keep counting and checking at key points (off and on the coach).
28. Keep your group together and keep pedestrian traffic flows clear.
29. Be proactive so as to try and avoid problems.
30. Use positive body language and maintain eye contact.
31. Develop a strong routine at the end to mark the final point of the tour.

SUMMARY AND CONCLUSIONS

This chapter examines the very nature of what it takes for a destination to be an appealing port of call that can be added to an itinerary. Thereafter, a number of theoretical approaches to analysing and evaluating destinations are suggested, alongside the need to consider tourist motivations. These approaches should be considered carefully to make sure that the theory selected meets the prospective task in hand. The reader is advised to undertake further literature review to examine the theories in more depth in order to make such a judgement. The chapter concludes by describing shore excursions as operated by cruise companies. This section of the chapter includes a critique of tour planning and tour management.

REFERENCES

1. Burton, R., *Travel Geography*. 2nd ed. 1995, London: Pitman.
2. Davidson, R. and R. Maitland, *Tourism Destinations*. 1997, London: Hodder and Stoughton.
3. *Lloyd's Cruise International*. 2003, London: Informa Publishing Group.
4. Lloyd's, 'Silversea', *Lloyd's Cruise International*. 2003.
5. Evans, N., D. Campbell and G. Stonehouse, *Strategic Management for Travel and Tourism*. 2003, Oxford: Butterworth-Heinemann. p. 120.
6. Melian-Gonzalez, A. and J.M. Garcia-Falcon, 'Competitive Potential of Tourism in

Destinations', *Annals of Tourism Research*, 2003. 30(3): p. 720–740.

7. Framke, W., 'The Destination as a Concept', *Scandinavian Journal of Hospitality and Tourism*, 2002. 2(2): p. 92–108.

8. Peattie, K. and L. Moutinho, 'The Marketing Environment for Travel and Tourism', *Strategic Management in Tourism*, L. Moutinho, ed. 2000, Wallingford: CABI Publishing.

9. Porter, M.E., *Competitive Strategy: Techniques for analyzing industries and competitors*. 1980, New York: Free Press.

10. Porter, M.E., *The Competitive Advantage of Nations*. 1990, New York: Free Press.

11. Wahab, S. and C. Cooper, 'Tourism Globalisation and the Competitive Advantage of Nations', *Tourism in the Age of Globalisation*, S. Wahab and C. Cooper, eds. 2001, London: Routledge.

12. Smeral, E., 'Globalisation and Changes in the Competitiveness of Tourism Destinations', *Globalisation and Tourism*. 1996, St Gallen, Switzerland: Editions AIEST.

13. Knowles, T., D. Diamantis and J.B. El-Mourhabi, *The Globalisation of Tourism and Hospitality: A strategic perspective*. 2nd ed. 2004, London: Thomson.

14. Butler, R., 'The Concept of a Tourist Area Cycle of Evolution', *Canadian Geographer*, 1980 (24).

15. Doxey, G.V., 'A Causation Theory of Visitor-Resident Irritants: Methodology and research inferences', *Travel and Tourism Research Associations Sixth Annual Conference Proceedings*. 1975. San Diego.

16. Shaw, G. and A.M. Williams, *Tourism and Tourism Spaces*. 2004, London: Sage.

17. Cooper, C., *et al.*, *Tourism Principles and Practices*. 1995, Harrow: Longman.

18. BTA, *The Sustainable Growth of Tourism to Britain*. 2001, London, British Tourist Authority.

19. Smith, M.K., *Issues in Cultural Tourism Studies*. 2003, London: Routledge.

20. McKercher, R. and H. du Cros, *Cultural Tourism: The partnership between tourism and cultural heritage management*. 2002, New York: Haworth Hospitality Press.

21. Lockyer, T., 'Understanding the Hotel Accommodation Purchase Decision', CHME conference. 2005, Bournemouth.

22. Maslow, A., *Motivation and Personality*. 2nd ed. 1970, New York: Harper & Row.

23. Cohen, E., 'Rethinking the Sociology of Tourism', *Annals of Tourism Research*, 1979. 6: p. 18–35.

24. Plog, S.C., 'Understanding Psychographics in Tourism Research', *Travel Tourism and Hospitality Research*, J.R. Brent Ritchie and C. Goeldner, eds. 1987, New York: Wiley. p. 203–214.

25. Dann, G., 'Tourist Motivation: An Appraisal', *Annals of Tourism Research*, 1981. 8: p. 187–219.

26. McIntosh, R. and C. Goeldner, *Tourism Principles, Practices, Philosophies*. 1986, New York: Wiley.

27. Moutinho, L., ed. *Strategic Management in Tourism*. 2000, Wallingford: CABI Publishing.

28. Goeldner, C. and J.R. Brent Ritchie, *Tourism: Principles, Practices and Philosophies*. 2003, New Jersey: John Wiley and Sons.

29. Laws, E., *Managing Packaged Tourism*. 1997, London: International Thomson Business Press.

30. CLIA, 'Committed to Keeping Passengers Safe and Secure'. 2011 [accessed October 2011]; Available from: http://www.cruising.org/regulatory/cruise-industry-policies/cruise-industrys-commitment-safety-security.

31. CLIA, 'Security'. 2011 [accessed April 2011]; Available from: http://www2.cruising. org/industry/security.cfm.

32. Europa, 'Free Movement of People'. 2011 [accessed October 2011]; Available from: http://europa.eu/legislation_summaries/justice_freedom security/free_movement_ of_persons_asylum_immigration/index_en.htm.

33. Pappas, S., 'Ticked off Travellers'. 2010 [accessed April 2011]; Available from: http:// www.cbsnews.com/8301-501465_162-20023698-501465.html.

34. Collins, V.R., *Becoming a Tour Guide*. 2000, London: Continuum.

6 Working onboard

This chapter examines staffing and personnel organizational structures and the concomitant roles and responsibilities onboard cruise ships. The role of the purser is considered and the hotel services department described to enable the reader to understand the lines of authority and criticality of human resource relationships onboard. Crewing is a complex issue for cruise operators and particular attention is given to the mechanisms that exist to support the management of hotel services crew, the sourcing of skilled, semi-skilled and unskilled labour for the hotel services department, and staff development. The organizations that exist to provide assistance and support to international crews, often in defence of the crew member's basic employment needs, are identified, together with a discussion relating to this sensitive employment issue [1].

By describing the purser's role and the onboard hotel services, a link is created in terms of introducing the range of products and services provided to customers and crew. This, in turn, introduces the distinct areas of operation that are defined as being hotel services, including customer services, bars, lounges, restaurants, bistros and sleeping accommodation. Those services that are concerned with customer entertainment, such as shops, casinos, entertainment casts and port lecturers, are also studied.

Cruise ships are likely to be heterogeneous – that is, containing a mixture of crew, with different nationalities, various ages, different backgrounds and prior learning, and varying needs and aspirations. The latter part of this chapter asks questions about managing such a multicultural and diverse crew situation and provides case studies that are intended to highlight crew perceptions about life onboard.

THE ROLES AND RESPONSIBILITIES ON A CRUISE SHIP

The majority of large cruise ships boast extensive facilities and activities. This, in turn, necessitates employing a virtual army of people to ensure the 'resort' operates to meet guests' needs. Traditionally, ships employed officers and ratings (non-officers) or crew who performed tasks related to the safe passage and commercial activity of the vessel within a hierarchical regime. This regime was often operated on a rotationary 'watch-keeping' basis, from which the term 'officer of the watch' is derived. Automation has, on many vessels, changed the strict pattern of 24-hour watch-keeping but for any ship there remains a need to maintain operational effectiveness, safety and security. Watch duties are traditionally four hours in duration: 0800 to 1200, 1200 to 1600, 1600 to 2000, 2000 to 2400, 2400 to 0400 and 0400 to 0800. Typically, a deck or engineering officer will undertake two 4-hour watches in a 24-hour period.

On cruise ships, the same hierarchical regime exists, for reasons that are explained later, but in comparison to a tanker or cargo vessel, the majority of employees are associated with customer services. In contemporary cruising, employees are designated officers, crew and staff [2]. Officers are employees with specific authority. They are located within four departments: deck, engineering, radio and hotel services. The crew is similarly divided between these four departments but in number this group represents the largest segment. The last group – staff – includes personnel, many of whom may be contracted to work onboard by a concessionaire, such

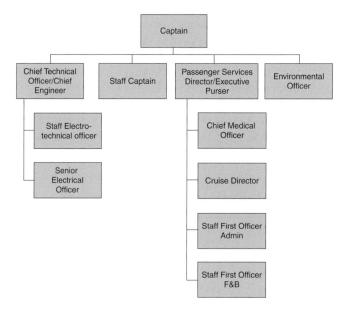

Figure 6.1 *Organizational chart – management structure*

as shop managers, hairdressers, beauticians, entertainers, casino staff and photographers. The organizational chart above is an example of the structure employed for managing a large cruise ship.

The resultant 'ship's company' is a large and diverse community that, because of scale and complexity, requires care in terms of management and coordination. A ship's Master has, according to Branch [3], absolute authority onboard a cruise ship. This authority, acting in lieu of the ship's owner, provides powers to act accordingly in cases where the ship, crew, customers and/or ship's contents are at risk. There is a subtle difference between this role and the post of Captain, which is deemed to be a rank, although frequently the Captain on a cruise ship will hold the position of Master. Other officers onboard may also hold the rank of Captain, e.g. the Staff Captain, who is charged with a responsibility relating to the crew, staff and customers onboard.

Some roles on the ship have cross-departmental responsibilities. The Environmental Officer has a direct responsibility to the Captain but an overarching responsibility to ensure company policies are adhered to in respect of regulations for environmental matters. Many ships also employ a Personnel and Training Officer with cross-departmental responsibility to ensure matters relating to training and personnel development are managed to meet company policies.

The deck department

The ship's Master is in charge of the ship but also oversees navigation and the deck department. On a day-to-day basis, the deck department is the responsibility of the Chief Officer or First Mate (First Officer). The larger the vessel, the more requirement for additional deck officers, who are termed Second, Third or Fourth Officer (the number depends on the size of the ship). This department oversees navigation and the care of the vessel. One of the senior officers in this department will also hold the position of Safety Officer. The deck officer's complement is frequently made up with junior officers in training, who are called 'cadets'.

Crew positions include: Chief Petty Officer (deck) and Petty Officers (deck), who supervise deck crew under the direction of deck officers; Deck Carpenter, who attends berthing and departure; Quartermaster or Coxswain, who is a senior rating responsible for steering; Junior Seamen, Seamen grade 2 and Seamen grade 1 – the latter two share look-out and steering duties with deck officers; the Bosun (boatswain), who is the deck hands overall foreman; and day workers employed in general duties. All seamen employed in the deck department who are not officers fall into the categories of ordinary seamen (OS), who are deemed to be unskilled, or able-bodied seamen (AB), who are considered skilled. The deck department can also include specific posts such as security.

Deck officers can be identified by their stripes, which are plain gold. Masters and Captains have four stripes, Chief Officers have three stripes, First Officers have two and a half stripes, Second Officers have two stripes, Third Officers have one and a half stripes and Fourth Officers have one stripe. Cadets frequently have either half or one stripe. The symbol for the deck department is a diamond. Security can be recognized by their brown stripes and their symbol – a capital 'S'. Most cruise ships appoint an Environmental Officer. This person is answerable to the ship's captain and is recognizable because he wears green and gold stripes.

The engine department

The engine room is the domain of the Chief Engineer, who is responsible to the Master for the vessel's propulsion, steering and power for auxiliary systems such as heating, ventilation, air conditioning, lighting and refrigeration. The Chief Engineer is also responsible for fuel, maintenance and repairs. Depending on both the size of the ship and the type of propulsion system, cruise ships may require additional engineering officers and cadets, including electrical engineers.

Crew positions in the engine department include: Chief Petty Officer (Motorman) and Petty Officer (Motorman) who supervise the engine room under the direction of engineer officers; Junior Motorman, Motorman grade 2 and Motorman grade 1. Some vessels have specific posts, such as electrician.

Chief Engineers have four stripes, which are gold and purple in alternate colours. The Chief Electrician has three stripes, the First Engineer has two and a half stripes, and the Second Engineer has two stripes. There are two symbols for this department; the propeller signifies technical and engineering, while an electric current motif is used for electrical officers.

The medical department

It is not surprising that, given the size of the community onboard, a cruise ship requires a medical team. The Principal Medical Officer (PMO) leads the team, supported by as many Medical Officers or doctors as are required. Thereafter, depending on the ship and the clientele, there may be a Senior Nurse or two or more nurses (usually at officer level). Some vessels also employ orderlies, who tend to be designated as ratings. The very largest of ships may also employ a Medical Dispenser, physiotherapists and dentists. Some ships have a morgue onboard.

The Medical Officer is usually identified by their three stripes, which are gold and red in colour. The symbol for this department is the *caduceus* (staff of Hermes). The provision of medical support onboard is a necessity for the well-being of the shipboard community. The medical team can also generate revenue in providing specialist support and, for that reason, some cruise companies locate the medical team under the management of the hotel services department.

The entertainment department

The Cruise Director, who tends to be an experienced professional from the world of entertainment, leads this department. As the departmental name implies, any aspect of entertaining customers (and crew) is managed from within this department. The range of employees can therefore include musicians, dancers, comedians, actors, singers, social hosts, sound and lighting crew, stage technicians, guest lecturers, port lecturers, health, fitness and sport instructors, children's staff and specialist experts.

A Deputy Cruise Director frequently assists the Cruise Director. The Cruise Director is usually regarded as having a rank equivalent to three stripes and is linked by association to the hotel services department.

The hotel department

Depending on the scale and size of operations, the hotel service team certainly may be extremely diverse, but that aside, for a cruise it dominates in terms of numbers of employees. An individual with the title of Hotel Manager, Director of Hotel Services, Passenger Services Director (PSD) or Executive Purser is usually in charge of the department. The term 'purser' is traditionally related to the controller of finances (hence derived from the word 'purse') but different cruise companies use the term in different ways. The senior officer in charge of hotel services will have four stripes, which are gold and white. The Executive Chef, the Food and Beverage Manager and/or Deputy Purser will have three stripes. The Senior Assistant Purser, Assistant Food and Beverage Manager, Bars Manager and Accommodation Manager (Housekeeper) will have two and a half stripes. The Second Purser will have two stripes. The symbol for this department is the cloverleaf.

Depending on the particular cruise company, their focus on core values, the type of passengers or customers and the product on offer, the hotel services department may be configured to reflect a bias somewhere between more traditional nautical lines and more contemporary hotel services, as seen shoreside. Because this department is the focus of this book, the various roles are outlined in more depth in the following section.

THE MANAGEMENT OF HOTEL SERVICES

Everything to do with managing hotel services on a cruise ship tends to be a reflection of the scale of the vessel and the labour intensity associated with product quality and service quality. In addition, if the ship and the tradition related to the development of cruising as a nautical enterprise are deemed to be a valuable marketing focus, the hotel services team is likely to be led by the Executive Purser; otherwise, the senior role might be identified as Passenger Services Director or Hotel Director. Thereafter, hotel services tend to be line managed by two or three senior managers, who may have the job title of Deputy Purser. These deputies focus on food and drink, passenger services (including accommodation) and finance. In turn, each deputy will lead a team that may comprise the following:

Food and drink: Executive Chef and kitchen brigade, including Bellbox chefs; Bars Manager, Bars Supervisors, Bar Stewards, Assistant Bar Stewards; *Maître d'Hôtel*, Restaurant Managers, Head Waiters, Head *Sommelier*, Assistant *Sommeliers*, Waiters and Assistant Waiters; Crew and Officer's Mess Chefs and Stewards and Utility Stewards.

Passenger services: Accommodation Manager, Accommodation Administration, Accommodation Supervisors, Public Area Supervisor (Decks), Public Area Supervisor (Lounges), Utility Stewards, Cabin Stewards, Butlers, Laundry Master, Assistant Laundry Master and Laundry Assistants.

Administration and personnel: Administration Manager/Assistant Purser Front Office, Assistant Administration Manager, Junior Assistant Pursers/Front Office Manager, Receptionists, Crew Assistant Purser, Shore Excursion Manager, Shore Excursion Assistant Purser and Junior Assistant Pursers.

Additional areas: Shops, florist, print shop, administration stores, art auctions, communication centre, beauty centre. Photography may also be located within the remit of the post holder.

Finance: Accounts Manager, Revenue Manager.

Various cruise companies operate hotel services managers to suit their strategic needs, so, for example, Princess Cruises recruit a team of Junior Assistant Pursers who are delegated to specific responsibilities, including reception, shore excursions, art auctions, food and beverage, and the crew office. They report to Assistant Pursers who are section assistant managers onboard, and in some cases, when the operation requires, the Assistant Pursers report to Senior Assistant Pursers.

The provision and orchestration of food and drink and accommodation are demanding from a human resource (HR) perspective. The effective performance of any cruise ship is irrevocably underpinned by the quality of service provided by people such as waiters, accommodation stewards, *sommeliers* and public service stewards. This presents a serious challenge to cruise companies. In periods of growth, cruise companies are faced with seemingly mind-boggling HR requirements. New mega cruise ships require in the region of 1,000 new personnel and, to staff a ship, contractual arrangements and the patterns of contracts need to be considered. These staff members require training, supervision and management.

Using experienced personnel to undertake training duties or to establish new vessels into service, dilutes the skills base on what may be a cruise ship with an impeccable reputation. The task of achieving minimum standards is never-ending. An example of an organizational chart for the Purser's department can be seen below (Figure 6.2). Note that many companies operate their hotel departments using alternative job titles.

In the galley, the team is frequently configured using a variant of more traditional approaches to the *hotelêrie* style brigade of chefs. This revolves around the Executive Chef supported by a team of Sous Chefs who control the hot plate (referred to as the 'hot press' on some vessels), where service takes place in the galley. These Sous Chefs may also be required for service to satellite restaurants, depending on the style of production and expectation for standards of food. Thereafter, the various sections in the galley are managed by *Chefs de Partie* such as: Larder Chef, Butcher, Sauce Chef, Grill Chef, Fish Chef and Pastry Chef, who work with their assistants. In addition there are Breakfast Chefs and Bellbox or Room Service Chefs. The latter produce food for room service from a pantry galley close to cabins or staterooms. Finally, it is very important to recognize that the officers, staff and crew also need to be fed and it is the job of the chefs who manage the crew and officers' messes (the name given to the ship's personnel dining areas onboard) to manage this complex and demanding task.

The restaurants on larger ships operate using an over-arching *Maître d'Hôtel* (*Maître d'*), who coordinates a team of Restaurant Managers. Each restaurant will employ a host to welcome guests and facilitate their entry and seating in the restaurant. Head Waiters are allocated to sections of larger restaurants (often up to

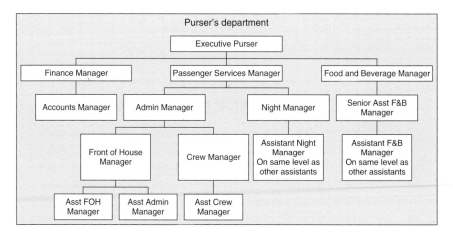

Figure 6.2 *Purser's department*

300 covers per section) where they have an overview of Waiters who work with an Assistant or 'Busboy' to serve 16–18 covers. These types of large restaurants will frequently employ a Head *Sommelier* and a team of Assistant *Sommeliers* to serve drinks and wine. Most mega-cruisers include a buffet service area as well as fast food outlets, such as pizza bars or burger bars. These are operated using a team of Assistant Buffet Stewards supervised by Head Waiters or Assistant Head Waiters.

The Bars Manager on a vessel organizes a multi-bar operation that can include: a dispense bar for restaurant drinks sales, show bars, cocktail bars, lounge bars, deck and pool bars, champagne and caviar bars, crew bars and, in some cases, an officers' mess bar. The bars are coordinated by Bars Supervisors who work with the individual Bar Stewards and their assistants.

Food and Beverage Managers working with Assistant Managers/Pursers liaise with the various managers to coordinate operations. Stores Managers receive, store and issue goods to the relevant personnel working in the galley, bars, restaurants or point of requisition.

THE SHIPBOARD CULTURE: MANAGING A MULTICULTURAL CREW

The crew onboard a mega-cruiser is likely to be diverse in terms of nationality and culture. For a vessel with approximately 2,000 passengers, there may be 900–1,000 crew members. On an early summer cruise in the Mediterranean on a Princess Cruises ship the make-up of the ship's company was as follows:

- Number of passengers – 2,054
- Number of crew – 980
- Nationalities – crew 54
- Nationalities – passengers 64

The following case studies present a synopsis of what it is like to work within this type of community. Names are disguised to preserve anonymity.

CASE STUDY: JUANITA, JUNIOR ASSISTANT PURSER

Juanita is Mexican. She came to work for Princess Cruises after studying business administration and tourism. She had an idea that she would progress to working in a hotel but became aware of the opportunities working at sea from a relative. She had always dreamed of travelling and, in particular, harboured a desire to go to Italy. She remembers now that she used to keep travel brochures so she could imagine different places around the world, and she even had a separate collection of Princess

Cruises brochures. Initially she started as an assistant buffet steward but eventually transferred to the Purser's desk where she is now employed as a Junior Assistant Purser. She really enjoys her life at sea, which she feels is a good experience for a single female and she has ambitions to progress in management onboard. One aspect of her work that she enjoys is the job rotation, which means she can be working in different areas, such as shore excursions or the crew office, on different contracts.

Juanita is fluent in English and Spanish, which is her mother tongue. She notes the diversity of nationalities and first languages onboard and says that she is amazed at how well people get on. She is friendly with people of all nationalities and declares that one critical factor for this intra-national situation is that the brain doesn't have a language. Rank may well create some separation but in general the crew work well together.

Work on the reception desk is demanding and challenging. This is where passengers head if they need information or if anything goes wrong. Juanita believes that reception staff need to be both strong and to care about people, with a 'how can I help' attitude. Problems have to be managed and passengers supported, and while outcomes are usually positive, the journey can be difficult. Juanita gets time off in port because the office team is large enough to allow for cover while maintaining appropriate staffing levels. However, it may not always be possible to go ashore on every occasion. Juanita has come to appreciate the advantages of learning other languages and being people oriented. This is the type of job where the people you work with are also the people you socialize with – this invariably means that you soon become friends with your colleagues and, at the end of the contract, you have the added bonus of being able to visit them all around the world. Juanita has been all over the world while working with Princess Cruises and recently she went to Italy for the first time.

CASE STUDY: JOHN, STAFF PURSER

From a career that commenced with hotels in the UK, John then moved on to cruise ships. He had the chance to join either P&O Cruises out of Southampton or Princess Cruises but chose the latter because he found the US style of service appealing. In his current position he is a senior manager with an ambition to progress to the post of Passenger Service Director (PSD) in the near future. He started work in reception as an Assistant Purser (AP) and was then promoted regularly until he achieved his current position. John now covers for the PSD. Up until five years ago, John believed that the company was very slow to promote on ability. The present situation has now changed and it is based on merit, informed by a sophisticated appraisal system. This change has meant that the company now has a large group of people in place who are very keen and extremely talented. In the shore-based office there were people who were used to the former and more traditional P&O Cruises purser model: P&O Cruises have since developed their approach to managing this department. John states that most managers are highly experienced in people management. He says that the responsibilities are demanding but the salaries reward this appropriately. This means that managers are unwilling to allow for any interference from secondary sources that can impact on the effectiveness and quality of operations.

Crew receive gratuities based on a point system, with 65% going to the food and beverage department and 35% going to the accommodation department (there is a per-day charge added to the passenger account to cover gratuities). Gratuities are awarded up to the Accommodation Manager and the *Maître d'*. The base salary is less than it has been in the past but John commented that the gratuity makes up for this. While passengers think this situation is not motivating, John declares that in reality it is. With 15% service being added to drinks sales, there is a visible impact on upselling and for staff to seek more training. Princess Cruises operate a credo using the acronym CRUISE, which stands for courtesy, respect, unfailing in service excellence. (At the time of the interview this had been operating for eight years and all staff appeared to be aware of it. Passenger satisfaction had leaped, too, from 82% to the point where the company was unhappy if it was less than 90%.)

In John's opinion, the current cruising season for the ship is going well, which can be attributed to many things, including the itinerary and an absence of unforeseen problems. The focus for managers onboard is predicated upon the need for awareness. It is better to predict and prevent problems rather than be faced with dealing with the repercussions. John's job means he has a wide remit of responsibilities, including the following: hotel key system (security), appraisals, line managing Senior Assistant Managers, gift salon, art manager, onboard sales, administration, hotel stores, florist, linen, photography, upholsterer, carpet, control for stores, review purchase orders (not shops), standards of performance, accommodation, compliance with regulations, indents, having the ship in readiness for dry dock, ensuring logistics embarkation and disembarkation, *Pratica* (dealing with port officials), security situation, tendering operations, the onboard newspaper (*Princess Patter*), overall printing, crew office, berthing and ship's crew welfare.

Cruise ship managers may well have more autonomy than was the case in the past, however, the vessels are not isolated islands operating independently of their corporate home base. Technology means that shore-based managers are aware of circumstances and events onboard, with the result that there is an immediacy required for dealing with critical issues identified ashore. In part this has come about because of the tendency for some to regard litigation as the most appropriate form of gaining a response to possible problems. However, ships are also subject to audits and inspection, which are in the public domain and can affect reputation.

John is a member of a number of committees: the executive committee, which used to be the PSD meeting, the captain's conference, and the task force meetings are all revenue related. In addition, there are meetings relating to the Norwalk (virus) action committee, the purser's office meetings (SAP), JAP meetings, hotel stores monthly meetings, which focus on costs and deal with any situation that could lead to excessive waste, and cruise meetings, which involve all departments and used to be known as the ship's committee meetings. The cruise ship is a lively community. People who are good at their job are noticed and rewards can be extremely high.

These cases draw attention to the demands of working in the hotel services department and highlight the differences in jobs and responsibility between a Junior Assistant Purser and Staff First Purser. Elements that are worth considering further include those community aspects that define the dynamics and atmosphere onboard, the attention to professionalism, the notion that this is an environment that is supported by individuals working in teams and the strength of opportunity for long-term careers.

WORKING ONBOARD: PRACTICAL CONSIDERATIONS

New employees who join a cruise ship can be, at first, somewhat overwhelmed by the environment. The scale of the ship, the way of life, the structures that support and inform crew, the disciplines of working at sea are all potentially alien and take some getting used to. Invariably, people work on cruise ships because they can travel but in addition there are advantages because of the types of jobs and levels of remuneration, opportunities for promotion and conditions of employment. There is no getting away from the fact that this is a unique job that entails long hours and long contracts. Hospitality businesses often cater for people who are socializing or purchasing services outside their normal work times, so it is not surprising that many people associate hospitality jobs with unsociable hours. This, however, ignores the sociability of hospitality work, the benefits in working when many people are playing, and playing when those same people are working [4]. The cruise setting provides a break from stereotypical work patterns that many find repetitive and tedious.

Conditions onboard will depend on the employer but the best provide excellent crew facilities and operate management regimes that are in tune with the personnel onboard. A successful cruise ship resonates with the harmony created by personnel who are proud of what they are doing, who know they are good at what they do and who enjoy what they do. Dining facilities revolve around a crew and officers' mess that is often serviced from the main galley, but has a separate Sous Chef and team to provide meals that may be specifically designed to meet the cultural and religious needs of specific groups of crew. Catering for crew is a major-scale, 24-hour operation. It is important to feed the crew well so they are happy with this element of their lives onboard. Some officers may be expected to eat with passengers as part of their public relations duties.

Going ashore will depend on operational circumstances. Where the team can cover the duties a split can be planned to create some time off for all members of a particular group or department. If the facility is closed and the personnel have no additional duties, time off can be organized: e.g. shop personnel. If duties are sufficiently demanding personnel may not be able to go ashore. Under maritime regulations ships must maintain minimum staffing levels for safety and security reasons.

If a member of the ship's complement is ill, they will be expected to see the ship's doctor and will be treated appropriately. In the worst-case scenario, a crew member may be sent ashore for further treatment and possibly repatriated. In less serious cases, after recuperation, the person will return to work. In the majority of situations, health and safety regulations prevent a person who is unwell from handling food and drink and serving passengers.

Crew members are generally accommodated in serviced and shared cabins. The more senior personnel are allocated larger cabins and over a certain rank, single en-suite cabins are provided. Space onboard any cruise ship is limited so crew members are advised to take care with what they bring onboard. The standard and specifications of crew accommodation varies depending on the cruise company and the ship. It is in the interests of the cruise company to provide the best standard of accommodation possible to ensure that crew are satisfied with this element of their life onboard, as with meals.

Social life is generally a high point onboard. Working and living in close proximity with colleagues invariably promotes a high level of camaraderie. Crew can spend time in the crew bar, officers' wardroom or social areas. Generally, prices of drinks are considerably lower than they would be in passenger areas. Most cruise ships have a crew club representative who organizes special events for the crew after consulting with the crew committee. The crew also has access to specific facilities that can include a pool, jacuzzi, gym and/or cinema. The ship's captain and senior officers manage discipline. When a crew member joins the ship, she/he signs on to confirm that they will comply with the regulations. Serious breaches of discipline can lead to instant dismissal.

RECRUITMENT PRACTICES

Finding a job on a cruise ship can take some investigation. Some companies are in business to act as a form of introductory agent, charging the applicant for the benefit of gaining access to potential employers. Others are genuine agents who are intermediaries in the recruitment process, often with offices located close to or within countries that are targets for employment. Some agents are actually secondary companies established by the cruise company to facilitate recruitment. Finally, some cruise companies employ directly. Trade journals, for either shipping and nautical matters or hospitality and catering, can be a useful source of information because major employers use these to gain access to a more specialized and experienced applicant. Managers in the Purser's department should have an appropriate undergraduate or postgraduate higher education qualification, which may be business-, hospitality- or tourism-based. Alternatively, many employers recognize professionals who have experience of working and managing in the hospitality industry but who may not have formal qualifications.

The University of Plymouth in the UK operates a three-year (or four with optional work placement) undergraduate degree – BSc (Hons) Cruise Management – that can help those who are seeking a hotel management position onboard a cruise ship to prepare and be qualified for this type of work [5]. Applicants should think more than twice before parting with money to secure an introduction or to get help with finding any type of job on a cruise ship. The best starting place for many appropriately qualified applicants is with the cruise companies themselves.

Finally, applicants should remember that the work and lifestyle might not suit everybody. There are many examples of potential crew members who were inappropriately prepared for their experiences onboard and who either had to be repatriated because they were unable to acclimatize, or worked their way through but left at the first chance. It is not in the best interests of a cruise company to be faced with serious human resource retention problems, because it is costly from a selection, recruitment and training point of view, potentially disruptive for other crew members and can impact on service quality. Klein [6] presents an interesting perspective, highlighting personnel problems on cruise ships. His study represents the negative position in regards to cruising. Many of the points raised in Klein's book are typical of comments made in opposition to globalization and capitalism as vehicles for a fair world and are punctuated by his stance of questioning the cruise industry as a socially and environmentally sustainable entity. He posits a view of the industry that at times suggests employers are oppressive or exploitative, and his work is an interesting read. He constructs a set of arguments that should be read by those who are seeking to work in this industry so they can consider the criticism and reflect on the balanced view of life and work for contemporary cruise companies. Research is presented in a later chapter on training that provides a contrasting view to that held by Klein.

CASE STUDY: INTERNS AT SEA – VICKY MORGAN

When Vicky was 14, her father, who she describes as being quite 'old fashioned', advised her to create a focus for her life. Vicky recalls that even at that relatively young age she said she would like to work on cruise ships. She had been on her first cruise, aboard *Canberra*, when she was nine months old and subsequently cruise holidays had punctuated her formative years. Vicky describes herself as a people person, and when she was at the stage of applying for a university course she had examined the prospectuses from a group of predominantly coastal universities. Her mother had spotted the Cruise degree at the University of Plymouth and Vicky now describes that moment as being, 'Victoria Morgan – this is your course, this is your life'. She believes that had she not found this course she would have selected a hospitality degree and targeted a career at sea. Vicky went to a relatively strict girls' school and remembers incurring some disquiet when she selected this course alone rather than the six options she was told to record on her application for university.

The course included a mix of people, some studying cruise management and others studying hospitality management, and Vicky appreciated this cross-fertilization of learning. She describes her first year as 'fabulous' – enjoying shared learning experiences with those outside the course too, with activities such as wine tasting – although it was also all new and difficult. Nevertheless, Vicky could see the logic of all her modules, and the way they could be applied to her career target. The best part of her degree was the work experience. Vicky was selected to work as a Trainee Hotel Manager by P&O Cruises. This experience took place just after her second year and she refers to it now as a time of maturation, as all her learning and experience began to come together and fit into place. She experienced all parts of the hotel department during her period at sea and gained a full understanding of operations.

Vicky worked in the galley preparing food, in reception dealing with enquiries, taking stocks in the bars: her complete immersion in hotel operations onboard was challenging but also highly relevant and, in the main, enjoyable. She is now employed as an Assistant Manager (Passenger Services) by P&O Cruises and she believes her training provided her with a serious advantage in terms of knowledge and confidence in 'doing the job'. She has carried out some very basic jobs – cleaning floors and filleting fish, for example – but she thinks these experiences have all gone towards making her a better manager. The advantages she gained in training include: familiarization with processes; comprehension of the onboard language; orientation – she can understand the complex geography onboard and fits more easily into it; float handling (she had experience of dealing with a £50,000 float when she spent time in the crew office during her training). At the point of employment post-graduation Vicky says she was easily 75% work-ready.

Her job as Assistant Manager is a responsible one – she looks after front of house and is responsible for supporting Passenger Service Assistants, complaint handling, organizing customer service questionnaires, disembarkation arrangements, passengers and tender operations. She states that her most challenging day is turn-around day, when the ship returns to home port and prepares for the next cruise, when she can average 12 to 14 hours of work. In terms of work–life balance, Vicky says you can't really compare the job to a 9–5 shoreside job but that she thinks the balance is acceptable. However, she does admit that her job wouldn't suit everyone. Furthermore, she notes that there are times when, dealing with difficult customers, it can be unpleasant. But there are also times when she can be sitting out on deck with a cocktail and it can seem like the best job in the world. More women are going to sea, particularly in the hotel department, and while many make a considered decision to spend a maximum number of years there, there are also increasingly more women achieving the most senior positions, as Executive Pursers. Her advice to future cruise management students is to be prepared to work hard but to remember that the benefits definitely outweigh the disadvantages.

CHALLENGES FOR LEADERS

Lukas [7] highlights the contextual, contractual and multinational issues that are critical for leaders on cruise ships. Working over many months in a highly charged, 'hot house' environment – one where the dynamic sense of change, travel and convenient social engagements dominate – flavours the professional and social lives of the employees. Change is all around. Every voyage means a new set of passengers or guests. While some cruise vessels operate a standard itinerary, many others change their patterns regularly. Cruise employees work to set contracts, so there are frequent comings and goings; new colleagues to become acquainted with and departing colleagues to say goodbye to. New managers set the pace and style of the working environment and it is not unusual to have managers casting a shadow over their teams because of a leadership style that might differ to that of their predecessor [8].

Developing this further, Yarnal and Kerstetter [9] discuss the implications of the difference in social 'feel' that comes about when people leave behind their state of being and join a cruise. This 'liminality' is said to also infect the crew in that lives shoreside and lives at sea are two contrasting realities. Beyond this sense of a new world are the demands of undertaking customer service consistently and constantly. Is this type of job, which requires a specific type of interaction with passengers, truly a form of emotional labour [10], or is it a reflection of the transactional nature of the workplace, where employees recognize that they are selling their labour and skills (both technical and interactive) in order to derive income and benefits [11]?

The implications for leaders are complex. Lukas [7] believes that those who seek to understand those complexities and to create the conditions for their employees

Figure 6.3 *Sous chefs onboard* Venture *undertaking a cookery demonstration*

to excel are most likely to succeed. However the author notes that in many senses the challenges for leaders are never-ending and the critical issue for many employees is to establish equilibrium within group dynamics so that professional practice operates in stabilized conditions [12].

SUMMARY AND CONCLUSIONS

The environment onboard a cruise ship is a society in microcosm. The society is one with a clear purpose; the operation of a cruise. Yet, as is the case in any society, there are subtleties and nuances involved because of the diversity of individuals, in managing this environment to create equilibrium. The command structure, as is described in this chapter, creates a framework in order to sustain management of operations. Thereafter, managers' actions to direct and support teams establish the normative conditions for working onboard. This chapter has highlighted some of these issues, which are, in turn, examined further in Chapters 11 and 12.

REFERENCES

1. Garrison, L., 'Finding a Job in the Cruise Industry'. 2005 [accessed May 2005]; Available from: http://cruises.about.com/cs/cruisejobs/a/cruisejobs.htm.

2. Bow, S., *Working on Cruise Ships*. 2002, Oxford: Vacation Work Publishing.

3. Branch, A.E., *Elements of Shipping*. 7th ed. 1996, Cheltenham: Nelson Thornes.

4. Douglas, N. and N. Douglas, *The Cruise Experience: Global and regional issues in cruising*. 2004, Frenchs Forest, Australia: Pearson Education.

5. University of Plymouth, *BSc (Hons) Cruise Operations Management*. 2005; [accessed April 2011]; Available from: http://www1.plymouth.ac.uk/courses/undergraduate/3697/Pages/CourseOverview.aspx.

6. Klein, R.A., *Cruise Ship Blues*. 2002, Gabriola Island: New Society Publishers.

7. Lukas, W., 'Leadership: Short termed, intercultural and performance oriented', *Cruise Sector Growth: Managing emerging markets, human resources, processes and systems*, ed. A. Papathanassis. 2009, Wiesbaden: Gabler.

8. Gibson, P., 'Cruising in the 21st Century: Who works while others play?', *International Journal of Hospitality Management*, 2008. 27(1): p. 42–52.

9. Yarnal, C.M. and D. Kerstetter, 'Casting Off', *Journal of Travel Research*, 2005. 43(4): p. 368.

10. Johansson, M. and L. Naslund, 'Welcome to Paradise. Customer experience design and emotional labour on a cruise ship', *International Journal of Work Organisation and Emotion*, 2009. 3(1): p. 40–55.

11. Brownell, J., 'Personality and Career Development: A study of gender differences', *Cornell Hotel and Restaurant Administration Quarterly*, 1994. 35(2): p. 36–43.

12. Gibson, P. 'Communities of Practice: Employment on cruise ships', *CHME Research Conference*. 2005. Bournemouth.

7 Customer services

By the end of this chapter the reader should be able to comprehend the importance of cruise-related operations and management on customer service, to describe the range of customer services, and to compare and contrast the internal and external factors that influence customer services. In addition, this chapter will examine customer service systems for cruise lines, discuss profiles of cruise customers and specific needs, and reflect on demography and segmentation.

SERVICE AND QUALITY

This chapter is concerned with customer service and the rather elusive issue of quality. The term 'quality' presents a number of complexities, starting with, at a basic level, the idea that it refers to a form of utopian excellence [1]. Consider, for example, what quality means from the perspective of an operational manager onboard a cruise ship? Harris [2] draws attention to the way that quality can correlate to prestige, relating to reputation, admiration, luxury and, as a result, the price – compare, for example, Silversea Cruises with Thomson Cruises – or that quality can be the way the customer views the service received against their perception of what was offered, or that quality is only concerned with ultimate customer satisfaction.

Taken a stage further, some authors suggest quality refers to a product or service, which is a combination of predictably uniform and reliable, suitable for the market and at the lowest cost [3]. Other theorists proclaim that it is more to do with the customer's perception of what is fit for purpose [4] or that quality can be to do with creating 'zero defects' and getting it right first time [5].

This debate indicates that managers should pay some attention to clarifying in their own minds what it is that they believe quality to be so they can create goals and targets. The implications for operations are critical in achieving the desired level of service together with the appropriate standard of product to budget. The subtleties in adopting an approach that strives at all times for excellence can create interesting operational dilemmas within a service organization that relies on staff and customer interaction, in terms of, for example, cost control and consistency of practice. Compare this to an organization that understands what its customer wants and designs the service to meet or even exceed this aim [6]. Wright [7, p. 186] declares that if an organization claims their service/product is quality, the implication is that so-called 'higher level benefits' such as attention to detail, high level of courtesy and those little, or sometimes not so little, important things that differentiate the business are evident, *as well as* the basic service/product specifications, the price and availability.

W. Edwards Deming, Philip Crosby and Joseph Juran are key sources who were involved in promoting a managerial stance when addressing quality. Their work, and the involvement of others, has led to the implementation of quality processes that are predicated upon the notion of researching quality, designing service quality as a fundamental for competitive differentiation, assessing perceptions of quality and making improvements [1]. Their particular views of quality in business embody subtle differences, yet they all share a common belief: that managers can make the difference; that improvements can only be achieved by involving stakeholders (e.g. suppliers, etc); that improving quality is not easy and that the process is continuous [6].

According to Dale [8], Total Quality Management (TQM) or Total Quality Control (TQC) was adopted in order to create continuous improvement, as a result of consultants from America, such as Deming, who contributed to the business renaissance in Japan during the 1950s and 60s. Their approach to achieve continuous improvements was to identify best practice, ensure it was established as best practice and train the workers to achieve that best practice. Tse [1] charts the progress of TQM as a management (and staff) philosophy within production-oriented companies through to its adoption by service companies. She lists the five guiding principles as: 'commit to quality, focus on customer satisfaction, assess organizational culture, empower employees and teams and measure quality efforts' [1, p. 303]. The implications are far reaching and, for some companies, change can be too slow [7]. However TQM can establish a particular approach for managers that is well suited to service organizations.

Proponents of TQM emphasize the fact that change for all organizations is inevitable and to strive for continuous improvement by embracing change is desirable. *Kaizen* is the word attributed to this process of continuous development, as taken from a Japanese term for steadfast day-by-day betterment. The word has entered the vocabulary of successful companies who have absorbed the *kaizen* approach into normal business practice [7].

Table 7.1 *Management of quality*

Quality theorists	Crosby	Juran	Deming
Key phrase	Zero defects. Right first time.	Fit for purpose.	Predictable degree of uniformity and dependability at low cost and suited to the market.
Key focus	Quality is established if the product or service conforms closely to customer requirements.	Quality can be set by stating goals and then aiming to achieve these goals.	Quality should be consistent, reliable and acceptable. Quality is everyone's business.
Implication	Time and resources are not spent on correcting errors.	Teams, groups and individuals should be appropriately organized and trained.	Customers have precise and clear needs and will go elsewhere if these are not met.
Management action	Confirm who is the customer and how they define quality in the setting. Senior managers are responsible for ensuring quality.	Managers would need to be clear about the purpose and what constitutes fitness for that purpose.	Managers should reduce delays, mistakes and defective work. Managers need to understand the market and how it is changing.

It is also useful to reflect on the causes of poor quality. Harris [2] lists some of the potential causes that have been prevalent and linked to claims of poor quality:

- A lack of concern for quality within the organization
- Elements of the organization omitted from the quality drive
- Incomplete or unavailable specifications for products, services and processes
- Badly designed operational methods

- Poor supervision and management leading to too much or too little discipline and control
- Poor supervision and management leading to poor morale
- Badly trained or untrained personnel
- Poor working conditions
- Poor job specifications
- Equipment and tools poorly maintained
- Materials not to purchase specification
- Ineffective audit or inspection
- Poor senior management control
- Lack of rewards and incentives

This list suggests that quality is highly complex and that circumstances where quality is at issue are highly individual. In addition, the variables connected to quality output are such that getting it right requires commitment, consistency and professionalism.

QUALITY FOR PRODUCTS AND SERVICES

Industry observers state that there are fundamental differences between products and services that are important when designing standards and establishing quality thresholds [6]. In essence they can be described as follows (Table 7.2).

Noting the points raised in the early part of this chapter, the key to ascertaining quality is to understand customer needs and wishes. However, at all times the arbiter for interpretation will be the provider of the service and this implies the poten-

Table 7.2 Defining products and services

Product	Service
A thing/object/device	A deed/performance/effort
Tangible	Intangible
Stand alone as an item	Requires people to take part
Customer not involved	Customer fully or partially involved
Standardized	Heterogeneous – different every time
Can be stored	Perishable
Can be tested prior to sale	Cannot be sampled prior to sale
Production often separated from consumption or usage	Production and consumption often occur simultaneously
Product purchase involves variable opportunity for reflection	Service encounter is a moment of truth

tial for misinterpretation. The problem can arise because, over time, elements (for example, people or processes) involved in a service can change, thus jeopardizing both the actual service quality and the understanding of customers' needs. A TQM approach stresses the need to continually appraise both aspects and to invest in training so as to ensure the consistent management of quality continuously. In this way, a cruise company can focus on identifying what the customer wants and then aim to provide that within a defined budget.

OPERATIONS AND MANAGEMENT

The success of a cruise business, in terms of securing repeat custom and capturing new business, is directly related to reputation. In turn, past and present customers and their perception of service and product quality directly inform that reputation. As discussed earlier, much is written about service quality and customer perceptions [8–11] and the notion that, to achieve quality, an organization must forever strive for continuous improvement and that ultimately the customer defines the level of service that is appropriate.

It follows that cruise companies who focus their attention on meeting and indeed exceeding customer expectations of service and product quality will be in a stronger position to retain existing customers and attract future customers. Companies invest time and money in order to prioritize their customer service programmes so that both staff and customers recognize the importance of getting customer service right. There may be, however, a yawning chasm between promoting customer service initiatives and delivering effective customer service initiatives and it is certainly not easy to deliver consistent high-level quality service. Disgruntled employees, an unexpected event such as an itinerary change, and production problems resulting in interruptions to service are among potential threats to maintaining service quality.

The formula for a successful cruise is demanding – getting everything right and exceeding expectations, and that means ensuring officers, managers, crew and staff are trained, are instinctively customer-oriented, are empowered to help customers if there is a problem, are aware of expected quality standards and capable of exceeding those standards. All this has to be done consistently and to a budget. A crew member who has been onboard for a nine-month contract has to be as fresh in her/his approach as an employee who is newly arrived.

Customer service presents serious challenges for managers at sea for a number of reasons. Staffing ratios of crew to customers can be high (almost 1:1 on luxury vessels) thus creating a requirement to ensure all crew who are in contact with customers are suitably customer-focused. Customers on large vessels may well be diverse in terms of country of origin and this can mean that expectations of quality

Figure 7.1 *Ensuring quality standards*

in customer service will vary. Contemporary cruise customers are demanding, in part because we live in a media-rich society that highlights consumer rights and advocates the benefits of complaining.

However, it should also be recognized that being at sea can create many positive customer service advantages. Staff are contracted to work onboard for a number of cruises. In this situation, the crew member cannot easily withdraw employment, nor can their performance be hidden from supervisors. The interaction onboard a cruise ship is complex. Customers and crew are together forming relationships for a number of days. In this situation, customer service is ongoing and cumulative and there are likely to be many occasions when crew members can provide moments of pleasure that may be important to ensure an ordinary vacation becomes special.

One additional element is worth considering in this regard. There are varying levels of labour intensity required on cruise ships for different activities. Food service and food production are examples of high labour intensity compared to the equivalent shore-based hotel model, where labour ratios of staff to customer have been reducing. In part this is influenced by the desire to differentiate and to maintain the 'service quality' but for cruise ships there are also important regulatory and safety issues to consider that impact on staff numbers.

Operations management in hotel services onboard cruise ships is configured to maintain optimum service contact strategies to meet service quality parameters. Decisions are taken to ensure service contact is essential and to make use of alternative approaches when appropriate [12] – for example, bookings for special services or shore excursions can be made prior to embarkation via the company website or via a travel agent, thus reducing the need for personal contact. This type of

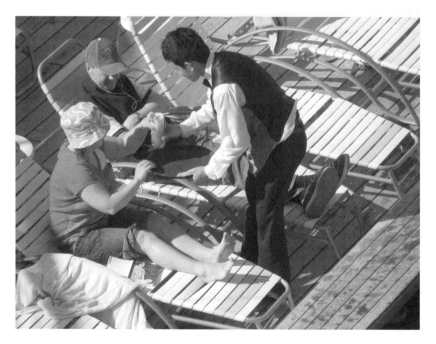

Figure 7.2 *Customer service on decks*

management action can reduce lines or queuing and congestion, and can increase customer satisfaction and staff job satisfaction.

In addition, consider events on a cruise ship that involve the potential for passengers to interact with crew and officers. These events may call for high contact to low contact. Strategies can be considered for reducing contact when the service quality is either unaffected or indeed improved, e.g., using in cabin on-screen account records reduces the number of passengers visiting the reception to collect and in some cases, query invoices or folios. At other times, careful organization of events such as the Captain's cocktail party or welcome meeting can create an impression of high-level contact without necessarily impacting on operational demands. Lovelock [12] believes that all service organizations can create operational improvements by reflecting on service contact by: considering decoupling services where it is of value within a service system; aim to reduce contact wherever possible by using appropriate strategies (see Table 7.3); where contact is inevitable, aim to enhance the contact to benefit all parties; examine low-contact areas to aim to address efficiency and quality improvement continuously.

The level and type of contact onboard a ship can vary from the personal service the passenger receives in the dining room, the interaction between cabin steward and passenger when they meet in the stateroom or cabin, passengers being joined by officers at their table in the restaurant (not practised on all ships) through to meeting officers in the bar and nightclub in the evening. Most passengers report that these forms of contacts and a broad range of other forms that are not described, are critical in maximizing the passenger experience [13]. It is also important to

Table 7.3 Contact strategies

Contact reduction strategy
Aim to use the phone, mail or other form of contact for most contacts
Introduce reservation and appointment systems
Create secondary information points to take pressure from main facility
Use drop-off points to collect customer information
Bring services to customers
Make use of roving greeters to control, entertain and give information
Use signs judiciously
Contact improvement strategy
Take a number system
Train contact personnel to deal with all situations they are likely to meet
Maintain consistent operating hours
Partition the back office from the reception area
Develop queuing or line patterns with signs

recognize that crew, staff and officers need to recharge and be able to spend time away from passengers in order to remain customer-focused.

MANAGING CUSTOMER SERVICES

The following section describes the typical range of services that may be available onboard a typical Grand class cruise ship catering for a US market. It is presented in chronological order as may be experienced by a passenger onboard. As cruising continues to grow, niche markets are targeted and innovative products and services are introduced accordingly, so this list is not exhaustive and is intended only as a guide.

INFORMATION

In any vessel with a large number of customers onboard, there is a need for information to be communicated accurately, effectively and in a timely fashion. Most cruise ships operate a purser's desk/office or a reception desk to provide a focal point for customers in need of information. Initially, when customers embark, there is a settling in period as they find their way about and orient themselves. Information will be provided to help with this task: pre-cruise information sent to the customer's home address, information pack in the staterooms or cabins, information posted at various key locations, and the daily publication, or cruise 'news'. Invariably, some customers will head for the reception desk to get answers. Some may use the telephone; others will stop and direct questions of crew members, whoever they may be.

From a customer service perspective there is much to be gained in predicting customer needs and while this approach is important throughout the cruise, there is evidence to suggest that first and last impressions are important in setting a template for service perceptions and sealing that set of perceptions of service experi-

Table 7.4 *Services onboard*

Embarkation	Butler service
Welcome onboard	Leisure services
Orientation and induction	Sport and recreation
Safety and lifeboat drills	Beauty and health
Food and drink service	treatments
Shops and boutiques	Entertainments
Medical service	Casino
Port lecturer and information services	Nightclub and disco
Accommodation services	Shore excursions
	Disembarkation services

Figure 7.3 *Reception – the information hub*

ences [14]. Equally, such predictions can help to establish a planned set of routines so that staffing levels at the reception desk, training of staff to deal with embarkation queries and production of printed material can be coordinated to best effect. The negative effect of poor customer service in dealing with information can lead to dissatisfaction, congestion and lines or queuing at information points such as the reception desk, overload of telephone enquiries creating non-response or late response to queries, a semblance of ineptitude or lack of both concern and professionalism.

INFLUENCES ON CUSTOMER SERVICES: TIPPING

Whether employed as a waiter, a cabin steward, a public room steward or a barperson, service staff who experience a direct customer interface are likely to receive gratuities or tips in the form of a financial reward. Throughout history, tipping has been a constant, yet sometimes awkward, element of the 'hospitality' guest–staff relationship. In European hotels and restaurants a system was devised called the *tronc* that created a model for distribution of shared tips, which was replicated for all hospitality businesses. This system allocated points based on a hierarchical reflection of status and rank in the service domain. Those on higher points such as the *maître d'hôtel*, (often referred to as the *maître d'*) or the restaurant managers received a larger slice of the total receipts. This system relied on those receiving the tip submitting the money to a central pot.

Cruise companies operate vastly different types of systems in relation to tips. In part this reflects cultural differences from the passenger point of view but there can also be other elements to note, such as the company or brand perspective. Thus, one company can proclaim that the ship is a no-tipping zone, as is the case with Seabourne Cruises, while Princess Cruises levies a $10 per day service charge to each passenger, which is then divided in *tronc*-like fashion. Passengers are also automatically charged 15% on every bar bill for the same reason. In both cases the service charge is stated as being optional and that the passenger should act to remove the charge if it is deemed inappropriate. P&O Cruises provide prospective passengers with a guide to tipping, so as to encourage passengers to provide a gratuity to specifically identified staff based on a formulaic approach.

It is useful to consider the different stakeholders in a scenario involving tipping. Each provides a different perspective on the transaction and the implication that arises from the act.

Stakeholder 1 – the passenger

Different passengers react to tipping in different ways. If a customer is used to tipping it becomes almost second nature. If a customer is used to tipping as a general exit strategy, the notion of reward for extra special service becomes rather less of an issue. Perhaps at times, the tip is in recognition that the server is in some way underpaid, so it is to right a wrong. Some passengers tip as an entry strategy. It is a message to the server to be attentive and that there is a promise for more to come. Some passengers identify a key individual, such as a head waiter, as the person to direct this entry strategy towards. Passengers are generally happy to pay a set amount per day as a service charge and to pay a percentage on top of all bar bills but some inevitably decline and act to remove the service charge because they think it is either unfair to them or not what they want to do.

Stakeholder 2 – the server

Money is money and, in a service job, tips can provide the bulk of income, thus making a job financially viable. At times the tip can be received in a spirit of genuine reward, as a thank you for making a vacation special. Other times, passengers may hide the tip in an envelope to disguise the fact that there are only a couple of dollars. Tipping can be incredibly unfair. Sometimes it depends who the customer is and the luck or bad luck of getting either 'Ms Generosity' or 'Mr Mean'. Passengers don't seem to understand what tipping really means to the server. Some are uncomfortable and get embarrassed, as if it is a dirty act. But it doesn't embarrass the server – it is too important for that. A managed system using fixed daily payments is fine, especially for supervisors, and there is the added benefit that tips may still be given in addition to the levy.

Stakeholder 3 – the employer

Tipping is an essential component of the cruise experience. It allows employers to pay minimum rates in the understanding that the actual income will be acceptable to the employee. If the money were not acceptable the staff wouldn't renew their contracts. That said, managed badly, tips can be a source of potential discord and disharmony. Staff notice what fellow employees receive and at times some servers can feel unhappy if they don't receive an anticipated tip. A managed tipping system using percentages and fixed payments gets around this problem but it is noticeable that some passengers still tip anyway and this can mean the problem is defrayed but doesn't really go away.

A tip-free environment is an interesting approach to managing the potential problem of passengers and crew reacting negatively to tipping from the other angle. In stating that tips are not expected and discouraged, a message is sent by the operator that tipping can be in some way unfair, that some customers can be uncomfortable about tipping and that they are above such petty matters. Furthermore, it appears the operator is suggesting that their staff don't require to be tipped (presumably they are appropriately rewarded through their payment), that staff are happy about this situation and that good service is not to be bought – it is all part of the package.

THE HUMAN SIDE OF SERVICE QUALITY

Customer service can be affected by personal factors related to life onboard. Cruise ships operate employment contracts for fixed terms. In some cases the contracts can be six, eight or ten months in duration. Crew work every day for these contracts and are expected to be consistently effective. Some cruise companies have the reputation for operating more 'enlightened' employment policies than their competitors. Those with better reputations ensure there is a fair and open approach to time off ashore, to covering for illness or unavoidable absences from the work area, and to maintaining a quality social environment for all onboard.

A factor to consider, however, is that customer service can be at risk if the server is unhappy for whatever reason and in need of a break. The nature of a shipboard community is that it can be a happy and almost sheltered environment where the people who work supportively together are friends and companions. If there is a breakdown in that arrangement it can be uncomfortable and so it is not in the interests of the cruise company for staff to be unhappy in either their social time or their work time.

Many cruise companies ensure that the crew elect or appoint a social club director to work with paid employees to construct a programme of events and activities. Despite the apparent monotony of having to work lengthy contracts, the reality for crew is invariably different. The attraction of travel and the places that crew visit coupled with the 'package' in terms of food, inexpensive drink, use of phones and the Internet as a means of staying in touch, entertainments and a lively social life can mean that life onboard is frequently more attractive than life at home. Many crew members report that after a month at home they were looking forward to returning to work.

CUSTOMER SERVICE SYSTEMS FOR CRUISE COMPANIES

Customer service strategies are often adopted to orient the brand from a holistic point of view and to clarify the brand's vision and mission in customers' minds. Examples include the following:

CRUISE: 'Princess Cruises' program (which stands for Courtesy, Respect, Unfailing In Service Excellence) recognizes and rewards shipboard personnel for developing solid customer relationships, for being proactive and responsive, and for going out of their way to meet our customers' needs with a smile.' (Princess Cruises, 2005) P&O Cruises also uses this acronym.

Gold Anchor Service: 'What is Gold Anchor Service? It's how we make your cruise adventure even more memorable. One thing that keeps our guests coming back again and again is our friendly and personal service. Maybe it's a server who remembers the name of your daughter's teddy bear. Or the bartender who remembers the extra olive. Or perhaps the housekeeper who reminds you of your dinner reservation time. Our unique style of service will enhance every aspect of your cruise. No matter where you are – the pool, the dining room, the spa or your room – get ready to be wowed! And we deliver it 24 hours a day. This is way beyond normal service. This is Gold Anchor Service.' (Royal Caribbean Cruise Lines, 2005)

Above and Beyond all Expectations: 'Silversea's service is simply the world's best. It is a philosophy, an attitude – complemented by distinctive European style and inherent in all that we do. Achieving perfection is driven by our desire to please. To see you smile. It begins the moment you step aboard with a warm welcome and a flute of champagne, and follows throughout your voyage with an unspoken anticipation of your needs. Sailing on Silversea's intimate ships is like visiting a friend's home; you're greeted by name and your personal preferences are always remembered.' (Silversea Cruises, 2005)

DEMOGRAPHY, PROFILES OF CRUISE CUSTOMERS AND SPECIFIC NEEDS

Cruise passengers are attracted by direct and targeted marketing. The product is designed specifically with people in mind and the cruise brands are very focused on the customers to whom they are selling. This creates excellent levels of knowledge about who is likely to be onboard but within the typical profiles that emerge there are likely to be a broad range of specific needs. Most of these specific needs can be predicted and catered for but there are always going to be unforeseen instances, individuals who bring something new in terms of a need or requirement that adds an extra challenge to operational management.

The cruising demography is changing annually, with lower age groups and a broader range of customer types beginning to have greater impact. In the past, the stereotypical cruise passenger may well have been of pensionnable age and female. Older passengers, passengers who may have a disability, passengers with specific preferences for food and drink, for entertainments onboard, for specific ports of call and specific shoreside activities, were understood and their needs addressed as well as could be achieved. Boat ports, with a tender from ship to quayside, always presented a problem for those passengers with a walking problem or who travelled in a wheelchair. Changing demography creates new demands, for example: a gym, children's nannies, computer games, action sports, more casual dining and larger nightclubs are symptomatic of this shift in profile.

Consider Table 7.5 and identify the types of needs each passenger is likely to possess.

According to the Cruise Line International Association (CLIA, 2005), there are a range of 'personas' or personalities, each with a particular set of attributes reflecting a psychographic inventory [15], who are synonymous with those types of people who cruise. These are: restless baby boomers, representing 33% of all

Table 7.5 *Passenger needs*

Profiles
Married couple in their 40s, both working, active lifestyles, enjoy finer things in life. Socially adept and aspirational, enjoy seeing new places and meeting new people.
Couple in late 20s with young family (son 6 and daughter 4). He is an Information Technology professional, she works part time from home as a telephone researcher. Want to relax and keep kids happy.
Single female, retired, aged 72. Fit, healthy and active. Likes dancing and meeting people. She is an experienced cruiser.

passengers, who, it is suggested, may find cost to be an impediment to trying different vacations; enthusiastic baby boomers representing 20% of cruisers, who are described as living a stressful life and seeking an opportunity to escape; the luxury seekers, 14% of all cruise passengers who unsurprisingly spend the most; consummate shoppers, 16% of passengers, who look for best value; 11% of cruisers are described as explorers who are well educated; and 6% are 'ship buffs', or seriously interested in and knowledgeable about cruise ships – the most senior segment.

PROVIDING CUSTOMER SERVICE

Customer service is a defining element of the cruise experience. The welcome and personal service in a restaurant, the care and empathy demonstrated by a room attendant, the friendly willingness of an Assistant Purser to turn a potential problem into a resounding success are momentous and memorable. The effect of great customer service can be to create loyal customers and the opposite is also true. In essence it is a form of public relations (PR) directly involving interaction with the passenger [16]. Customer service involves high-level communication and an ability to tune in to the needs of customers.

Johns [17] declares that businesses get the customers they deserve – in other words, the business that loses customers should look internally to identify the reason. All employees should practise customer service in business, although the front-line staff should be trained to exhibit and implement the critical skills that can make a difference. Cruise companies build their brands on quality customer service to underpin the tangible elements of the cruise product. Invariably, customer service is itself built on certain critical components, such as ability to communicate, product and service knowledge, and interpersonal skills. The simplest singular element that appears to play a disproportionate part in the customer service process is the ability of the individual staff member to smile at the right time [18]. Clark believes this is because it is a human action that is universal – it sends a positive message and signals a willingness to interact in a friendly manner.

WHAT IS GOOD PRACTICE FOR CUSTOMER SERVICE?

Customer service is subjective and will be uniquely understood by the customer. By its nature, generally involving a discussion between two parties, it can be highly personal and things can go wrong. An experienced front-line staff member will adapt what they know to personalize each customer service event so as to aim to create the best outcome, suiting both the customer and the company.

It is often difficult to remember that an unhappy customer is invariably not making a personal verbal attack on a front-line member of staff. Difficult customers who bring negative attitudes don't tend to create the best conditions under which to find a positive outcome. Yet, difficult customers are relatively common. People learn to complain by observation and practice. Our media-driven society creates many opportunities for people to hone these skills and some level in the attempt to turn the skill into an art [19]. Dealing badly with a negative customer can spread the negativity (to as many as five people, according to studies). Dealing positively with complaints on a cruse ship can turn a dissatisfied client into a satisfied client and can generate positive PR, lead to increased sales and help to improve working life for many personnel along the way.

ORIENTATION FOR CUSTOMER SERVICE

Creating the right attitude
Good front-line staff know when to talk and when to listen. Listening skills involve concentration and good eye contact (attending), careful use of nods and gestures as well as occasional probe questions or paraphrasing (following) and summarizing or confirming understanding (reflecting) [18]. In addition, it is important to adopt the right attitude and to aim to be open minded before dealing with any contact. The setting is important, as it is better for the clients to be able to express themselves without concern and to contain situations that may create unwarranted audiences for potentially distressing situations. This can work both ways, protecting the image and reputation of both the customer and the company.

Letting the customer talk
It is always best to assume that the customer is truthful and not to try and find flaws or holes in their story. It is important to remember that a complaint is a problem-solving issue and not a battle. The customer will believe she or he is right and sometimes that position may appear unmoveable. Talking allows the customer to get the problem over to the person that should receive the information. It is important to enable the employee to gather facts and it helps the customer to compose and settle. This can defuse emotions and create a platform for negotiating the next stage.

Empathy
If the member of staff expresses that she/he understands how the customer feels, they are not necessarily agreeing or admitting guilt in the face of a complaint. By using language, voice projection, modulation and tone with care the mood is established and the server can be positive in affirming the desire to deal with the situation by working with the customer. At this stage the employee can check facts that are unclear and order the information systematically to make sense of what is said.

Problem solving
When problem solving, it is bad practice to say 'no'. It is good practice to find out what the customer wants. Present options to the customer and examine and explore

options to ensure that both parties can end up with an acceptable outcome. Options for dealing with the problem will depend on company policy. A justifiable complaint may require a gesture to be made that acknowledges the situation and provides some form of restitution. The amount of leeway will be a matter for policy to decide – for example, if a head waiter can offer a bottle of wine to apologize for a serious delay in service or if $100 credit can be provided by the Senior Assistant Purser to a client's account to compensate for damage to personal property.

Most companies will not allow for refunds to be offered onboard and will expect that a customer file is sent to the appropriate department ashore so any claim can be properly considered. Gestures of goodwill onboard involving consumables or spending onboard can be offset against the fact that, while the selling price is not achieved, the loss in real terms is the cost of sale.

Follow up
A complaint may seem traumatic for the staff but it must be remembered that it is possibly equally or more traumatic for the customer. In addition, the complaint may draw attention to a symptom that is indicative of larger problem. In this respect, the company should welcome all complaints and the front-line staff should be open in their gratitude to the customer. Any action point should be followed up without delay. Even if no follow up contact is suggested, it is still good practice to get in touch with the passenger to inform them about what you did and to check that all is well.

Action and resolution
This will involve recording the problem and creating a log of events to chart how the problem was resolved. It may be important to disseminate details of the problem more widely so that appropriate colleagues are informed and to monitor the situation more closely. Patterns or trends may exist which are not widely understood. Many problems are a matter of poor communication and most suggest lessons for better practice. It is better to prevent problems than to aim to repair them [5].

Important exceptions
If a client departs from what is held as reasonable behaviour and starts to threaten or abuse either verbally or physically, policy should dictate the next step. This may require summoning a senior officer or immediately calling for help. No employee should feel that they are open to abuse and they should feel secure and safe while doing their job. Incidents such as this are extremely rare.

Personnel should take care when speaking with a customer not to use certain inflammatory phrases. Depending on the situation, these can include:

- 'You must be mistaken'
- 'I can't help you' or 'I don't know'

- 'Calm down' or 'Don't shout'
- 'That's never happened before'
- 'It wasn't me'
- 'Sorry, that is not my problem'

If the customer service staff show boredom, are distracted by a colleague when in the middle of a complaint or adopt a patronizing tone of voice, then there is the chance that this may also inflame the situation. Staff should aim to provide realistic promises that identify worst-case scenarios from a time perspective. Customers are impressed by service recovery that improves on a stated target. It is good practice to under-promise and over-deliver.

SUMMARY AND CONCLUSIONS

This chapter has investigated a number of theories related to service quality and has applied these theories to the context of cruise ships. Good managers make the difference to service quality but the complex environment of a mega cruise ship is such that there are numerous fault lines that can emerge. Growth for a cruise company can be positive, exciting and rewarding, yet critical qualities can be threatened when new staff are poorly trained and prepared, experienced staff are stretched or asked to do more and corporate planners ignore the operational tensions arising from growth.

REFERENCES

1. Tse, E.C., 'Towards a Strategic Total Quality Framework for Hospitality Firms', *Service Quality in Hospitality Organisations*, M.D. Olsen, R. Tear and E. Gummesson, eds. 1996, London: Cassell. p. 316.
2. Harris, N.D., *Service Operations Management*. 1989, London: Cassell. p. 288.
3. Deming, W.E., *Out of the Crisis*. 2000, Cambridge, MA; London: MIT Press. p. 507.
4. Juran, J.M., *Quality Planning and Analysis: From product development*. 2nd ed. 1980, New York: McGraw-Hill. xvii, 629.
5. Crosby, P., *Quality is Still Free: Making quality certain in uncertain*. 1996, New York: McGraw-Hill. p. 264.
6. Harrington, D. and T. Lenehan, *Managing Quality in Tourism: Theory and practice*. 1998, Dublin: Oak Tree Press. p. 302.
7. Wright, J.N., *The Management of Service Operations*. 2001, London: Continuum. p. 239.
8. Dale, B.G., *Managing Quality*. 2nd ed. 1999, Hemel Hempstead: Prentice-Hall.
9. Williams, C. and J. Buswell, *Service Quality in Leisure and Tourism*. 2003, Wallingford: CABI Publishing.
10. Peters, T., *Thriving on Chaos*. 1987, London: Pan.
11. Wyckov, D.D., 'New Tools for Achieving Service Quality', *Managing Services: Marketing, operations and human resources*, C.H. Lovelock, ed. 1982, Hemel Hempstead: Prentice-Hall.
12. Lovelock, C.H., *Managing Services*. 1992, New Jersey: Prentice-Hall.

13. Douglas, N. and N. Douglas, *The Cruise Experience: Global and regional issues in cruising*. 2004, Frenchs Forest, Australia: Pearson Education.
14. Office of Quality Management, 'Quality Bytes: managing perception points to make service perceptions last'. 2005 [accessed August 2005]; Available from: http://www.nus.edu.sg/oqm/news/qbytes/archive/issue0013/.
15. Williams, A., *Understanding the Hospitality Consumer*. 2002, Oxford: Butterworth-Heinemann.
16. Kudrle, A.E. and M. Sandler, *Public Relations for Hospitality Managers*. 1995, New York: John Wiley and Sons.
17. Johns, T., *Perfect Customer Care*. 1994, London: Arrow Business Books.
18. Clark, M., *Interpersonal Skills for Hospitality Management*. 1995, London: Chapman and Hall.
19. Williams, T., *Dealing with Customer Complaints*. 1996, Aldershot: Gower.

8 Managing food and drink operations

INTRODUCTION

In this chapter the reader is introduced to the way that food and drink operations are managed onboard a cruise ship. This will entail examining the supply chain, considering how stores and supplies are managed, and reflecting on the systems approach to managing food and drink. Finally, organizational issues are discussed in order to achieve a comprehensive overview of this complex and important element of the cruise vacation.

FOOD AND DRINK ONBOARD

There are few more complex or demanding food and drink operations than those that are operated on a high-specification contemporary cruise ship. Yet, at a time when comparable shore-based operations are locked in a constant struggle to achieve the highest standards of output within a trading environment that demands a regime of cost cutting, together with a reliance on de-skilling and centralized production, in the main, the calibre of provision of food and drink on these types of cruise ships is a veritable beacon of excellence.

Kirk and Laffin [1] describe the unique problems faced by those who are involved in general terms in 'travel catering' and, more specifically, in cruise ship catering. Among the points they raise are the following:

- The quality of the food onboard is critical for the success of the cruise, yet the food product is not the main reason for the purchase decision of the vacation.
- The price of the vacation includes the provision of food (and sometimes drink).
- Cruise ships operate a variety of restaurants to meet diverse customer requirements.

- There may be complicated logistics involved in setting up a supply chain.
- The facilities for dining are managed to achieve the highest possible standards.
- Passenger-to-crew ratios can be low, meaning potentially the levels of service are correspondingly high.
- Crew are expected to work long hours, for seven days a week and for several months at a time.
- Crew rewards can be high because of tips, tax-free wages and the opportunity to travel.

Kirk and Laffin [1] note that the layout of galleys onboard tends to be similar to more conventional kitchens ashore. They further identify that space is less of a problem than for other travel options, such as aircraft. However, new generations of cruise ships are forging ahead in terms of galley design to the extent that comparison with shore-based operators is fast becoming anomalous. Galleys on cruise ships are constructed to effectively meet the unique demands that are posed in producing high-volume, high-calibre meals safely, effectively and consistently.

In some respects, the constraints of operating a food and beverage operation on a cruise ship at sea provides certain compelling advantages. The ship's staffing levels (the ship's complement) must be geared so as to meet both statutory legal requirements and operating needs at full capacity. Staffing levels cannot be reduced or increased suddenly, although changes to staffing can be put in place on a cruise-by-cruise basis if essential and subject to minimum requirements for safety reasons. The optimum levels of staffing need to fit all circumstances. Planning needs to take account of contingency issues. There are serious implications if a ship is not appropriately serviced and in receipt of consumables. The logistical exercise of supplying stores to a ship is thus influenced by a need to ensure that operations are not jeopardized by an unexpected occurrence, such as a technical delay, change of itinerary or bad weather.

SUPPLIES AND SERVICES

The world's famous transatlantic liners were designed to be self-contained entities. The ships were away from home ports and at sea for lengthy periods so, in effect, the ships were floating cargo as well as passenger carriers. Frequently ships called in to certain ports to purchase indigenous goods that were then stored and taken back to the home port for distribution to other ships in the fleet. An example of this is the port of Auckland for New Zealand lamb. Storage on these vessels was designed to meet these needs with cavernous freezer storage, refrigerated spaces and dry goods areas located on lower decks, in close proximity to loading bays.

Contemporary cruise ships are different. They are designed with certain features in mind, as has been discussed earlier. Usually they are not intended to sail in difficult sea conditions and the maximum space is provided for passenger areas so as to create as much income from cabins or staterooms, bars and other revenue-generating areas as possible. The primary purpose of the ship is to generate profits for the company. Therefore, in designing the ship, care has to be taken to ensure that space is not wasted. Space is allocated to be optimal. If the ship is designed to undertake ten-day cruises, storage is allocated accordingly. At the beginning of such a cruise, the ship's storage areas will be stacked to the limit and at the end, the stock holding will be minimal.

The business of managing a ship's food and beverage supplies can be highly technical and highly specialized. For a major cruise company the process commences at the head office and involves consultation with a number of key professionals on ship and ashore. Planning involves reflecting on prior patterns of consumption, identifying changes to expected routines, menu planning for passenger types and itineraries and forecasting quantity. Contracts are offered on the basis of ability to supply, quality and price. The size of the contracts means this business is highly lucrative and attractive but the scale of operations invariably means that some suppliers are unable to meet the criteria for the contract tender.

A Head Storekeeper or Stores Manager manages stores onboard and, depending on the size of the ship, is often helped by an assistant and an administrator. In addition, ships frequently employ a Cellar Master, who is responsible for beverages. These employees report to the Food and Beverage Manager, or equivalent, and work closely with the Head Chef and/or the Bars Manager. The routine of receiving and storing goods generally commences on arrival at the port of departure. This may be the home port or the port that is selected for embarking and disembarking passengers for a series of cruises.

On the dockside, goods are held in a container that is sealed by the supplier and checked by customs officers prior to the arrival of the ship. When the ship ties up and has been cleared by customs or port officials, goods can be loaded. This is usually undertaken using forklift trucks and pallets, although conveyor belt systems are often utilized onboard. Most large contemporary vessels are loaded via doorways that are located at the quayside level. These are frequently referred to as 'gun port doors', utilizing a historical nautical term. On the quayside Stevedores supervise a team of dockside labourers to deliver goods to the ship and onboard general assistants are deployed to ensure the various supplies are stored correctly. Stores Managers check the items arriving for accuracy and quality. Goods can be rejected if the quality is below specification.

Figure 8.1 *Beverages being loaded onboard* Balmoral

Most cruise companies operate a computerized stock management system. This allows goods to be controlled accurately. Requisitions can be undertaken electronically from the Chef's office or from the Bar Manager's office and stock is then collected and checked against the requisition. The stock management system allows the inventory or stock holding in the stores, cellar or bars to be easily checked against the record to ensure there are no discrepancies.

Stores Managers are responsible for the safe and accurate management of stores in their areas. This means that stores assistants and anyone involved in handling goods must be trained to undertake this task safely. The volume of stores arriving can mean that there is pressure to ensure that the storing process is undertaken as quickly as possible. But health and safety considerations are paramount to make sure personnel lift heavy goods without damaging themselves and handle items in an appropriate, safe and hygienic fashion. Goods must be stacked or stored securely so that they don't get damaged or cause accidents to individuals if the ship moves or because of the general conditions of storage. Goods that are perishable must be rotated to ensure that wastage is minimized and that the highest quality of produce is supplied.

Some stores items require careful treatment because of their prestige value (caviar, vintage champagne, etc) and may be stored more securely. Other items, such as

Figure 8.2 *Beer stored in cellar (courtesy of Tom Hunter)*

fresh vegetables, may be stored in order to maintain or develop their condition of readiness to use or consume. The purchasing specification provided to the supplier will outline the expected condition of the produce (e.g. state of ripeness for fresh produce). When items are requisitioned from stores they are then transported to the next stage in the process. Drink products may be distributed to bars or the restaurant dispense bar. Food items may go to preparation rooms in the galley or to the bellbox (room service galley) or the main galley itself.

FOOD PRODUCTION AND SERVICE DELIVERY SYSTEMS

According to Ball *et al.* [2], hospitality organizations provide excellent examples for considering systems theory. This is because systems theory helps to explain complex situations [3]. Systems can be subdivided into 'hard' systems, which are technologically based, and 'soft' systems, which are to do with people. Ball *et al.* [2], describe a system as 'a set of components and the relations between them, usually configured to produce a desired set of outputs, operating in the context of its environment'. The study of systems enables managers to deconstruct a process and potentially make improvements or to introduce a new system with due regard to planning, structure and relevance.

The authors identify a number of principles that they feel are valuable when reflecting on systems theory [2].

- Systems are most at risk during periods of change, because there appears to be a feeling that change is generally resisted.
- Systems and interacting systems are complex and some elements of a system appear to be more risk prone or 'dispersive' while other elements are stable or 'cohesive'. It is important to develop a balance to ensure the dispersive elements don't disrupt and ultimately undermine the system.
- Systems must adapt at the same rate as the environment changes in order to maintain cohesion and balance. The authors suggest that in complex settings where systems interact with other systems, a higher degree of stability occurs when the interaction is between a larger number and more varied type of systems.
- Systems have a limitation in terms of variety that is predicated by the environment.
- Systems may not be totally standardized across a group, yet they may be stable and unique within individual settings.

Interconnected systems appear to undergo a cyclic progression from the point where the system variety is generated, the emergence of a dominant approach, suppression of variety, the breakdown of the dominant approach and the re-emergence of surviving variety.

Ultimately, systems theory develops a logical approach that for food and beverage operational management on a cruise ship may be described as the Food Production System, involving food preparation and production, holding and transportation, and the Food and Drink Service System, involving food service and dining, clearing and dishwashing and bars. According to Davis *et al.* [4], food production is the process concerned with converting raw, semi-prepared or pre-prepared materials into ready-to-consume items. The system's effectiveness and efficiency are reflected in both the relationship between inputs and outputs (waste, energy efficiency and labour efficiency) and service delivery factors (customer satisfaction, perception of quality and service issues) [2].

The production system on a cruise ship has three key elements: the policy relating to catering onboard (variety of outlets, variables in terms of demand, type of catering operations, timing of services), the menus (style and quality factors, implication for production if *à la carte* or *table d'hôte,* number, variety and standard of dishes, preparation of food, noting standardized recipes, volumes, implication for service and portion control) and galley or kitchen design.

Contemporary cruise ship galleys appear at first sight to be vast areas of stainless steel populated by chefs working away in their gleaming white uniforms to produce culinary works of art as if by some kind of magic. The production system on most ships is a derivation and development of the traditional French *partie* system, where *mise en place* (preparation) is undertaken in relative isolation, only to come together at the time of service in an orchestrated manner. The *partie* on cruise ships is less reliant on French culinary terminology, such as *garde manger* for the larder or *saucier* for the soups and sauces, but the compartmentalization is effective nevertheless, using terms more relevant to the type of menus (e.g. fish, pastry, butcher, soups and pasta). This approach is less visible on cruise ships because the preparation stages take place in closed areas to prevent contamination and to maintain high levels of hygiene control.

The main galley is designed to enable the assembling of the prepared items in a logical manner so that they can be collected by waiters and served efficiently to customers without any degradation of quality in terms of appearance, temperature or taste. The location of the galley is therfore crucial. It is best located adjacent to the preparation rooms and the restaurants that it is servicing. Ideally it should be on the same level, although lifts are frequently utilized for transporting food from preparation rooms to satellite restaurant galleys on ships where there are bistro or speciality restaurants. In these cases the lifts are prioritized for the specific use of carrying foodstuffs and treated accordingly. The location aspects also apply to crew dining and the location of wash up and storage areas.

Galleys require good and effective ventilation to ensure that working conditions are comfortable, that condensation is minimized and cooking odours are controlled [2]. In addition the galley requires cold water supplies for drinking, cooking or food preparation and washing up, and hot water for various purposes. The galley must have adequate drainage, a safe, user-friendly, durable and hygienic floor surface, suitable lighting and hygienic, safe and easy-to-use work surfaces.

The Food and Drink Service System is concerned with delivering food and drink to the customer [4]. The way that this is done is, of course, vital in satisfying the

Figure 8.3 *Table setting,* Carnival Destiny

customer and demonstrates the inseparability of food service from food production and vice versa. Indeed, on some cruise ships there is a blurring of the edges in terms of the location for food production as can be seen in some restaurants on cruise ships where *flambé*, or the cooking and flaming of food, is undertaken in theatrical fashion at the table. This is sometimes referred to as *guéridon* work, after the name given to the trolley and lamp. Safety devices on ship prevent the use of gas fuels to cook at the table. High-powered electric elements are used instead. Alternatively, restaurants may showcase national styles of cuisines, such as Crystal Cruises' sushi and sashimi bar, and P&O Cruises' celebrity chef-inspired Indian restaurant, Sindhu.

Food service systems take account of the time (when the customer wants the service or when the service is scheduled to take place), location (restaurants, buffet service, room service) and customers' specific needs (e.g. silver service, semi-silver service, plated service and degree of social interaction between staff and customers). Service system types are usually hybridized versions that have emerged from historical service methods. Thus in formal dining areas, plated service or semi-silver service may be used to serve food to the table using waiters and assistant waiters, while for informal buffets, a combination of table service and self-service may be utilized. The hybridization relates to the way the service style has been adapted to suit customers and to create a service routine.

The service system process involves *mise en place* (preparation), when the room is prepared and thoroughly cleaned, tables are laid, cutlery and glassware polished, the serviettes or napkins folded, cruet sets filled and the appearance of each table's setting is carefully checked to make sure it is uniform, attractive and appropriately prepared. Waiters and assistant waiters work from sideboards that contain the various items that may become necessary during the service, including water, glassware, spare cutlery, bread rolls, various sauces, pepper mills, and these also need preparation before service begins. Wine waiters, or *sommeliers*, prepare any items they may require, such as decanters that are used to decant wines that throw a sediment (not common), spare glasses, liqueur trolleys and ice buckets. The buffet also needs preparation to ensure customer tables, buffet areas, beverage points and clearing areas are ready for service.

Service follows a pattern dictated by the arrival of guests (whether one or two sittings or flexible dining). Experience informs the managers as to the type of traffic flow to expect within the time constraints of the meal. Often, customers tend to eat early if the ship has been in a port with a late afternoon departure, or if a show is scheduled that is attracting interest. The meals onboard most cruise ships tend to be included in the price and it can be difficult for staff to treat requests for a customer's third serving of lobster without batting an eye. Some restaurants on

Figure 8.4 *Table setting, Fred Olsen's* Balmoral

Figure 8.5 *Sir Samuel's Bar,* Queen Mary 2

cruise ships have a certain cachet or prestige value because, as on Cunard's *Queen Mary 2*, it relates to the grade of cabin and the menu and service is available on a similarly graduated scale. Other restaurants are made available at a supplement to reflect a speciality. The menu may be designed and branded by a celebrity chef or the style of restaurant may be in some way unique.

The Bar Service System is designed for the 'purpose of dispensing and consuming alcoholic and non-alcoholic beverage' [2]. Most cruise ships with American clientele adopt an approach to controlling the bar area that is in keeping with licensing in the US. Thus anyone under 21 is unable to purchase and consume alcoholic beverages. The same rule is not applied on ships with predominantly Italian, Spanish, Australian, German or British clientele, which serve anyone over the age of 18. Alcohol is potentially dangerous and bar staff are trained to comply with company policy regarding its sale to safeguard passenger interests.

The sale of drinks involves a bar with a counter. The back area of the bar is used to display the various beverages that are available, while the under-counter area houses glassware, preparation areas, refrigeration units, ice containers, cocktail-making equipment, sinks and so on. The theory is that functional items should be hidden from view while items for sale should be easily seen. Different types of bars are fitted to meet different purposes. A sports bar may have greater volumes

Figure 8.6 *Show bar on a Carnival Cruises ship*

of draft beer sales compared to a champagne bar, while a cocktail bar may serve more after-dinner cocktails than a pool bar. Seating and layouts are also highly individual. It is normal practice to design bars that have a view from the front or back of the ship over the sea (commonly named the lookout bar, the crow's nest bar or the ocean bar) and the design can frequently use split levels to maximize the number of seating and table configurations that are in 'pole position'. Some bars are designed with intimate areas, others with 'see and be seen' areas. Cruise ships tend to favour table service rather than service at the bar counter as a way of maximizing sales, making sure the customer enjoys a feeling of being looked after and keeping crowds or lines to a minimum.

In common with both the galley and the restaurants, the drinks and bar service system also involves *mise en place*, with the preparation of beverages, glassware, displays, ingredients, decorations and garnishes. The preparation of the bar area in general includes the cleaning and polishing of tables and counter surfaces, positioning of the appropriate items on the tables (various bar lists, promotional tent-cards and drinks coasters) the bar (display areas) and the bar counter. The bar is a focal point and is highly effective in generating sales. Tactics employed can include careful positioning of premium products, promotional displays, a raised floor area behind the bar to highlight the bar staff and give them enhanced view of their trading area, and raised lighting behind the bar to increase impact and visibility of the area.

Figure 8.7 *Bar preparation and service area,* Balmoral

ORGANIZING PEOPLE, PRODUCTS, PROCESSES, PREMISES AND PLANT

It is a function of Food and Beverage management [4] to coordinate the organization of teams, to monitor and review the production and service of products, to implement and evaluate processes, as laid down by standard operational procedures, and to maintain an overview of the method of operations that impact on premises and plant so as to achieve effectiveness and efficiency.

Food and Beverage personnel operate in teams. The activities demanded within the Food and Beverage areas are such that teamwork [2] ensures volume can be achieved with greater job satisfaction (there is less repetition when tasks are shared, there is the potential for a higher degree of interaction and communication in the work area, and individuals in teams can support each other), with more efficiency (production systems and service routines can deal with higher units of output when people work together, health and safety can be managed and monitored more effectively within an open team environment) and with greater effectiveness (quality control is overt in a team setting, the aforementioned support can lead to higher levels of competence and shared good practice). Correspondingly, there is a need to ensure the teams are nurtured to ensure working relations are maximized and company targets are achieved.

In monitoring and reviewing the production and service of products, the Food and Beverage Manager acts as the arbiter of quality, providing a lead in raising standards, creating clarity of purpose and focus for fellow managers, supervisors and operatives, and maintaining a highly visible presence as a key individual within a team. Complex Food and Beverage operations that have multiple outlets and continuous, frequently high-volume production and service routines require constant attention to ensure that consistent high-standard practices are maintained. The part played by managers in this sense is pivotal to assuring quality. The manager is a conductor, loyal, caring and sensitive to the component parts of the operation; a highly proficient communicator capable of motivating teams and individuals, and yet unyielding in an expectation of high-quality output and health and safety compliance.

As has been indicated earlier, systems evolve within a setting and, in many respects, the evolution can be positive. However, it is the Food and Beverage Manager's role to assess processes in consultation with key colleagues so as to address potential problems or issues. Because Food and Drink Systems are frequently integrated and reliant on groups of people, Food and Beverage Managers must be diligent in observing operational routines to identify emerging or inherent flaws or risks in these routines. A manager in this position can only make decisions about remedying problems from a position of strength, experience and knowledge.

Figure 8.8 *Stainless steel work surface in galley*

Standard Operational Procedures provide a framework that guides the Food and Beverage Manager and helps to establish minimum standards but interpreting the framework is a human activity that requires conscientiousness.

The organization of Food and Beverage focuses on a unique, carefully designed setting – that is, in the case of the service areas, simultaneously a place of work and a place of entertainment and, in the case of a production area, a potentially dangerous and high-octane environment. In the former position, Food and Drink emulates theatre. The staff members are actors who integrate with the audience, performing their duties and, if successful, creating customer satisfaction. Managing the environment is complicated by this need to maintain the theatricality of the setting. The mechanics of production and much of the work associated with service are hidden from view in a desire to present an experience that is desirable and appreciated by the customer. The manager has a responsibility in making sure the environment is not compromised by rogue practice or deterioration of the premises or plant. The efficient operation of equipment is paramount in preventing unwarranted damage and unnecessary cost. This aspect of a manager's job is termed asset protection [5].

CUSTOMER DEMANDS AND OPERATIONAL CAPABILITIES

Ask any Food and Beverage Manager how they know what the customer wants and, invariably, the reply will be along the lines of, 'years of cumulative experience'. Yet dining experiences are changing in line with the types of demography now experienced onboard and with contemporary fashion trends in relation to eating out. With cruise brands targeting new market sectors, the product designers are being faced with different challenges to satisfy customer demands and expectations.

Roy Wood [6] doubts that the hospitality industry knows that much about people's eating needs today. Yet the cruise industry seems to get it right. The individual brands develop products that are elements of the brand identity. Some British vessels may emulate a more traditional dining pattern with the type of food seen in high-class, sometimes more formal restaurants (e.g. Cunard Line). Some US-based vessels adopt a casual pseudo-Italian approach to dining, reflecting a friendly and informal approach to meal time (e.g. Princess Cruises). The origins of the 'product' appear to be traceable. With Cunard, the 'Britishness' of the dining experience and indeed the 'Britishness' of the cruise is the Unique Selling Proposition (USP) that attracted UK and US passengers to the early cruise ships. The tradition, once established, is protected (often fiercely) in order to establish and maintain the company's branding or perception of identity.

This same reflective analysis can be done with Princess Cruises. The company absorbed 'Sitmar', an Italian brand, during what was an important formative development period for the cruise company. The resultant influx of Italian staff, and their establishment within the new 'Princess' brand, led to the development of the Italian/American emphasis on food and menus. Subsequent growth has been bolstered from within by the company, in terms of promotion of highly skilled and experienced Food and Beverage Managers and because of a consolidation of the strategic vision regarding the concept and delivery of food and beverage as part of a brand identity.

The product and product design has, for many brands, emerged as an evolving developmental process. New ideas can be tested on ships before being rolled out across the brand. Cultural elements, including ports on an itinerary, predominant crew nationality, predominant existing passenger and new passenger nationalities, all play a part in creating the changing setting and in stimulating new ideas for developing the food and drink on offer. Consideration of the passenger service questionnaire and the high degree of interaction between passenger and staff means that awareness about perceptions to do with the product is indeed a matter of cumulative experience.

Operational capability is tied into the basic concepts associated with the notion of food and drink as elements of the brand. Style of service, skills acquisitions, knowledge and learning and the need to deliver food and drink to standard and within a

Figure 8.9 Restaurant on P&O Cruises' Aurora

budget form the other elements of the equation. The number of people to serve in a given time is modified by the service routine and the product specification.

There are a number of different types of operational problems that can require attention when food and drink planning is changed. For example, establishing an *al fresco* dining area seems to create an excellent passenger option that capitalizes on the location of open areas on decks and provides an alternative choice. Typically, however, the distance from finishing galley to restaurant needs to be surveyed to make sure the food can be delivered safely and to standard.

CONTROL ACTIONS FOR FOOD AND DRINK OPERATIONS

According to Davis *et al.* [4], there is a need for systematic quality management in the provision of food and beverage which should include inspection, analysis, the design of proactive problem-preventing systems and processes and a team-focused, quality-oriented approach. Quality control can stem from the way that a team embraces the critical elements that help the company to produce and serve food and beverage to meet or exceed customer expectations, safely and to a budget. For a barperson quality may be reflected in the taste and appearance of the product coupled with the ambience of the room and the service skills involved in delivering the product to the customer. The quality may well be undone if portions are inaccurate and profitability is undermined.

The balance onboard a cruise ship is producing food without wastage. Producing food to a pattern based on historical data and supplying products to customers to meet reasonable expectations achieve this balancing act. Portions on the plate are designed to look good and to satisfy expectations. Some customers may eat more than others but that is managed by delivering acceptable portions, which can, if necessary, be increased on request.

Over the years, the cruise product has evolved so that for many premium and economy brands food has remained as one of the elements of the all-inclusive package. On luxury brands all inclusive can mean all main-brand alcoholic beverages and all food in all restaurants. For those brands where dining options are diverse there is an opportunity to increase revenues by charging a supplement. Increasingly cruise brands have experimented with the use of celebrity chefs in order to attach a cachet to optional dining outlets. The menus and dining experiences are designed in conjunction with the cruise food and beverage departments and the celebrity chefs make guest appearances to reinforce their celebrity brand status.

In addition, cruise brands subscribe to further sub-branding in terms of food and drink by buying in well-known brands that add value. This can be for ice cream products, coffee or other items. In this way brands such as Ben and Jerry, Costa Coffee and Starbucks are becoming more prevalent. Thus branding has become a

Figure 8.10 *Food plated to appeal to the eye (courtesy of Tom Hunter)*

multilayered affair, with cruise passengers faced with the cruise brand presenting them with other franchised brands or celebrity brands that are often used to generate additional revenues for the company.

FOOD SAFETY, HEALTH AND SAFETY AND CONSUMER PROTECTION

Production and service of food and drink can be compromised by poor safety and hygiene. Therefore, cruise ships are vigilant to ensure the management of food and beverage areas is undertaken to promote best practice. In addition, port health authorities undertake inspections that are highly visible and can be important for a cruise ship's reputation. In the US, the Centers for Disease Control and Prevention operate the Vessel Sanitation Program (VSP) and have done so for almost 35 years. This government agency inspects water, food, spas, pools, employee hygiene and general cleanliness onboard cruise ships that carry 13 or more passengers bi-annually to provide a score out of a total 100. In addition, the CDC provides an annual summary known as the 'Green Sheet' to highlight issues and make recommendations.

In undertaking the review, the CDC examines potable (consumable) water supplies to make sure the storage and transfer equipment is clean and that the water is microbiologically analysed to ensure it is safe for consumption. Pools and spas are checked to ensure they are safe and well maintained. Personnel are checked to highlight infections, management of hygiene, staff knowledge relating to hygiene, monitoring of food safety and compliance with recommendations for safe hygiene practices and training plans are examined.

Food products are inspected, storage or holding temperatures examined, thawing practices noted, cross contamination checked and general practices such as the protection of food, storage containers, labelling and dispense is monitored. Equipment such as food contact surfaces, production equipment, washing equipment, and utensils are all examined. Chefs' or food handlers' uniforms and cloths or towels are inspected and hand-washing facilities carefully examined. The inspection goes to considerable depth, even checking bulkheads (ceilings) and deck heads (floors). Medical records are also noted as part of the process. Any ship scoring less than 86 is deemed to have failed.

PLANNING WINE LISTS

Wine is perceived as a highly desirable adjunct to, or component of, the meal experience. The consumption of wine appears to be more socially acceptable than say drinking beer or spirits because, according to Ravenscroft and van Westering [7], the product embodies connotations of knowledge and connoisseurship. Therefore, there is much to be gained in selling wines, either as a beverage during social interaction or as part of the meal experience, because of the customer perception of what wine is and what it is for.

That said, for many, the topic creates fear. Prial [8] recognizes that some people, who may be seen as generally rational individuals, appear to find the notion of buying wine too complex and, as a result, they avoid the process. Wine as a subject is laden with theory and, for those in the business of selling wine, there are critical aspects to note when designing wine lists and making sales. Cruise brands have the potential of selling large quantities of wine and the very diversity of wine as a product creates potential for matching products to settings and to client types. The following section is intended to provide some guidance relating to the selection of wines for selling onboard.

Cruise brands are in strong positions because of their cumulative knowledge about which wines to stock and sell. Yet, like food, a broad range of elements that can affect both the fashionability and acceptability of wine types affect wine trends. Those elements can include the passengers' diversity and variability by cruise of aspects such as age and demography, socio-economic background, wine knowledge and social and cultural circumstances.

A starting point could well consider the logic and practicality of constructing individual wine lists for each cruise. This might enable greater sales by ensuring products are made available and sold in line with predicted demand. The alternative approach is to offer as wide a range of wines as possible to suit the market in its broadest sense. Constraints on range include: availability of storage space; potential of being left with redundant and/or deteriorating stock; availability and continuity of supply; complexity of managing a wine cellar onboard a ship; and the investment cost of holding large supplies.

The logical progression of this argument suggests that a contemporary cruise brand with a definable clientele may opt to develop a standard wine list that can be amended if required. The wine list will form the basis of supplementary lists (for speciality restaurants) or offers (wines of the day) and be the product of close consultation between the cruise brand purchasing team and an identified wine supplier. There are certain truths that are self-evident when purchasing wine in large volume. Continuity of supply is predicated upon quantity of production. The wines on a wine list that is replicated across a fleet will have been sourced from wine producers who are in the business of producing high volumes. This implies that smaller producers, who may well have excellent reputations for the quality of their product, are generally unable to be considered.

Selecting wine types is often a matter of dividing wines by colour (red, white or pink/rosé), by production method (still, sparkling or fortified), by body (full through to light) or by acid/sugar content (dry through to sweet). This process helps to create a range that is sufficiently diverse to meet clients' needs and expectations. Some cruise brands may be required to stock products for sale that have a higher degree of prestige value, which might translate into the need to hold vintage champagnes, expensive clarets from France, cult wines from California or famous wines from Australia. Inevitably, however, the sales patterns that occur for most cruise brands will reflect in a balanced stock-holding that is biased towards less expensive products.

Points to note that can help when planning a wine list are as follows:

- The list should have a logic that is easily understood by the client. White and red may be sufficient to delineate initial options, followed by identity by country or area. More traditional approaches can be taken to list countries by significance from a 'sales on board' perspective. Shorter lists are easier to digest but the list may lack impact or image if too constrained.
- Wines should be selected that are consistent in quality and availability. Quality is implied by the information on the label that, depending on the wine and country, could identify and guarantee the derivation of the contents. Quality is subjective, yet careful selection by tasting wine samples can help to make critical decisions. When purchasing from volume suppliers, it is useful to assess quality regularly to ensure that standards are consistency.

- Vintages (year of the grape harvest) are important for most wines. The year can be indicative of the potential for longevity and may be a warning about potential 'sell by date' quality. Some wines – mainly reds and some sparkling wines, such as vintage champagnes – are capable of aging because they are made with grapes in such a way that they will mature in the bottle. Other wines, mainly whites and some light-bodied reds, are best consumed within one or two years of bottling.

- Wine connoisseurs and novice drinkers like to recognize familiar wines. These can create a point of reference and help to make the novice more comfortable and the connoisseur more trusting. Wine lists can be a mix of these familiar names together with others that are deemed reliable. Wines can be named after grape varieties such as riesling, sauvignon blanc, chardonnay, pinot gris, viognier, pinot noir, shiraz (syrah) or cabernet sauvignon (to name but a few). This is a common approach that can help consumers who feel able to identify the properties of wines that are varietal by nature. Others are named after a brand or place, e.g. Beaujolais (a town in Burgundy, France), Sancerre (a town in Loire, France), Cuvé Napa (a brand incorporating Napa Valley, California), Barolo (a town in Piedmont in Italy) and Villa Maria (a brand from New Zealand).

- The Selling Price (SP) is important. Some clients may not be inhibited by price, yet in most cases clients will have an understanding about the relationship between value and SP. Compared to food, it appears that little is done to wine overtly in terms of service to enhance the value. For some this can mean that they have a perception that the product can represent poor value if much above retail pricing. Some cruise passengers are aware that previous cruising price structures offered drinks onboard to achieve lower margins because the basic cruise price returned considerably higher margins than is currently the case. Wine products can create good returns but investment in glassware, equipment and staff need to be noted.

- The wine list should achieve a balance to ensure the wines offered represent an amalgam of products by type, by source of origin (noting connections with the itinerary), by price range (noting client types) and should offer alternatives such as half bottles (for those who may not wish to consume a whole bottle), wines by the glass and low or no alcohol wines. It is also common practice for passengers to order a bottle of wine but to then send it back for storage rather than purchase wine by the glass or half bottle.

- Finally, the skills and knowledge of working with wines are worthy of discussion. A good wine waiter, or *sommelier*, will have accrued years of knowledge and experience. The subject is, as was stated earlier, weighty but interest in the topic of wine among the general public remains high. Wine knowledge and skills require investment in order to meet possible demand onboard and to ensure wine sales are effective. Some products require a higher degree of care than others. Interestingly, these products tend to be those that require one thing a cruise ship may struggle to offer – a stable cellar. It is still possible to stock products that require processes such as decanting (to remove sediment from aging wines) although it is more common to avoid this by stocking wines that don't require this action.

Figure 8.11 Salads ready to serve

CASE STUDY: THE EXECUTIVE CORPORATE CHEF AND MENU PLANNING

Planning menus and food on the *Star Princess* is an exercise in systematicism. For the cruise that this case study relates to, there is a 12-day cyclical menu. The company has menus that can span cruises that are 3 days to 30 days in duration. Menus are sensitive to the nationality of passengers so as to satisfy their preferences.

The main restaurants on the *Star Princess* serve exactly the same food and therefore, for a 12-day cruise, that means there are menus for 12 breakfasts, 12 lunches and 12 dinners. The actual menus are laid out to a pattern in exactly the same way so that the passengers are, firstly, not confused and, secondly, can quickly become familiar with the format.

On the lunch menu, the first page presents the beverage suggestions, which can include cocktails, wine by the glass, beer and mineral water. These are followed by appetizers and a soup, then by a salad and 'always available' items, such as hamburgers and cheeseburgers. The second page includes 'favorites' in the form of two pasta dishes, followed by a range of main courses to include one fish item, one meat item, one poultry item, one main course salad and one vegetarian dish. Desserts follow with three ice creams, two frozen yogurts, jelly and cheeses.

The dinner menu has a different format. Page one presents a complete healthy-choice three-course meal. This menu indicates that the proposed items will be lower in fat. This is followed by a complete six-course vegetarian meal. Standard dishes that always appear on the menu are listed, such as classic Caesar salad and plain grilled fish, chicken and beef. Page two commences with the appetizers or hors d'oeuvres, which include three food items that may be fish, meat, vegetables or fruit. The soups and salad section offers three soups – one cream, one consommé and one a chilled soup – and a salad dish. There is then a main-course pasta dish and a range of main courses that are selected from fish, shellfish, an alternative meat such as veal, pork or lamb, a red meat dish and a poultry dish. Desserts are presented on a separate dessert menu to include a selection of ice creams, pastry items, fruit items, hot desserts and cheese.

The crew also require to be fed. The Executive Chef plans a 30-day menu that caters for their needs. The menu is constructed bearing in mind advice from nutritionalists and input from crew representatives. This ensures that crew members, who may have a special preference or diet because of their nationality, cultural background or religion, are appropriately catered for. The crew menu will include a standard hamburger, a vegetarian dish, cold cuts, soup, rice, pasta, plus two main-course dishes (meat or poultry) in the evening. At lunchtime fruit, cheese and ice cream is offered and for dinner a dessert dish is offered in place of ice cream.

Figure 8.12 The wash up area

CASE STUDY: ROSS SAUNDERS – FOOD AND DRINK ASSISTANT MANAGER, CARNIVAL UK

Ross completed a work placement at Princess Cruises while still a student at the University of Plymouth but then, after graduating and having spent a brief time in management for a major restaurant and licensed retailer, he accepted a position working for Carnival UK as a Food & Beverage Assistant Manager based in their Southampton offices.

The majority of Ross's focus is on beverages. He works in a team that provides shoreside support and undertakes planning and strategic decision making in respect of the food and beverage operation onboard P&O Cruises and Cunard Line. The majority of his focus is on P&O Cruises, for whom he has recently been involved in a benchmarking project to identify the usual patterns of where typical P&O Cruises passengers tend to drink and how much they pay for their drinks. The passengers on a cruise ship are a captive market, yet the planners realize that it would be counterproductive to load prices too highly or to restrict their buying behaviour simply because of this point, so the benchmarking project is useful in determining the appropriate price point to adopt.

Ross has a demanding job. He is under pressure to complete a number of tasks in relatively short time and he is always working to deadlines. He notes that when he first started it was sobering to have to deal with very expensive items such as a 1981 Chateau Lafitte, which sells at just under $3,000 onboard Cunard ships. He notes that when calculating cost and selling prices a decimal point in the wrong place can be critical for this type of item.

One of the biggest challenges to Ross and his colleagues relates to pricing. This tends to occur at the start of the year, when they are calculating the pricing for the season. The company deals with the travel retail market, which supplies duty-free products, and if a product is de-listed it can have repercussions, particularly if that item is high volume. The alternative would be to obtain the item from a different source, which may well be duty paid and therefore considerably more expensive. In relation to suppliers, at one point Carnival UK had 30 beverage suppliers but now that is down to 8. This has the benefit of ensuring suppliers provide better prices but also means the suppliers are motivated to provide more support.

Another challenge relates to the pattern of work onboard ships. With crew constantly changing there is a continuous requirement to ensure the crew onboard are fully trained, that information is distributed and that key employees are knowledgeable about the products they are selling. To deal with this challenge, suppliers travel with the ship for a few days to train the crew and then fly home. However, any cabin that is taken by a non-paying guest means that revenue is being lost and because entertainers and contractors also require accommodation this can be a significant problem.

The culinary team comprises the Culinary Manager, the Corporate Chef and the Executive Development Chef. They are constantly travelling, seeking out new ideas and developing menus. P&O Cruises works with Michelin-starred celebrity chefs such as Marco Pierre White and Atul Kochhar in order to create highly desirable alternative dining options onboard. These options are very popular with the passengers and, because they attract a supplement, they also generate considerable revenue and help to promote sales of wine. As time has gone by some ships have been configured to cater for either family or adult-only markets. The implications from a food and drink perspective are negligible, although buffets on adult-only ships may be smaller in size and main dining rooms tend to get used more. In addition, where there is a family market the company introduces a separate kids' teatime menu.

The company has developed a number of different approaches to encourage sales onboard, such as the use of drinks packages and the creation of a cabin wine line to pre-sell wines and deliver to the table. Most importantly the company aims to predict market trends. Recently Ross was involved in a wine tasting to select a new rosé wine for the P&O Cruises wine list. This involved suppliers providing a range of wines that were then checked for temperature and grouped to represent grape variety and country of origin or geographical area. Wine tastings take place in the morning in a room where the light is carefully checked so a full organoleptic experience can be analysed. The task is to evaluate rapidly and to narrow down wines for selection in an effective and efficient way. Taste and price are important within the target selling price range – less than £20 for the majority of P&O Cruises wines. The benchmarking exercise revealed that most passengers base their judgement of wines on prior experiences, which include consuming brands such as Hardys (Australia) and Gallo or Blossom Hill (California).

Ross says there are few problems with the sale of alcohol onboard. Great care is taken to ensure people under the age of 18 are not served alcoholic drinks and the crew are trained to ensure that alcoholic drinks are sold responsibly.

SUMMARY AND CONCLUSIONS

Food and drink are vital elements for a cruise. Passengers put considerable emphasis on the provision and perceived quality (and sometimes quantity) of food and drink, both in terms of feedback provided in questionnaires and when relating verbal accounts to friends, acquaintances and/or family. This is an area of provision that is not outsourced (as can be the case for operating tours ashore); it requires very high staffing levels (the majority of crew work in this department) and it deals in high volumes (the largest ships are now feeding up to 8,000 people at least three times a day). This type of operation must be systematic, carefully planned to emulate a military campaign and consistently monitored to ensure it is under control.

Managing food and drink is highly specialized, requiring a combination of skills and knowledge. Such individuals should have an appreciation concerning the art as well as the science of producing food and drink. The Food and Beverage Manager is like a theatre director, ensuring people, plans and conditions are in place for a finely tuned performance that meets and exceeds the audience's expectation. Finally, the manager has a responsibility to assure that the provision of food and drink is achieved safely and within budget. The next chapter considers a parallel role: that of Facility Management.

REFERENCES

1. Kirk, D. and D. Laffin, 'Travel Catering', *Introduction to Hospitality Operations*, P. Jones, ed. 2000, London: Continuum.
2. Ball, S., P. Jones, D. Kirk and A. Lockwood, *Hospitality Operations: A Systems Approach*. 2003, London: Continuum.
3. Kirk, D., 'Hard and Soft Systems: A common paradigm for operations management', *International Journal of Contemporary Hospitality Management*, 1995. 7(5): p. 13–16.
4. Davis, B., A. Lockwood and S. Stone, *Food and Beverage Management*. 3rd ed. 1999, Oxford: Butterworth-Heinemann.
5. Verginis, C.S. and R.C. Wood, eds., *Accommodation Management: Perspectives for the international hotel industry*. 1999, London: Thomson.
6. Wood, R.C., ed., *Strategic Questions in Food and Beverage Management*. 2000, Oxford: Butterworth-Heinemann.
7. Ravenscroft, N. and J. van Westering, 'Wine Tourism, Culture and the Everyday: A theoretical note', *Tourism & Hospitality Research*, 2001. 3(2): p. 149–163.
8. Prial, F.J., 'What Is It With Wine?', *Journal of Gastronomy*, 1990. 6(3): p. 3.

9 Managing facilities

INTRODUCTION

This chapter deals with the effective management of accommodation onboard, including cabins, public areas, crew areas and deck areas. In examining this department, a number of issues are considered, including administration, yield management, design aspects, routines and schedules, and environmental issues [1]. The constraints on planning accommodation that were discussed earlier, namely, the need to utilize space economically, the increasing demand for enhanced passenger facilities and the current trend to ensure cruise ships sail on full capacity, all play a part for operational managers in this department.

Figure 9.1 *Stateroom on Arcadia*

When considering space management, there can be problems for this department with passengers embarking with large quantities of luggage, both in terms of the implications of moving the luggage from shore to ship to cabin and vice versa, and in storing personal belongings within the cabin. Passengers make comparisons between cabin/stateroom accommodation onboard and hotel accommodation ashore. There is an expectation that the look and feel of the accommodation will be appropriate for the style of cruise, the image presented by the brand, the price paid, the advertised product offer and similar shore-based products. While passengers acknowledge the constraints in terms of space, as well as recognizing that the attractions onboard mean that proportionately little time may spent in the cabin/stateroom, the expectation regarding the product offer can be high. The lack of alternative accommodation space presents problems for managers faced with critical events that may necessitate temporary or permanent reallocation of accommodation.

REVENUE OR YIELD MANAGEMENT

Revenue Management (RM) is the practice of offering the correct type of inventory (cabins/staterooms) at the appropriate price in order to maximize revenue [2]. RM is a practice that is undertaken in a number of industries to ensure that the passage of time together with the selling strategy are utilized effectively so as to generate the best 'yield' [3]. Yield is the function of both the price the cruise company charges for differentiated service options (pricing) and the number of cabins or staterooms sold at each price (seat inventory control). The perishability of the inventory, whether that inventory is cabins on cruise ships, seats on aircraft, hotel rooms or theatre tickets, drives the RM policy and provides a focus for the company to aim for in order to optimize profitability.

RM includes the construction and implementation of policies related to the formulation and alignment of price, product and buyer that will lead to profitability. In this way RM utilizes predictions regarding inventory and market segments and optimum pricing in order to create an increase in net yield. Typically, RM is applied when service organizations have a fixed capacity (as is determined by a cruise ship or a fleet of ships) and when success or failure is dependent on how this capacity is made use of. These organizations frequently have high fixed costs that are covered when a certain level of sales is achieved. In making an additional sale on top of this break-even point has a marginal impact on costs in comparison to the impact on revenue.

COSTS, SALES AND MARKETS

The cruise business is investment heavy in terms of the ship itself, the fixtures and fittings, the technical and operational aspects of maintaining the ship, the labour element involved and providing services onboard. Once in service, it is difficult to adjust the capacity of a cruise ship and so the critical factor is to ensure the ship sails on full or as close to full capacity as can be achieved. The costs of adding any extra passenger to reduce unused capacity is, in relative terms, inexpensive and so cruise companies can view actual selling prices with an open mind. It benefits cruise companies to sell inventory as quickly as possible so that they can:

- Gain early access to passengers' money (deposits)
- Be able to ascertain demand at an early stage so as to formulate a robust strategy for dealing with maximizing yield
- Can make decisions to decrease time uncertainty relating to demand

This means that cruise companies derive advantages from operating initiatives designed to attract early booking. Typical initiatives include: time-constrained discounts, free upgrades for early booking, additional incentives for early booking (e.g. transport to port or onboard credit), loyalty club membership with access to advance notice with a range of early-booking benefits.

In order to make critical decisions about RM, the cruise company needs to be aware of:

- Market segments and consumer buying behaviour
- Specific markets to be targeted for specific vacations
- Historical demand and booking patterns
- Pricing knowledge (competitors' rates and/or rate ranges)

It is becoming increasingly possible for cruises to be overbooked. This occurs because, based on analysis of trading patterns, cruise operators make predictions about what is likely to happen in relation to cancellations and no-shows. A calculation is made to ensure that overbookings are made to compensate for last moment non-arrivals. The overbooking policy is designed to identify actions, including compensation, that are available if an overbooking remains in place.

An additional element to be considered by the cruise operator is the multiplier effect. This implies that revenue can be generated onboard after the booking is made and therefore the RM system needs to be concerned with a yield that notes the opportunity to attract income through sales onboard. This model will very much depend on the nature of the 'package' on offer. The trend for vessels over recent years has been to maximize occupancy rates by reducing prices, while increasing yield through the combination of volume sales of cruise vacations and revenue generated onboard. Sales figures represent the percentage of lower berths that are sold onboard. Many operators offer four-berth cabins to single passengers willing to share or family groups who are travelling together. This, in turn, can increase the occupancy percentage. In combination with the overbooking policy, ships can sail with a stated occupancy level that is greater than 100%.

Other features of RM worth considering:

- A complex pricing structure that changes can alienate passengers and cause confusion.
- Passengers in this position may seek alternatives.
- The RM system relies on the yield manager knowing the true availability of inventory.
- The distribution system must be reliable.
- RM requires that the company can forecast accurately (forecasting includes knowledge of customers, booking patterns, no-shows and cancellations, supply factors and market assessment).
- RM is a strategic decision-making process that needs to take into account alternative scenarios.
- RM is a team activity that utilizes software to analyse complex data.

According to Toh *et al.* [4] there are a number of features that differentiate cruise bookings from hotel bookings. These include the fact that the booking window is longer for the cruise industry, that the 'wave period' from January to March is the busiest peak for cruise bookings, that the cheapest and most expensive staterooms tend to book first and that canny bookers often take out no-deposit options on a number of cruises while they make up their mind.

The patterns change as different economic situations prevail but Toh *et al.* [4] note that there is a pattern of cancellations, which means that cruise reservations managers tend to overbook to try to compensate and achieve full capacity. Sailing at full capacity has consequences apart from the obvious one of greater onboard sales. While a half-full aircraft is viewed positively by a traveller, a half-full ship could be inferred to imply an unpopular cruise or even a bad purchase decision. First-time cruise passengers are perceived positively by the industry because experience has shown that cruise passengers become loyal repeat customers.

ADMINISTERING ACCOMMODATION

For the reasons explained above, it is possible to achieve capacity for a vessel that exceeds 100%. The process of managing accommodation onboard is greatly complicated by an inflexibility when it comes to dealing with accidents or problems. Most situations are dealt with at the purser's desk or reception. To be able to deal with these problems the ship's manager/officer needs to be able to make a judgement about the nature of the case in hand, the options available for solving the problem and be able to make a choice from these options to arrive at the solution that is most beneficial for both the passenger and the cruise company.

In the first instance the purser's department requires accurate information about cabins and passengers. This database, supplied from the sales office ashore, is crucial as it provides intelligence relating to the passenger that may inform the manager further about the background of any potential problem. The database may also inform heads of department about any surplus inventory that can be utilized in the event that a change of cabin is unavoidable. Secondly, the purser's office needs to be aware of the policy for dealing with problems so that she/he is appropriately empowered to make decisions and act accordingly. Thirdly, the manager needs to be able to communicate with all parties to access more information when necessary and seek advice when appropriate. A constant channel of communication is maintained between the purser's department and the accommodation manager to facilitate this type of problem solving. The updated information database is critical for administering the accommodation department, to generate accurate passenger accounts or folios and to produce information about passengers onboard for port authorities.

AESTHETICS AND ERGONOMICS

The design of cabin or stateroom spaces, public areas and crew accommodation is undertaken with a view to ensuring that the resultant product:

- Is suitable for the purpose for which it is designed
- Is acceptable to the user in terms of appearance and functionability
- Meets the needs of the user in terms of quality
- Meets the health and safety requirements that are required onboard
- Is maintainable and serviceable
- Is congruent with the brand and brand values

Therefore, the furnishings, fittings, lighting, décor and quality of air (air condition) are, in totality, the product with which passengers and crew interact. The calibre of the linen, the colour and texture of the fabrics, the weave of the carpets, the sheen of the wood finish, the size and feel of the bed are but a small sample of the variables that contribute to the overall design. Bitner [5] emphasizes how this collection of variables plays a vital part in influencing both staff and customer when she describes her ideas on servicescapes. In terms of a cruise ship, the totality of the servicescape performs a range of functions that include: underpinning the 'offering' that will be provided by the cruise brand; creating a setting to encourage interactivity, guest to guest and guest to staff; and providing a setting where the guest and staff are helped to achieve their personal targets, whether that be enjoying the cruise or performing their professional duties respectively.

The word 'aesthetics' refers to the concept of beauty or taste while 'ergonomics' is the study of the relationship of people with their environment [6] and, in this context, it is reasonable to reflect on the balance that can be achieved when designing the interior of a cabin so that the appearance portrays the essential attractiveness that the passenger may desire while remaining intelligently practical for the

Figure 9.2 *Double bed*

purposes of, among other things, resting, sleeping, changing clothes, reading and relaxing (from the passenger's perspective), and cleaning, tidying and servicing (from the cabin steward's perspective).

Many difficulties can arise from the ergonomical aspects, or when taking anthropometrics [7] – the measurement of human dimensions – into account, when aiming to design a product that fits all types of people irrespective of their dimensions. In much the same way that an airline is faced with problems if a passenger is too large for a standard seat, the cruise company may have problems if, for example, the passenger has difficulty in being able to get around in a cabin with limited space. However, specially adapted cabins are available for passengers with certain special needs and most cruise companies are careful to ensure that they welcome, rather than discriminate against, such passengers.

ACCOMMODATION SYSTEMS

Housekeeping in any accommodation- and facility-oriented business is, according to Ball *et al.* [8], fundamental for a successful operation. On a cruise ship, the cabin or stateroom is the singlemost utilized area for the passenger and, as a result, will potentially be examined more frequently and in more detail than any other

Figure 9.3 *Space limitations*

area on the ship. The personnel working in this area have a distinct advantage over those working in equivalent jobs in hotels, because they will have a higher profile and greater opportunity for interface with the passenger. For this reason, the aforementioned success is not simply a reflection of the perceived quality of the physical product but also a measure of the service skills in terms of the interaction with the cabin steward.

Ball *et al.* [8] state that the system for housekeeping: ensures that all rooms are cleaned ready for occupation and/or use; ensures that all rooms are serviced during occupation and or use; provides uniforms and laundry services; creates an element of security for guests and their property and maintains standards of decoration. There is an overlap between the accommodation office and other departments that provide technical support for repairs and servicing. Frequently, galley cleaning is not part of the housekeeping function but is managed internally by galley staff.

Cabin or stateroom service work requires a lot of attention to detail and, because of the amount of handling and carrying, it can be physically demanding. The number of cabins or staterooms that are serviced by a steward will often depend on the type of ship, type of passenger and type of cabin. On the *QM2*, more experienced stewards service the higher-grade cabins. Larger cabins and cabins with balconies

Figure 9.4 *Cabins with balconies*

require more time to undertake the routines and smaller cabins less time. Some ships require stewards to service the cabins and provide room service duties; others do not. Typically a cabin steward may have to service approximately 12 cabins.

Teamwork in this department is of importance to ensure tasks are achieved effectively, to standard and within the appropriate time parameters. Cabin servicing may well be an independent activity but, when stewards cooperate and form close working groups, they can support each other and deal with the types of tasks that arise that are better shared. Teams are most effective in dealing with servicing of large areas, such as the inside and outside public areas. The laundry is an important facility for any cruise ship. It functions under the direction of the laundry master supported by a team.

WORK SCHEDULES AND ROUTINES

The tasks involved in serving accommodation fall under different categories:

- Routine daily tasks, which include vacuuming floors, cleaning bathrooms, making beds, tidying surfaces, changing dirty towels.
- Regular tasks, which include changing linen (sometimes twice per ten-day cruise), cleaning walls (bulkheads), ceilings (deck heads), windows and

Figure 9.5 *The laundry*

mirrors.
- Periodical tasks, which include deep cleaning, shampooing carpets and soft furnishings.

Routines are established to deal with all routine tasks and to create a balanced workload that is fair and equitable to the personnel involved. Thereafter, routines are established to ensure that all regular and periodical tasks are undertaken so as to maintain the desired standards. According to Adamo [1], the maintenance procedures for accommodation can be identified as:

- Non-Routine Maintenance (NRM): e.g. dealing with leaking taps, bulb blowouts.
- Emergency Response Maintenance (ERM): e.g. responding to leaks, heating problems.
- Cyclical Planned Maintenance (CPM): cleaning or servicing items on a regular basis.
- Preventive Planned Maintenance (PPM): e.g. including inspections and planning for maintenance.

Standard operational procedures (SOPs) are communicated from the cruise company head office to ships in order to establish the standardized model onboard.

Figure 9.6 *Processing laundry*

This takes the form of photographs of, for example, standard lay-ups, cabin con-figuration and vanity tray set-ups, supported by text that describes details. The SOPs are prescriptive and communicated from managers to supervisors to staff.

DRYDOCK

For hard-working ships on relentless itineraries and satisfying the needs of thou-sands of demanding passengers there is a need to schedule in a 'pitstop'. A dry-dock period may be required for a cruise ship for the following reasons:

- To attend to and rectify the constant wear and tear on the vessel's furnishings and fittings and the ship in general.
- To service and maintain the ship's power and propulsion systems, technical and electrical equipment, and navigation and maritime equipment.
- To remove the build up of algae and other marine growth that can affect fuel efficiency.
- To convert or upgrade the ship's facilities.
- To ensure the vessel complies with international regulations.

Most drydock facilities allow for complex work to be scheduled to ensure the ship can face the next period of operation in the best condition possible. This will mean

Figure 9.7 *Ship in drydock (courtesy of Tom Hunter)*

employing contractors and sub-contractors who are faced with the challenge of completing complex tasks in difficult working conditions to a strict deadline. Drydock facilities can be found around the world and frequently ships are scheduled into a drydock that is convenient (e.g. the drydock facility in the Grand Bahamas is centrally located to service ships located in the Caribbean).

As technology develops there are contrasting demands. New types of surface paints mean that ships' hulls are able to be left for longer without attention, thus reducing the time the ship requires to be out of service and out of the water. Larger ships with more facilities mean that wear and tear is constant. Changes to international regulations, relating to the management of safety systems or prevention of pollution, can often lead to pressure on cruise operators to modify practices, retrofitting new technical systems or upgrading IT systems.

ENVIRONMENTAL ISSUES

Ecological concerns present a serious issue when managing facilities. Adamo [1] identifies the typical problems faced by companies aiming to operate to an environmental agenda within a consumer-led society that appears to ignore the ecological impacts connected to the excesses of consumption. The hospitality industry is a volume user of water, energy, consumer goods in general and scarce luxury items, and the cruise industry can be included in this statement. In addition, the cruise industry has to cope with managing waste products to meet merchant shipping regulations and providing a duty of care to the environment.

Most cruise brands employ an Environmental Officer, who reports directly to the ship's Master to address environmental matters. Davies and Cahill [9] describe two drivers for environmental friendliness. Those referred to as 'upstream' impacts relate to the influence that can be placed by cruise companies on their suppliers to make sure supplies meet appropriate environmental criteria, while 'downstream' impacts are more related to the education of customers and clients. The authors suggest both are within the remit of the cruise industry.

CASE STUDY: MANAGING ACCOMMODATION ON A GRAND CLASS SHIP

Edward Green has worked in the cruise industry for 18 years. While he has been predominantly a Princess Cruises employee, in the past he has also worked for other cruise companies. As Accommodation Manager, he reports to the Staff First Purser (Admin) and then the Passenger Services Director. His rank is equivalent to a Senior Assistant Purser (two stripes), although this aspect is underplayed because Princess consciously chooses to emphasize the hotel or resort aspect of the vacation rather than the maritime element with its almost pseudo-military connotations.

The vessel weighs in at 109,000 GRTs and carries 2,600 passengers when full. In order to maintain the high standards expected onboard, Edward's team is both diverse and large. The statistics are as follows:

- Total employees: 188
- Accommodation manager: 1
- Supervisors: 9
- Administration assistant: 1

- Deck supervisors: 3
- Stateroom stewards: 72
- Inside public area supervisor: 1
- Outside public area supervisor: 1
- Inside public area accommodation attendants (ACATs): 38
- Outside public area accommodation attendants (ACATs): 12
- Utility cleaners: 27
- Bellbox supervisor: 1
- Bellbox staff: 7
- Laundry supervisor 2
- Laundry staff: 23
- Numbers of cabins serviced by stateroom stewards: 18/19
- Nationalities of accommodation personnel: Filipino approx. 50%, E. Europe (Hungary, Slovakia, Poland and Romania) approx. 25%, Thai approx. 25% (also a few Portuguese and Mexican)
- Duration of contracts by nationality: Accommodation Manager 6 months, Filipino 10 months, Thai 10 months, Mexican 9 months and Portuguese 7 months
- Number Bellbox (room service): 1
- Number of Pantries: 30

The department operates around a set of routines and procedures that are to be completed to standards as are laid out by head office:

- Stateroom stewards servicing cabins, suites and mini-suites; they look after 18/19 staterooms each, which might be a mix of suites and cabins. Although suites take longer to service than cabins, the allocation is rotated to make sure the balance of work is fair.
- ACATs ensure public rooms and toilets are serviced. In addition to routine tasks, they undertake scheduled deep cleaning and shampooing of public-area furniture carpets and drapes. They also deal with accidents, which may result in soiled carpets or soft furnishings.
- ACATs (pool boys) service passenger areas out on decks, looking after open-deck furniture and any cleaning duties that are required.
- Utility cleaners service crew areas such as alleyways, bulkheads, crew mess, officers' mess and act as officers' stewards.
- Bellbox room service teamwork from the bellbox and deck pantries to deliver room service to cabins, suites and mini-suites.

The job managing accommodation is demanding but because of the good working relationships both onboard and ashore the incidence of problems are few and far between. On each cruise there are meetings to examine performance and to consider emerging issues. The brand head office in Santa Clarida keeps in regular and close contact with managers onboard to advise about changes or updates to policy and procedures. Systems are in place for a range of eventualities. For passengers with special requests, lists are generated to ensure the request is distributed to the correct department and personnel for action to be taken. For cruises where passenger profiles are different to the norm, patterns are identified to ensure plans are in place to deal with, for example, a greater demand for cribs and high chairs. A reporting mechanism is in place to ensure defects are identified, reported and appropriately dealt with. Quality control is practised by all personnel, and the Accommodation Manager undertakes regular checks that involve random sampling.

Increasingly, passengers report allergies or special needs and when this occurs plans are put in place to meet their requirements. There are neither smoking nor non-smoking cabins onboard, so a passenger stating an allergy to cigarette smoke would be allocated a cabin that had been deep cleaned to remove potential problems. For most general deck areas and public rooms onboard, on the port side (left) passengers may smoke, while the starboard side (right) is non-smoking. Smoking is not allowed in certain lounges and outside decks where there is a potential hazard.

In the main the Accommodation Manager is responsible for all aspects of managing the department. The department relies on good-quality supervisors being in place who have operational experience and strong interpersonal skills. As Edward states, when commenting upon the management skills of his supervisors, 'you don't want supervisors who scream and bawl!' In a growing fleet, getting the right supervisors and managers in place can be a potential problem, although experience has shown that the *Star Princess*, as one of many new large ships joining the Princess brand over a relatively short space of time, has quickly become operationally effective to the required standard. The impetus on head office to source and then schedule key staff was crucial in achieving this aim. Training onboard is continuous with, much of the time, personnel learning on the job and being coached by more experienced personnel. Promotion tends to be from within, thus continually

Figure 9.8 *Public areas – swimming pool (courtesy of Tom Hunter)*

building a model of competence based on shared knowledge.

Interesting problems do emerge from time to time, like the very tall passenger who didn't fit into his standard 6 ft 6 inch bed. In this situation a bed extender was built at short notice by the joiner. Normally the ship would get advanced warning about this and similar problems. There are ADA (American Disability Aid) cabins onboard, with doors that can allow easy access for a wheelchair and ramps to get onto the balcony.

Norwalk-like viruses (NLV; see also Chapter 10) have been around for a long time and the company has produced an in-depth handbook that is regularly updated, which contains guidelines. Thus if any suspected incident is reported, it is dealt with as a matter of routine. For example, if the doctor advises that a Junior Assistant Purser has symptoms (not full), the Accommodation Manager will contact the crew supervisor, who has a trained 'hit squad' of 15 people on 24-hours availability to sanitize the cabin. The procedure involves isolating the person with the reported problem so as to contain any potential risk. Fleet cabins – crew cabins that are allocated for training purposes – are used to cope with the problem to ensure the ill person does not come in contact with others.

On arrival and departure days the accommodation department manages baggage onboard. Around 129 baggage cages are filled with the departing passengers' luggage and taken ashore; joining passengers' luggage is boarded using a similar system. ACATs, utility cleaners and bellbox staff handle the baggage, collecting, distributing and offloading as may be required. Stateroom stewards are not involved in this process. A turnaround in Venice or Barcelona is easier to manage because the ship has a three-day lay-over. The Caribbean, with a one-day turnaround, is more difficult, especially on two-week cruises when passengers take more luggage.

Figure 9.9 *Loading luggage*

In Edward's opinion, the US Port Health inspection is not really a problem because onboard standards are very high. The biggest area for this inspection is the galley but for his department Port Health officers will look at pantries, onboard cleaning routines for dishwashers and the logs and records related to these areas. They will check that jacuzzis are sanitized once every seven days, potable water is monitored and in perfect condition, and swimming pools are thoroughly tested. Swimming pools and jacuzzis are tested by a pool boy every four hours to take readings, a copy of which are taken to the engine control room. The pool boy will highlight any discrepancies but engineers will deal with the problem. In the main, general housekeeping doesn't hold dangerous chemicals. The ship's Environmental Officer, who reports directly to the captain, monitors all potential risk areas, from an environmental safety or compliance point of view.

Edward is very aware that soft skills are vital when managing accommodation services – being able to construct and motivate a team, treating people with respect and understanding their cultural differences are each important elements in the complex task of managing a working community at sea. One example Edward notes is that some nationalities seem more aggressive; they are not necessarily aggressive but they may come across as such because this is the way they do things. People who work on a cruise ship need to get on with both crew and passengers. He says it can be a long time for some to be away from home and over the years the routines have changed – for example, on the *Island Princess* stateroom stewards used to service 12 cabins with room service; now they service 19 cabins with balconies. Edward also suggests that over the years he has been at sea, passengers have become more demanding, influenced partly by demographical changes, depending on the time of year and the cruising season. Also, as cruise companies have merged, cost control and budgets have been managed more effectively.

Princess Cruises operates a passenger service 'credo' called CRUISE, which has evolved and been amplified over the years since it was first introduced. This stands for 'Courtesy, Respect, Unfailing in Service Excellence'. It is intended to create a culture of friendly care within an environment where the crew strive for the best level of service. Edward wholeheartedly supports the strategy but highlights those repeat passengers who know the credo and who place additional burdens on the cruise ship personnel as a result. In particular, when the ship is full – which is becoming more frequent – cabin moves are a problem.

Question 1
How is quality addressed in the accommodation department?

Question 2
What are the critical issues to consider when managing this department?

SUMMARY AND CONCLUSIONS

In the conclusion to the last chapter, this role was introduced as being parallel to that of the Food and Beverage Manager. There are many similarities, such as the constant demand for service that is high-volume and potentially 24-hour, the highly visible nature of the job, the high expectation held by passengers and the need for systematism in operations. There are also unique aspects, such as the key points during the day, and having to accommodate periods of heavy and lighter demands. Turnaround day is always hectic.

This chapter has highlighted key issues connected with accommodation, such as revenue management and how it impacts on sales, administration and the link with accommodation management, the part played by aesthetics and ergonomics, and the criticality of environmental concerns. Some of these points re-emerge in the next chapter, which addresses health, safety and security.

REFERENCES

1. Adamo, A., 'Hotel Engineering and Maintenance', *Accommodation Management: Perspectives for the international hotel industry*, C.S. Verginis and R.C. Wood, eds. 1999, London: Thomson.
2. Yeoman, I. and A. Ingold, eds., *Yield Management: Strategies for the service industries*. 1997, London: Cassell.
3. Donaghy, K., U. McMahan-Beattie and D. McDowell, 'Yield Management Practices', *Yield Management: Strategies for the service industries*, Yeoman, I. and A. Ingold, eds. 1997, London: Cassell.
4. Toh, R.S., M.J. Rivers and T.W. Ling, 'Room Occupancies: Cruise lines out-do the hotels', *International Journal of Hospitality Management*, 2005. 24(1): p. 121–135.
5. Bitner, M.J., 'Servicescapes: The impact of physical surroundings on customers and employees', *The Journal of Marketing*, 1992. 56(2): p. 57–71.
6. Collins, *Concise English Dictionary*. 1987, London: Guild Publishing.
7. Pheasant, S. and C.M. Haslegrave, *Bodyspace: Anthropometry, ergonomics, and the design of work*. 2006, Boca Raton Fl: CRC Press.
8. Ball, S., P. Jones, D. Kirk and A. Lockwood, *Hospitality Operations: A systems approach*. 2003, London: Continuum.
9. Davies, T. and S. Cahill, 'Environmental Implications of the Tourism Industry'. 2000 [accessed January 2005]; Available from: http://www.eldis.org/static/DOC10089.htm.

10 Health, safety and security

INTRODUCTION

By the end of this chapter the reader should be able to appreciate the range of issues that can affect health, safety and security for people on cruise ships. The chapter will include an overview of the US Public Health Service Vessel Sanitation Program (VSP) operated by the Centers for Disease Control and Protection (CDC) and a discussion of food hygiene in relation to cruise ship operators. This will allow for reflection on the regulatory framework and the implications for cruise operators in relation to port health authorities. In terms of security, the International Ship and Port Facility Security Code (ISPS Code) will be considered. Finally, the chapter will conclude by examining issues relating to providing a service to customers who have special needs.

TRAVELLING SAFELY

The image of cruising reflects a picture of what many would perceive as a leisure-focused utopian dream. However, in common with most popular travel-based vacations, there are distinct and diverse perils that can exist and that demand attention. This chapter is designed to assist the reader to appreciate the range of issues that can potentially affect health, safety and security for people on cruise ships. These complex subjects pose serious challenges for society and the ramifications for many industries involved in travel, tourism and leisure have been severe. In the first instance, medical cases concerning the health of passengers are highly visible and attract widespread media attention. The norovirus, also referred to as the Norwalk-like virus, can be a concern and organizations such as the US Port Health have been active in working with the cruise industry and other industries to address the problems that can arise. Although highly visible in the media, this health issue is not the only medical problem that can be faced by cruise operators.

The US Public Health Service's Vessel Sanitation Program (VSP), operated by the Centers for Disease Control and Protection (CDC), plays a significant role in helping to make cruise ships safe and hygienic [1]. This organization promotes good practice, provides information and training, and identifies potential hazards that could lead to the emergence of risk for passengers and crew.

Security onboard is paramount. The cruise industry has expanded and become more successful by presenting itself as a secure option for a vacation. The International Maritime Organization (IMO) has taken the lead in aiming to provide an international framework to ensure that safety and security remain appropriately centre stage. The introduction of the International Ship and Port Facility Security Code (ISPS Code) was a move to react to the heightened tensions relating to potential threats for shipping in general.

Health, safety and security are, as it has been claimed, complex subjects and it is not possible to cover every aspect of this subject in detail here. Readers are therefore prompted to undertake further study to develop their understanding of these areas and to make sure that they remain vigilant to ensure their learning is in line with current best practice. This chapter deals with the issue of security in general terms. Much of what is done in securing a vessel is, understandably, a matter of confidentiality and comments made in this section reflect plans and action that will not compromise this confidentiality.

CENTERS FOR DISEASE CONTROL AND PROTECTION – VESSEL SANITATION PROGRAM

The US Public Health Service's Centers for Disease Control and Protection (CDC) introduced the Vessel Sanitation Program (VSP) in the early 1970s because of several disease outbreaks on cruise ships. The VSP primarily targets gastrointestinal illnesses (GI) so as to protect the health of passengers and crew. Over the years, the relationship with the cruise industry has matured and although the CDC is still seen as a powerful agency in terms of control and regulation, it has evolved to provide assistance and training in order to achieve best practice [1].

The CDC is best known for its sanitation inspections, which result in cruise ships being graded with 'scores' out of 100. Vessels that fail to achieve 86 or more are deemed to have failed the inspection. Ships that score an 85 or lower are therefore declared to have an unsatisfactory sanitation level and will be re-inspected, usually within 30–45 days to determine if conditions have improved. The CDC assert that in general terms a ship with a lower score is likely to have a lower level of sanitation, although that doesn't automatically imply an imminent risk for GI. The CDC declares that since the programme began, the number of disease outbreaks on ships has declined even though the number of ships sailing and the number of passengers carried has increased significantly [2].

VESSEL SANITATION INSPECTION REPORT

Vessel Name	Inspection Date	Port	Results Presented to	Score:
Cruise Line	No. Pax. / No. Crew	Inspection Type	Inspected by	

Item No. / Point Value / Description   **Bold** = Critical Item

DISEASE REPORTING

01	4	**Disease reporting**
02	1	Medical logs maintenance

POTABLE WATER

03	5	**Bunker / production source; Halogen residual**
04	5	**Distribution system halogen residual**
05	2	Distribution system halogen analyzer calibrated
06	2	Halogen analyzer chart recorder maintenance, operation, records; Micro sampling, records
07	3	**System protection cross-connections, backflow; Disinfection**
08	1	Filling hoses, caps, connections, procedures; Sample records, valves; System construction, maintenance

SWIMMING POOLS, SPAS

09	3	**Swimming pools / spas halogen residuals**
10	2	Swimming pools / spas maintenance, safety equipment

FOOD SAFETY

PERSONNEL

11	5	**Food handlers infections, communicable diseases**
12	4	**Hands washed; Hygienic practices**
13	3	**Management, knowledge, monitoring**
14	1	Outer clothing clean; Jewelry, hair, hand sanitizers

FOOD

15	5	**Food source, sound condition; Food re-service**
16	5	**Potentially hazardous food temperatures**
17	2	Temperature practices; Thawing
18	3	**Cross-contamination**
19	2	Food protection; Original containers; labeling; In-use food dispensing, preparation utensils

MEDICAL LOG REVIEW

Cruise – Start / End / Port / PAX / ILL / CREW / ILL

1.
2.
3.
4.
5.

EQUIPMENT

20	2	PHF temperature maintenance facilities; Food-contact surfaces; Food TMD's
21	1	Nonfood-contact surfaces; Ambient TMD's
22	2	Warewashing facilities; TMD's; Test kits
23	2	Pre-wash; Wash and rinse solutions
24	3	**Sanitizing rinse**
25	1	Wiping cloths / chef's towels
26	3	**Food-contact surfaces equipment / utensils clean; Safe materials**
27	1	Non-food contact surfaces equipment / utensils clean
28	2	Equipment / utensil / linen / single / service storage handling dispensing ; Cleaning frequency

TOILET AND HANDWASHING FACILITIES

29	3	**Facilities convenient, accessible, design, installation**
30	1	Hand cleanser, sanitary towels, waste receptacles. Handwashing signs; Maintenance

TOXIC SUBSTANCES

31	3	**Toxic Items**

FACILITIES

32	1	Solid waste containers
33	1	Decks / bulkheads / deckheads
34	1	Plumbing fixtures / supply lines / drain lines / drains
35	2	Liquid waste disposal
36	1	Lighting
37	1	Rooms / equipment venting
38	1	Unnecessary articles, cleaning equipment; Unauthorized personnel

ENVIRONMENTAL HEALTH

39	3	**IPM program effective; Approved pesticide application**
40	1	IPM procedures; Outer openings protection
41	2	Housekeeping
42	1	Child activity centers
43	1	Ventilation

KNOWLEDGE

44	2	Person in charge, Knowledge

Figure 10.1 CDC final draft inspection checklist, VSP [3]

The VSP undertakes targeted surveys to identify problems relating to gastrointestinal illness. This attention is triggered if the total number of passengers or crew members with such an illness reaches 2% of the total passengers or crew members onboard. An investigation may also be undertaken if an unusual pattern or characteristic associated to GI is found. To achieve this, ships are required to maintain a log of passengers and crew who have reported symptoms for GI and who may have requested medicines to treat diarrhoea. If a case emerges from the data that causes concern, the VSP wil analyse the risk associated to any outbreak, review practices onboard, aim to identify infectious agents, develop a prevention and control response, and evaluate the implemented response. The action of the VSP is undertaken so as to identify the problem, deal with the problem and make sure the problem does not re-emerge.

The CDC also assists when a new-build or upgraded vessel is being planned and constructed. This ensures the vessel is in an optimum position to meet public health requirements, and can help with issues such as the correct location of hand-washing facilities, the correct way to design and construct storage and preparation areas for food and drink (including potable water supplies) and temperature control management when storing and holding foods. The organization offers training for cruise staff from its facilities in Florida, covering recommended standards, the reasons for the standards and how to comply with them. The following points are covered by their training programmes: water storage, distribution, protection and disinfection; food protection during storage, preparation, cooking and service; employee practices and personal hygiene; general cleanliness, facility repair and vector control (a vector is any insect or arthropod, rodent or other animal of public health significance capable of harbouring or transmitting the causative agents of disease to humans); and potential for contamination of food and water.

The latest CDC VSP handbook extends to approximately 300 pages and goes into great depth about the process of inspection [3]. Much importance is attributed to work of the CDC [2] and the incidence of outbreak of any form of communicable disease is seen to be of importance in terms of the way that passengers perceive the implications of such an outbreak on their holiday [4]. The most high-profile cases relating to such outbreaks tend to be associated to the norovirus, which is discussed in the next section.

THE NOROVIRUS

The norovirus was previously known as the Norwalk-like virus [5] after a virus that was first identified in 1972 following an outbreak of G.I. in Norwalk, Ohio. Norovirus is a collective name for a group of viruses that can affect the stomach and intestines. In some cases, these viruses can cause gastroenteritis, an inflammation of the stomach and the large intestines. While gastroenteritis is frequently known as a calicivirus infection or a form of food poisoning, it may not always be related to food. Norovirus is sometimes also called 'stomach flu', although it is not related to the 'flu, or the '24-hour stomach bug'.

People who contract a norovirus tend to present symptoms such as vomiting, diarrhoea and stomach cramps [6]. Children may vomit more than adults. In some cases people may also develop low-grade fever, chills, headache, muscle aches, nausea, and tiredness or fatigue. The illness can begin quite rapidly and the infected person may feel very unwell. The illness tends to last for one or two days. Noroviruses are found in the stool or vomit of infected people. They can also be present on surfaces that have been touched by people with the symptoms who are infected. Critically, outbreaks have occurred more often where relatively large numbers of people are contained in a small area, such as trains, buses, schools, army barracks, restaurants, hospitals, nursing homes, catered events and cruise ships [7]. The illness can be incubated for 24–48 hours and have a duration of between 12–60 hours [8].

Noroviruses are often most readily connected with cruise ships [9] but this is incorrect. There are many more cases ashore than at sea. The reporting mechanism connected to the VSP and the work of health officials who track illnesses on cruise ships mean that shipboard problem are identified and dealt with more effectively than they are ashore. Often the problem emerges because the illness is carried onboard and then subsequently spread by passengers. The layout of a cruise ship with accommodation configured in close proximity is thought to contribute to the amount of interaction and person-to-person contact.

People can become infected with the virus in a number of ways, as can be identified in the list below. It is important to note that the virus is more likely to originate ashore than onboard a cruise ship and to identify that this is a people problem not a cruise problem – although of course the industry must deal with the consequences.

- The virus can infect food and drink, which can be consumed. In particular, ready-to-eat foods such as shellfish, deli foods, sandwiches, dips, salads, peeled fruits and communal foods that require handling can be affected. The food may have been contaminated before purchase. Contaminated water can also cause a threat. This may be because of inferior sewage treatment, contamination in pools, rivers or swimming pools, well water or ice.
- A person can inadvertently touch a surface or object that is infected with noroviruses and then touch her/his own mouth, nose or eyes.
- One to one contact (with a norovirus-infected person) can occur by being in the immediate vicinity while someone is vomiting, which suggests that there is an airborne risk. It can also occur when caring for an infected person or

using the same utensil to share food with an infected person. It can even occur when shaking hands (this explains why some staff on cruise ships have been known to replace the ritual of shaking hands with touching elbows).
• Not washing hands after using the bathroom or changing nappies and before eating or preparing food.

Noroviruses are highly contagious but are not generally regarded as being serious [10]. The symptoms are uncomfortable and can be distressing but there are usually no long-term adverse health effects. Anyone who contracts the virus is advised to contact the doctor or medical staff, to drink fluids (because they may be dehydrated from vomiting or the effects of diarrhoea) and to be particularly careful to wash hands frequently. Practice onboard ship is sensitive to outbreaks [11]. Crew and passengers are advised to wash their hands often. This should be done after using the toilet, after sneezing or coughing, changing a baby's nappy or before eating, drinking or preparing food or smoking. Frequency of hand washing should increase if someone is unwell. Passengers and crew are advised to wash their hands with soap and water for at least 20 seconds before rinsing them thoroughly. Passengers and crew are also advised not to touch their mouths because of the risk of infection. An alcohol-based hand sanitizer can be used along with hand washing [12] and this is usually located at the entrance to a buffet service area or restaurant.

Regimes onboard cruise ships are directed towards prevention, surveillance and response. The onboard plan is based on isolation, containment, disinfection, investigation and information/education [13].

Isolation
This is interpreted as confining the infected person to quarters for three days after the symptoms have ended. Care is recommended in terms of locating the person in relation to other people who may share the accommodation. Full instructions should be provided to the infected person about personal hygiene.

Containment
The area that may be affected should be dealt with by a specially trained, equipped and prepared hit squad. Access to the area should be carefully restricted. Infected people should be treated by medical or care staff who wear universal precaution protocols (gown, gloves and mask). It is recommended that passengers are not charged for this care.

Disinfection
Disinfectants such as CDC-recommended virucidal agents and bleach can be used to eradicate the virus in a specific location. Areas and objects that are likely to receive a significant amount of touching by hand should be targeted – railings, banisters, handles, pens, pencils, tables and counter chips in the casino; the list is

endless. Indoor and outdoor facilities and all public areas such as lounges or bars, toilets, buffets and restaurants may be affected.

Investigation

A full history should be taken to identify potential causes.

Information/education

This involves informing the crew and passengers about any outbreak, telling them what the outbreak is and what it means. Give advice about how to deal with the situation, reporting problems and taking precautions. The crew should be fully trained to understand the issues before commencing work, either through an induction event or a training programme.

VESSEL SANITATION PROGRAM INSPECTION

The VSP calls for all cruise ships with a foreign itinerary calling into the US and carrying more than 13 people to be inspected twice yearly by a team of environmental health officers. Inspection details are described in the VSP manual [1]. The VSP operations manual was revised in 2005 and again in 2011 [3] to take account of new technology, advances in food hygiene and emerging biological agents that can cause disease to humans. The manual is used to guide and educate cruise ship operators and crew and as a focus for the CDC in their inspection routines. The following points are summarized from the manual.

Water

Potable water refers to drinking water. The process of pumping water from shore to ship is known as bunkering (this can also be the term used when fuel and stores are taken onboard). Drinking water is expected to meet World Health Organization (WHO) standards. It should be regularly sampled (every 30 days or less) and tested to provide a microbiological report to confirm it meets expected standards. The ship will retain records on testing for 12 months. Generally, water cannot be produced (reverse osmosis, distillation or other process) onboard when the ship is at anchor, in polluted areas or in harbour. The manual provides full technical information relating to water and water systems onboard.

Swimming pools

Flow through seawater pools may only be used when the ship is underway and at sea beyond 12 kilometres from land. The pool shall be drained prior to arrival in port and remain empty while in port. In some circumstances a pool may be left full as long as appropriate procedures are in place to disconnect the filling system and to provide appropriate filtration and halogenation. Water-safety tests must meet desired levels before bathers can use the pool. Recirculating pools must be effectively filtered in accordance with the filtration manufacturer's instructions. Water quality must be monitored and exceed expected minimum standards.

Whirlpool water will be filtered. The filters must be inspected regularly and changed every six months. Water will be changed daily. Safety signs and depth markings for pools must be displayed prominently. Temperature controls must prevent the water exceeding 40 degrees Centigrade. Safety equipment must be provided as directed. Babies or young children in nappies or, who are not toilet trained, are not permitted in the pool.

Food safety

The person in charge of food production and food safety onboard will possess an appropriate level of knowledge about food-borne disease prevention, Hazard Analysis Critical Control Point (HACCP) principles and the VSP food safety guidelines. Appropriate certification from the US or overseas is acceptable evidence in part, although evidence will also be demonstrated through practice observed onboard and the ability to answer questions during the inspection (see Table 10.1).

Table 10.1 *Guidelines for food safety [1, p. 51]*

The person in charge of the food operations on the vessel shall ensure that:

(1) Food operations are not conducted in a room used as living or sleeping quarters;

(2) Persons unnecessary to the food operation are not allowed in the food preparation, food storage, or warewashing areas, except that brief visits and tours may be authorized if steps are taken to ensure that exposed food; clean equipment, utensils, and linens; and unwrapped single-service and single-use articles are protected from contamination;

(3) Employees and other persons such as delivery and maintenance persons and pesticide applicators entering the food preparation, food storage, and warewashing areas comply with the guidelines in this manual;

(4) Food employees are effectively cleaning their hands, by routinely monitoring the employees' handwashing;

(5) Employees are observing foods as they are received to determine that they are from approved sources, delivered at the required temperatures, protected from contamination, unadulterated, and accurately presented, by routinely monitoring the employees' observations and periodically evaluating foods upon their receipt;

Table 10.1 *Continued*

(6) Employees are properly cooking potentially hazardous food, being particularly careful in cooking foods known to cause severe food-borne illness and death, such as eggs and comminuted meats, through daily oversight of the employees' routine monitoring of the cooking temperatures using appropriate temperature measuring devices properly scaled and calibrated;

(7) Employees are using proper methods to rapidly cool potentially hazardous foods that are not held hot or are not for consumption within 4 hours, through daily oversight of the employees' routine monitoring of food temperatures during cooling;

(8) Consumers who order raw or partially cooked ready-to-eat foods of animal origin are informed that the food is not cooked sufficiently to ensure its safety;

(9) Employees are properly sanitizing cleaned multiuse equipment and utensils before they are reused, through routine monitoring of solution temperature and exposure time for hot water sanitizing, and chemical concentration, pH, temperature, and exposure time for chemical sanitizing;

(10) Consumers are notified that clean tableware is to be used when they return to self-service areas such as salad bars and buffets;

(11) Employees are preventing cross-contamination of ready-to-eat food with bare hands by properly using suitable utensils such as deli tissue, spatulas, tongs, single-use gloves, or dispensing equipment; and

(12) Employees are properly trained in food safety as it relates to their assigned duties.

In this context knowledge encompasses: personal hygiene and how that impacts on prevention of food-borne disease; the areas of responsibility held by a manager in charge of a food production team; the symptoms associated with food-borne diseases; the criticality of holding time and temperature control for potentially hazardous food; the hazards related to raw or undercooked eggs, meat, poultry and fish; safe cooking times for potentially hazardous food; management and control concerning cross contamination, hand contact with ready-to-eat foods, hand washing and general hygiene; food safety; provision of equipment in appropriate condition; procedures for cleaning and sanitizing; storage, usage and handling of toxic or poisonous materials; and operational management and control of production to service routines to prevent problems associated with food hygiene and safety.

Managers are expected to ensure that their staff adopt safe and hygienic practices as laid down by the manual. In general terms all food must be safe, unadulterated and sourced appropriately to meet guidelines. Potentially hazardous foods must be received at a temperature of 7° C or below. Food will be protected from contamination by being stored in a clean, dry location, 15 centimetres above the deck in a location where it will not be contaminated. Food may not be stored in places such as locker rooms, toilets, dressing rooms, garbage rooms, mechanical rooms and under open stairwells. Food on display shall be protected from contamination.

Cooking times:

- A temperature for raw eggs of 63° C or above must be held for a minimum of 15 seconds
- A temperature for ratites (ostrich, emu and rhea) and injected meats of 68° C or above must be held for a minimum of 15 seconds
- A temperature for poultry and wild game of 74° C or above must be held for a minimum of 15 seconds
- A temperature for whole roasts of 63° C or above must be held for a minimum of 15 seconds (note there are alternative conditions for rare meat cooking and for preparation of other foods noted in the VSP manual).

Food cooling

Potentially hazardous food shall be cooled:

- within 2 hours from 60° C to 21° C and
- within 4 hours from 21° C to 5° C or less.

Holding temperatures

Potentially hazardous food shall be held at:

- 60° C or above (except roasts which may be held at 54° C or above) or
- at 5°C or less.

Full details relating to food storage, handling, service, equipment and equipment care, cleaning, sanitizing and managing the vessel, the galley and associated areas from a food safety and hygiene perspective can be seen in the VSP operations manual [1]. It is possible for operators to apply to the CDC to seek variances to requirements. These variances may be granted if evidence is provided to show that the request is reasonable and will not jeopardize crew and passenger health.

There are a number of ports that, when visited, are likely to prompt a visit from the national port health authorities. In the main, the requirements overlap those that are operated by the VSP.

The process of inspection identifies that it is good practice to adopt a Hazard Analysis and Critical Control Point (HACCP) approach for food and drink. This approach involves seven principles:

Table 10.2 *The seven principles of HACCP [14]*

1 Analyse hazards. Potential hazards associated with a food and measures to control those hazards are identified. The hazard could be biological, such as a microbe; chemical, such as a toxin; or physical, such as ground glass or metal fragments.

2 Identify critical control points. These are points in a food's production– from its raw state through processing and shipping to consumption by the consumer–at which the potential hazard can be controlled or eliminated. Examples are cooking, cooling, packaging, and metal detection.

3 Establish preventive measures with critical limits for each control point. For a cooked food, for example, this might include setting the minimum cooking temperature and time required to ensure the elimination of any harmful microbes.

4 Establish procedures to monitor the critical control points. Such procedures might include determining how and by whom cooking time and temperature should be monitored.

5 Establish corrective actions to be taken when monitoring shows that a critical limit has not been met–for example, reprocessing or disposing of food if the minimum cooking temperature is not met.

6 Establish procedures to verify that the system is working properly–for example, testing time-and-temperature recording devices to verify that a cooking unit is working properly.

7 Establish effective record keeping to document the HACCP system. This would include records of hazards and their control methods, the monitoring of safety requirements and action taken to correct potential problems. Each of these principles must be backed by sound scientific knowledge: for example, published microbiological studies on time and temperature factors for controlling food-borne pathogens.

SAFETY AT SEA

For a significant number of people, the threat of terrorism presents major concerns. Since 9/11, the apparent safety and relative peace enjoyed by those in the wealthier nations of the world has been compromised as governments have taken steps to challenge those who harbour terrorists or condone terrorism. The corollary to this situation has been increased vigilance at borders and increased security in general. The security implications have actually helped the cruise industry, which can capitalize on flexibility of itinerary planning and opportunity to move in and out of world regions depending on risk [15]. The downside is more bureaucracy, longer queues for passengers and crew at security desks, higher levels of intrusion into individuals' lives, increased costs and greater complexity when planning. Nevertheless, cruise passengers are said to have accepted the implications of the heightened security as a normal consequence of the type of vacation in current circumstances [16].

Under the watchful eye of the IMO, shipping has operated to a framework that raises the bar in terms of the operation of vessels in safety. SOLAS and MARSEC are key elements of marine safety and security (see Chapter 3). In December 2002, a conference attended by 108 Contracting Governments to the 1974 SOLAS Convention, observers from two IMO Member States and observers from the two IMO Associate Members was held [17]. The attending representatives agreed to a series of measures intended to strengthen marine security and aimed at preventing and suppressing terrorism acts against shipping. The resultant code is an amendment to the SOLAS agreement, and is known as the International Ship and Port Facility Security (ISPS). ISPS provides detailed security-related requirements for governments, port authorities and shipping companies in a mandatory section, together with a series of guidelines about how to meet these requirements in a second, non-mandatory section.

Table 10.3 *ISPS Process*

Contracting government risk assessment

1) Identify and evaluate important assets and infrastructures that are critical to the port facility

2) Assessment must identify the actual threats to those critical assets and infrastructure in order to prioritize security measures

3) Assessment must address vulnerability of the port facility by identifying its weaknesses in physical security, structural integrity, protection systems, procedural policies, communications systems, transportation infrastructure, utilities, and other areas within a port facility that may be a likely target

4) The port facility are required to develop port facility security plans, to appoint port facility security officers and to have access to certain security equipment

Company and ship

1) Company is required to appoint a designated Company Security Officer (CSO)

2) Ship is required to appoint a Ship Security Officer (SSO)

3) CSO to prepare Ship Security Plans for approval

4) The ship is required to have in place ship security plans, to appoint ship security officers and company security officers and to have access to certain onboard equipment

The target date for implementing ISPS was 1 July 2004 and although some contracting states did not achieve compliance, the majority have [18]. The implications for a ship visiting a port that does not comply can be serious as it can mean that the next port of call on the route may view the ship as being contaminated from a security point of view. This could result in raised security measures or even, in a worst case scenario, refusal for entry.

Contracting Governments set the risk level that is appropriate for a port facility or for a ship. The levels are designed to create a clear message and for easy communication. The levels correspond to the basic assumption that a hazard with a low probability is a low risk and a hazard with a high probability is a high risk [19].

Both ship and port facility are responsible for monitoring and controlling access, monitoring the activities of people and cargo, and ensuring security communications are readily available. The SSO is accountable to the ship's Master. This notes the Master's ultimate responsibility for ship safety and security. On cruise ships the SSO manages a team of security professionals who are frequently sourced

Table 10.4 *levels of risk and action*

Risk and action	Level one – normal threat	Level two – medium threat	Level three – high threat
Port facility	Minimum operational and physical security measures the port facility has established as essential.	The additional, or intensified, security measures the port facility can take to move to when instructed to do so.	The possible preparatory actions the port facility could take to allow prompt response to the instructions that may be issued.
Ship	Minimum operational and physical security measures the CSO has established as essential.	The additional, or intensified, security measures the ship itself can take to move to and operate at.	The possible preparatory actions the ship could take to allow prompt response to instructions that may be issued to the ship.

from the armed forces or police. Ships are required to carry an International Ship Security Certificate and to establish a security alert communication system that can be activated from the bridge and another location onboard to identify if and when a serious breach of security is at hand. This alert is to be communicated without sounding any alarm on the ship itself.

Parker [15] notes that although security associated with cruise ships is often reliant on technology such as X-ray machines and scanners, higher levels of security are achieved by creating a 'security philosophy and mindset' among the crew, staff and officers. This suggests that a well-trained crew, which is aware, observant and alert to potential security issues, is an advantage in aiming to control risk.

ASSESSING RISK

The terminology associated with this subject identifies that: 'a hazard (causal) is a potential threat to humans and their welfare; a risk (likely consequence) is the probability of a hazard occurring and creating loss; disaster (actual consequence) is the realization of a hazard' [19, p.12]. According to Faulkner [20], tourism disaster management should be a matter that involves coordination, consultation with all parties, commitment, risk assessment, prioritization, the development of protocols, a capability audit, a command centre in the event of a disaster, a media communication strategy, a warning system and some flexibility. Risk is a term that is frequently reflected on, in relation to consequence and likelihood.

The nature of this topic is such that one's attention is immediately drawn to the high-impact, high-profile events that can dominate world attention for lengthy periods, yet risks may be small by nature or start small and ultimately conclude with a disproportionately damaging outcome. It is useful to make a distinction between a crisis and a disaster in this sense; a crisis is said to be an issue emerging from poor or ineffective planning and management, while a disaster is thought to be relatively unavoidable because of natural events [20]. Incidentally, Smith [19] draws attention to the notion that a disaster is a social phenomenon, i.e. if humans aren't involved the critical event is not viewed as a disaster. Planning for risk is common sense but it is also good business sense. The logic of this type of planning can make the difference for a company and can demonstrate the way the company values its clientele and staff, the commitment it has to its business and the maturity it shows in dealing with some of today's potentially chilling realities.

The types of hazards that exist can be categorized as natural (environmental), which can include severe storms, earthquakes, flooding; biological; technological; and what Smith [19: p8] calls 'new concern threats', which allude to matters such as terrorism. These hazards can have implications for humans, goods and property or the environment and, in terms of risk, can expose vulnerability that can test human resilience or responsiveness to recovering from the event and also test the reliability of measures that are put in place to address the event [19].

When commenting on risk and risk assessment, Lois *et al.* [21] identify that a cruise ship in its general sense has two types of facilities: the hotel facilities and ship facilities. The hotel and ship facilities can be disaggregated to identify components, as is portrayed in Table 10.5.

Table 10.5 *Facilities onboard by type*

Hotel facilities		Ship facilities	
Passenger facilities	Staterooms/cabins Stairways and halls Public areas Public areas (outdoor)	Comfort system	Air conditioning Water and sewage Stores
Crew facilities	Crew cabins Crew messes and bars Crew common areas Crew stairs and corridors	Machinery	Engine room Pump room Steering and thrusters
Task-related facilities	Tender boats Stern marina Special attractions	Tanks/Voids	Fuel and oil Water and sewage Ballast and voids
Entertainment facilities	Casino Swimming pool Jacuzzi Cabaret Games areas Nightclub Shore excursions Office	Safety	Life boat Life raft Sprinklers Detectors and alarms Low-level lighting Life jackets
Service facilities	Passenger service Catering production and service areas Hotel service areas		
Others	Shops Beauty salon Medical centre Photo Shop Internet		

In addition, Lois *et al.* [21] describe cruise shipping as differing from other shipping because: the passengers' needs must be accommodated in the ship's design and structure (i.e. requirement for appropriate traffic lanes, division of accommodation for crew and passengers, etc.); appropriateness of docking facilities or support for tendering; servicing for supply, fuel and waste management; the itinerary based on passenger demand; terminal facilities required to process people and provide shoreside facilities and services; and the need to have access to a transport infrastructure for home ports or turnaround ports and destinations. These characteristics play a part in the exercise of analysing risk for the context of a cruise ship.

The IMO has proposed that shipping companies adopt Formal Safety Assessment (FSA). FSA is described as a structured and systematic approach to risk analysis and a tool for interpreting the rules and regulations that must be implemented by those responsible in relation to safety for shipping. The methodology aims to create a balance between technical, operational and human factors and a balance in terms maritime safety, environmental concerns and cost factors.

The FSA recommends these five steps in the process of risk analysis:

- Hazard identification (based on potential and relevant accident scenarios that could occur together with likely causes and outcomes);
- Risk assessment (evaluation of risk factors);
- Options for controlling risk (devising measures to control and/or reduce the identified risks);
- Cost benefit assessment (calculating cost effectiveness of each risk control option);
- Establishing recommendations for decision making (making an informed decision, taking all the facts into account).

Lois *et al.* [21], counsel that hazard identification can emerge in a number of ways including: brainstorming by utilizing a team of experts; formal studies of operations based on systematic reflection; analysis of failure mode and effects concentrating on known potential defects or problems; and analysis using a flow chart. The last option can result in a model that recognizes five logical phases for a cruise: the embarkation (passenger arrival, checking in, establishing onboard account, information and key or keycard and photo opportunity); getting underway (welcoming passengers, directing to cabins, luggage delivery, safety information); the cruise (normal cruising routines, daily programme); docking or tendering (shore excursions in destination; transit prior to disembarkation); and disembarkation (managing passengers, managing luggage, transport coordination). This enables a study to be undertaken that recognizes the complex situated factors that can impact on a cruise (see Table 10.6).

Table 10.6 *Analyzing risk*

Point on scale	Outcome	Implication
1	Negligible	No first aid, no delay to voyage, no environmental impact, no cosmetic damage to vessel.
2	Minor	Some first aid, some cosmetic damage, no environmental impact, some delay to vessel.
3	Significant	More treatment than first aid required, vessel damage, some missed voyages, some environmental impact.
4	Critical	Severe injury, major damage to vessel, major environmental damage, cancelled voyage.
5	Catastrophic	Loss of life, loss of vessel, extreme environmental damage, cancelled voyages.

Using this approach a matrix can be constructed to quantitatively analyse risk. Note that hazard analysis can be gauged according to frequency using a five-point scale, where

1 = remote
2 = occasional
3 = likely
4 = probable
5 = frequent

In terms of consequence a five-point scale is also used to reflect outcome.

Risk assessment develops the interpretation of factors that impact on hazards at each level to examine implications when, for example, training of crew, design, maintenance routines or communication are changed or improved. This consideration of influences can lead to the creation of 'what if' scenarios. In effect this overview enables a systematic process of assessment of those circumstances, influences and faults that can lead to an event in order to make a judgement about relative risk. This analysis can be undertaken against a PESTLE model (see Chapter 5) or, as Lois *et al.* [21] suggest, using the contexts of commercial, regulatory, technical and social or environmental.

Causal chains can be useful devices to identify a chain of events associated with a hazard and to construct a list of countermeasures that can avoid, or mitigate against, the hazard based on interventions that could involve human resources, physical resources or systems or processes. Risk control options suggest: interventions that can remove a cause, by focusing on the setting and conditions within the setting; interventions before a prospective incident by considering ways the emerging issue can be identified in timely fashion and an alert raised to prompt action; interventions before an accident such as training for drills or special incident protocols; and interventions before the outcome such as response plans.

It is also possible to measure a risk in terms of cost and balance that against the benefit. The cost-benefit assessment technique can address action from a causal chain, the events that can lead up to and create a hazard, assess them on a five-point scale for benefit and a five-point scale for cost to calculate a result on the basis of benefit divided by cost.

This sequence of analysis is employed in Table 10.6, which uses a hypothetical situation that is unlikely to be encountered on many ships but provides a graphic representation of the process:

Hazard – drunk passenger causes fight in bar: frequency rating 2 (occasional,

Table 10.7 Risk assessment and cost benefit analysis

	Cause	Incident	Accident	Consequence
Causal chain	Passenger consumes too much alcohol	Passenger starts a fight	Crew or passenger injury	Damage to company reputation Lowers staff morale
Interventions by stage	Intervention to remove cause	Intervention before incident	Intervention before accident	Intervention before outcome
Potential interventions	A Training B Develop policy for sale of alcohol	A Security staff in area B Design of bar area (mirrors for line of sight, etc) C Early warning protocols	A Procedure for dealing with difficult and unruly individuals	A Response plan
Cost benefit ratings (1 – very low to 5 – very high)	A – Cost 3 medium A – Benefit 5 very high (Result 1.66) B – Cost 2 low B – Benefit 5 very high (Result 2.5)	A – Cost 5 very high A – Benefit 4 high (Result 0.8) B – Cost 4 high B – Benefit 4 very high (Result 1)	A – Cost 3 medium A – Benefit 4 high (Result 1.33.)	A – Cost 3 medium A – Benefit 4 high (Result 1.33)

once or twice a month), consequence rating 2 (possible first aid and damage to bar furniture and glassware).

In terms of decision making, this implies that managers will be in a position to arrive at an informed decision based on this type of analysis, which can take into account complex situated factors and can lead to a prioritization for action in a logical manner. The table (above) suggests, for example, that there are considerable advantages to be accrued in focusing on the causes as a priority in terms of cost benefit.

PROVIDING A SERVICE TO CUSTOMERS WHO HAVE SPECIAL NEEDS

The Americans with Disabilities Act (ADA) is a powerful piece of legislation that protects the rights of US citizens who may have a disability and aims to protect them from discrimination [22]. With reference to the cruise industry, the legislation affects any cruise company where the vessel is registered in the US or where the ship uses US ports. In the UK there is similar legislation in place to protect those who may be discriminated against in this way [23]. It makes good business sense to ensure provision is made for all guests with due regard to these laws in order to be compliant but also to be seen as a responsible business that cares about its customers.

In general terms, the needs of people who have a disability are summarized in the requirement to have equal treatment, the ability to gain equality of access and the need to remove any barriers that may inhibit access. For cruise companies this can start with design and construction and the need to ensure that ADA-compliant staterooms are provided and that facilities take the ADA guidelines into account.

Cruise ships vary in terms of when they were constructed, their target market, the types of itinerary they cover, the range and scale of facilities, the carrying capacity and so on. Inevitably this implies that passengers should consult carefully with their travel agents to ensure that they are happy with the provision that is being offered. An example of advice provided to passengers by Princess Cruises can be seen in Table 10.8.

SUMMARY AND CONCLUSIONS

This chapter provides insight into a number of critical issues affecting the cruise industry. In particular, the role of the CDC and the VSP are examined to help develop understanding about the implications and actions that arise from the inspection regime. The norovirus is also discussed to place the risk associated with the problem in context and to reflect on good practice. It is important for

Table 10.8 *Princess Access – adapted from Princess Cruises [24].*

PRINCESS ACCESS

Princess makes every effort to accommodate our passengers with disabilities. Just be sure your travel agent notifies us of your wheelchair usage and/or any other special needs prior to sailing. We have wheelchair-accessible staterooms on all Princess ships. Each ship has a limited number of wheelchairs available to pre-reserve, but please be aware they must be confirmed in advance. Wheelchairs reserved for onboard use cannot be used for pre- and/or post-cruise land tours or hotel packages. If you require a mobility device in those instances, you must provide your own. When bringing your own wheelchair, we highly recommend collapsible wheelchairs, as the width of stateroom doors varies. Some Princess ships have areas that are not wheelchair accessible.

Accessibility varies widely on pre- and post-cruise land tours and hotel packages. Not all products have lift-equipped transportation options available and, when available, arrangements must be secured in advance to accommodate your needs for pre- or post-cruise land tours. To ensure we can accommodate your needs, please call the Tour Quality Department at XXXXXXXXXXX.

If you have purchased a Princess Transfer at the start or end of the cruise, be aware that lift-equipped transportation may be available in your port of embarkation or disembarkation. When available, arrangements must be secured in advance to accommodate your needs. To ensure we can accommodate your needs, we ask that you contact us at XXXXXXXXXXXX.

Passengers utilizing mobility devices with batteries are advised that the batteries must be of a dry cell type and they will be required to be stored and recharged in the individual staterooms. Scooters and or wheelchairs may not be left in hallways. Because we are not staffed with specially trained personnel to assist passengers with physical challenges, we recommend you be accompanied by someone who is physically able, to assist you both ashore and onboard if necessary. Travellers with disabilities should check in with the on-board Tour Office to ensure all pre-reserved tours can accommodate their needs. Not all port facilities are easily accessible for those using mobility devices.

Ports of call may be accessed by a variety of methods including, but not limited to, a ramped gangway, series of steps or by tender. In some cases, you may be able to access the tender; however, the shoreside facility is not accessible. With your safety and comfort in mind, the decision to permit or prohibit passengers from going ashore will be made on each occasion by the ship's Captain, and the decision is final. Those ports, which normally utilize tenders to access the shore, are noted on the itinerary. In many ports of call a mechanism known as a stair climber is used to assist passengers up and down the gangway. The

Table 10.8 *Continued*

stair climber requires passengers transfer to a Princess wheelchair, which is then connected to the stair climber and operated by the ship's personnel. If you cannot transfer or your personal mobility device cannot be easily disembarked due to size or weight, you may be precluded from going ashore.

If you are travelling with a service animal, please be aware Princess requires notice in advance. Entry regulations vary from port to port and there are some ports that prohibit the landing of animals altogether. Passengers are advised to consult the local authorities at each port of call prior to departure for the necessary documentation.

Princess does not provide food for service animals.

---

future cruise managers to appreciate these elements of health and safety and also to refer to updates relating to the development of good practice. Much is said about security in our modern world. All aspects of our societies are affected and the cruise industry is no exception. This is reflected upon in this chapter, along with risk assessment and safety at sea. A cruise ship is a complex machine, yet increasingly there are people wishing to cruise who may have disabilities. This creates a dilemma for the cruise operator, who must meet all individual passenger needs despite the constraints imposed by being onboard a cruise ship with gangways, tender operations (boat ports), safety and emergency drills and the implications of weather at sea. This chapter has considered some of the points concerning ADA in this respect.

REFERENCES

1. US Public Health Service, *Vessel Sanitation Program – Operations Manual*. 2005, Centers for Disease Control and Prevention, National Center for Environmental Health: Atlanta.
2. Cramer, E.H., C.J. Blanton and C. Otto, 'Shipshape: Sanitation inspections on cruise ships, 1990–2005', Vessel Sanitation Program, Centers for Disease Control and Prevention, *Journal of Environmental Health*, 2008. 70(7): p. 15–22.
3. Centers for Disease Control and Prevention. *Vessel Sanitation Program*. 2011; [accessed April 2011] Available from: http://www.cdc.gov/nceh/vsp/default.htm.
4. Neri, A.J., *et al.*, 'Passenger Behaviors During Norovirus Outbreaks on Cruise Ships', *Journal of Travel Medicine*, 2008. 15(3): p. 172–176.
5. Anon, 'Outbreaks of Gastroenteritis Associated with Noroviruses on Cruise Ships–United States', 2002. MMWR. *Morbidity and Mortality Weekly Report*, 2002. 51(49): p. 1112–1115.
6. Widdowson, M.-A., *et al.*, 'Outbreaks of Acute Gastroenteritis on Cruise Ships and on Land: Identification of a predominant circulating strain of norovirus – United States', 2002. *Journal of Infectious Diseases*, 2004. 190(1): p. 27–36.

7. Cramer, E.H., D.X. Gu and R.E. Durbin, 'Diarrheal Disease on Cruise Ships, 1990–2000', *American Journal of Preventive Medicine*, 2003. 24(3): p. 227–233.

8. Centers for Disease Control and Prevention, *Facts About Noroviruses on Cruise Ships*, CDC, ed. 2004, Health and Human Services: US.

9. Ramilo, P.B., M. Augenbraun and M.R. Hammerschlag, 'Recent Outbreaks on Cruise Ships', *Infections in Medicine*, 2004. 21(1): p. 14–17.

10. Lindesmith, L., *et al.*., 'Human Susceptibility and Resistance to Norwalk Virus Infection', *Nature Medicine*, 2003. 9(5): p. 548–553.

11. Sternstein, A., 'How Good is Health Care on Those Big Cruise Lines?', *Forbes*, 2003. 171(8): p. 249–251.

12. US Public Health Service, 'Noroviruses'. 2005 [accessed June 2005]; Available from: http://www.cdc.gov/nceh/vsp/pub/Norovirus/Norovirus.htm.

13. Gibson, P., 'Understanding the Norovirus: A guide for managers', *IoH Management Guides*, Institute of Hospitality, ed. 2007.

14. Food and Drug Administration, 'Hazard Analysis & Critical Control Points (HACCP)'. 2011 [accessed October 2011]; Available from: http://www.cfsan.fda.gov/~lrd/bghaccp.html.

15. Parker, S., 'Adopting a Security Mindset', *Lloyd's Cruise International*. 2004. p. 14–15.

16. Scorza, A., 'Euro Cruise Shipping: Paying the price for peace of mind', *Fairplay International Shipping Weekly*, 2004.

17. IMO, 'Conference of Contracting Governments to the International Convention for the Safety of Life at Sea, 1974: 9–13 December 2002'. 2002 [accessed June 2005]; Available from: http://www.imo.org/Pages/home.aspx.

18. NSnet, News archive. 2004 [accessed June 2005]; Available from: http://www.nsnet.com/archive-1-2004-06.html.

19. Smith, K., *Environmental Hazards*. 4th ed. 2004, London: Routledge.

20. Faulkner, B., 'Towards a Framework for Tourism Disaster Management', *Tourism Management*, 2001. 22(2): p. 135–147.

21. Lois, P., T. Ruxton, A. Wall and J. Wang, 'Formal Safety Assessment of Cruise Ships', *Tourism Management*, 2004. 25(1): p. 93–109.

22. US Department of Justice, 'A Guide to Disability Rights Laws'. 2004 [accessed June 2005]; Available from: http://www.usdoj.gov/crt/ada/cguide.htm.

23. UK Government, 'Changes to the Disability Discrimination Act'. 2005 [accessed June 2005]; Available from: http://www.direct.gov.uk/en/DisabledPeople/index.htm.

24. Princess Cruises, *Cruise Answer Book*. 2005 [accessed June 2005]; Available from: www.princess.com/learn/answer/pdf/2009_Cruise_Answer.pdf.

Training and learning onboard

INTRODUCTION

This chapter is designed to help the reader appreciate issues concerning training and learning, reflecting on the importance of cultures in the setting and learning cultures in relation to professional development. The chapter also includes a section on how to understand Training Needs Analysis (TNA) before concluding with a variety of approaches to skills development, including training, coaching and mentoring.

What is discussed here is the nature of skills development onboard. Training is both essential for operational effectiveness and continuous improvement and development – it is an element of onboard practice that can never be ignored. Training is often identified as a process that is managed by the Human Resources (HR) department but frequently it is seen more broadly as an operational routine. This implies that training plays a strategic role in achieving a brand's vision. Training is an activity that appears inseparable from the term 'service quality' – a company that seeks to achieve excellence in service quality must wholeheartedly embrace training as a key strategic activity.

The provision of training is an investment and as such there is constant attention on outcomes and benefits, cost effectiveness and value for money. However, while it is relatively easy to survey passenger feedback about services, and to generate 'scores' that reflect on satisfaction levels, it can be difficult to measure the impacts of training. It is tempting to ascribe interpretations for changes to feedback patterns to single reason factors such as training, when the reality may be more complex, with a multiplicity of issues to be considered. However, training can mean the difference between satisfaction and dissatisfaction, stability and instability, risk and confidence, safety and danger, and/or profit and loss and it is a brave or foolish organization that ignores these salient facts. In real terms, by planning and implementing continuous, effective training, significant improvements may occur incrementally.

Training differs from learning in that the former is employer-directed and the latter is employee-motivated. Contemporary practice focuses on the way that organizations can move from being modelled on a traditional training regime, which seeks to establish a 'one size fits all' approach to training, towards a learning organization. Learning is the responsibility of the learner and this latter approach radically changes an organizational culture by recognizing the natural predilection of people to learn and the way that the individual can be encouraged to take responsibility for learning in the workplace so as to benefit the individual and the company [1].

In identifying key issues relating to training and learning, this chapter will consider training needs onboard mega cruise ships and the interface between organizational culture and learning organizations. In addition a variety of approaches to skills development will be proposed, including training, coaching and mentoring. Motivation for learning is also considered before finally a case study is presented, which considers a cruise company's training provision.

TRAINING AND LEARNING

The task of developing a competent, effective, committed and passenger-focused workforce onboard a cruise ship is demanding. The growth in the industry means that new ships are constantly being constructed, passenger numbers are increasing, passengers' needs are continuously changing, and the need to source the right type of workforce is overwhelming [2]. Cruise ships adopt flags or national registrations to create flexibility of approach and to limit external control so as to manage costs effectively. This practice is widespread, although by no means universal, and it ensures, among other things, that the labour bill is minimized and, in turn, that the product is available at a price that is acceptable to the customer. The sourcing of labour from favoured countries by using agents has been discussed in an earlier chapter. Frequently the countries selected provide labour that has been plentiful and where the types of potential employees are suited to customer service tasks [3].

With the pattern of demand for labour, a danger exists that workforce availability will become more problematic, leading to shortages. These shortages mean that HR departments are likely to widen their search for employees, looking at emerging sources. Recent patterns have seen employees sourced from the Philippines, India, Mexico and Eastern Europe. Developing sources are likely to include various South American countries, China, Vietnam and other Asian countries [4].

Customer service posts such as cabin stewards and buffet assistants or waiters often receive elementary training ashore that is designed to check that the applicant possesses the desired minimum level of dexterity and has a good manner with customers, and also to help the employee to adapt to operations when they join the ship. Chefs are frequently sourced from training colleges, although the skills levels achieved may well be rudimentary. Invariably, selection and recruitment practice result in the contracting of service staff, who arrive onboard needing to develop their skills and abilities in the workplace. Standards are attained by a number of interventions including: employing key experienced staff in supervisory posts; by constructing manuals that define service and product standards; and by training on and off the job to ensure service staff meet prescribed standards. The value of a shoreside training team coupled with peripatetic trainers who travel with ships and undertake targeted training can add significant value in this effort [3].

Workplace competence is critical for delivering service excellence but onboard a cruise ship it is only one part of the training equation. Crew must be trained initially to fit in with the shipboard way of life, to orient themselves and find their way around, to settle into the job and then, to understand and comply with relevant regulations, to develop product knowledge, to deliver expected levels of customer service, to adopt the company and/or brand culture, to learn how systems work, to know the part they are to play within a team and to deal with change. The list is long and challenging. Regulations are vital for safe and secure practice, as are the safety routines associated with emergency drills, and these areas provide a prominent focus for training onboard and an overarching commitment to training across departments.

LEARNING CULTURES

According to Simmonds [1], trainers play a large part in helping to transform a company from a training-led entity to a learning organization. The subtle advantage in encouraging the individual to: take responsibility for their personal development; to seek opportunities to learn and develop themselves within the organization; and to identify their learning needs, creates a paradigm shift that can have far-reaching positive effects. Such an individual is more likely to have high expectations for her/his employment, which should mean that barriers for progression or promotion are removed. A learning organization has a specific philosophical approach that is best understood by considering Table 11.1.

This table suggests that a learning organization is one which possesses: a vision that is understood and shared by the employees; employees who are constantly seeking to create improvements; and a strategic aim that seeks to support people as they change and grow. In this organizational climate, employees are valued, supported, rewarded and appreciated. The organization is sold on the idea of learning and development for all, who are, in turn, encouraged to introduce ideas. The organization is also open to the adoption of externally generated ideas.

Table 11.1 *The learning organization, adapted from Honey (2005)*

Beliefs that help define a learning organization

- You cannot make people learn; only make it more likely that they learn
- Learning and continuous development are too important to leave to chance
- Complacency is the biggest enemy of continuous improvement/development
- Most organizations unintentionally reinforce many unwanted behaviours (e.g. deference, blaming, covering up mistakes)
- People learn, not organizations
- Learning is our core purpose and we sell the results of that learning
- Learning is the only sustainable competitive advantage
- Learning has occurred when people can show that they know something they didn't know before and/or can do something they couldn't do before

Beliefs that hinder when creating a learning organization

- Most of what people learn 'just happens' as a natural consequence of doing things and keeping busy
- The experiences I learn most from are the experiences others will learn most from
- It is more important to learn from mistakes than to learn from successes
- Learning from experience mostly happens intuitively (i.e. it isn't necessary to do it deliberately or consciously)
- Developing people is a primary responsibility of any manager
- The more senior you are, the less you need to learn
- The learning organization is doomed unless it is done top down
- Learning is best done at courses, conferences, seminars and workshops

It may seem almost incongruous that organizations, modelled on former hierarchical pseudo-militaristic, class-divided structures, which now appear to utilize labour sources in part because of cost benefits, should adopt a learning organization approach. Yet the evidence suggests that enlightened cruise companies are moving towards this approach in order to derive competitive advantage from their increasingly much-treasured human resource. For example, Princess Cruises encourages employees to seek career development promotions and the organization has many examples of individuals who have created opportunities for themselves by seeking to take ownership of their career trajectory and learning opportunities. Within this particular organization, employees can access learning opportunities by signing up for training or using online learning facilities.

The culture of an organization can be described in a number of ways. For example, Evans *et al.* [6, p. 81] describe the 'cultural web' as relating to:

- Stories that surround the organization that might help to define the people, the successes or the characteristics.
- Routines and rituals, which for a shipping company might related to the annual Christmas celebration for crew and officers, the crossing the line (equator) ceremony or the launching of a new vessel. Equally it can relate to the company's way of achieving service quality through some form of customer service strategy and a correlating system of rewards.
- The symbols, logos, flags and images relating to sea-going, the use of semiotics or the symbolic representation of signs – even the shape and colour of the ship can present symbolisms.
- Structure, the way the ship is organized in teams, departments and groups of teams, the informal social structures that exist onboard and the structure of shoreside organization.
- Control systems. This includes budgetary control, quality control and operational control and can refer to what Hofstede [7] refers to as power-distance. In this sense a small power-distance environment creates a more liberal, tolerant and equal society while a large power-distance environment has a strict hierarchy with a less liberal regime. Cruise ship societies from different companies can be located along a continuum that extends from one power-distance to the other. Power structures, the location of the head office, the owner of the company and the prevailing management style can all fed into this element of the cultural web.

This cultural web, seen in its entirety, can present a holistic view of an organizational culture. Other views of culture emerge when reflecting back on work undertaken by Handy [8], who stated that there are four distinct cultural types:

- Power cultures tend to be dominated by an individual or group of people who retain overall control. This type of organization relies on the quality of those key people and it will depend on one or a few people as to whether the organization can respond to change.
- Role cultures are frequently hierarchical and give credence to often long-standing, well-established procedures and policies. These organizations can appear bureaucratic and can be slow to adopt change.
- Task cultures are often team based and are found when the day-to-day routines are replaced by projects or one-off events. The teams are often multi-skilled and flexible so as to respond to the demands they face.
- Person cultures are there to support an individual. In this sense such a culture might be a trade union.

Miles and Snow [9], describe culture for organizations by the way they react strategically. They identify 'defenders' as organizations that are generally found in stable, mature markets that are frequently niche by nature. These types of businesses defend their territory by targeting costs or making service improvements. Miles and Snow state that such organizations have limited flexibility because of their rather hierarchical style and strict, unyielding control processes. The authors describe 'prospectors' as innovators that seek new markets. The organization is aware of the market environment and values flexibility in order to respond with appropriate speed to opportunities. 'Analyzers' are careful in approaching the market. This type of culture exists when the business follows the lead of others. Mistakes are avoided by carefully examining data. Finally, 'reactors' also take a lead from others but this cultural type is prone to repeating errors. Such a business tends to have poor leadership and unsatisfactory systems.

TRAINING NEEDS ANALYSIS/ASSESSMENT (TNA)

Training Needs Analysis or Assessment can be undertaken for a number of reasons: to remedy a problem, to identify a problem or state of effectiveness, or as part of an ongoing process built on the need to develop continuous improvement. In the case of the first two reasons, the implication that a firm has a training need may suggest that there is an underlying performance problem. Therefore, for such a situation, TNA can be a form of research undertaken to identify and then address underlying or root causes that can create symptoms for problems. TNA can be undertaken by an external agency in the form of a consultancy service in order that the assessment is conducted objectively, without bias and unfettered by prior or preconceived expectations. It can be undertaken to reflect on critical actions to achieve corporate change, to examine competence levels for potential progression or to measure the impact of training.

Chiu and Thompson [10] point out that TNA tends to focus on four distinctive methods of data collection – surveys, individual interviews, focus groups and on-site observations. In their reflection on TNA, the authors note that action research methods, which can capture the true essence of training needs by considering work place dynamics, are less commonly found, despite the potential benefits for an organization that is focused on achieving best levels of performance and meeting strategic objectives. Chiu and Thompson believe that the individual's learning needs are frequently discounted in this type of TNA exercise but that this is a critical issue because a learning organization cannot afford to lose sight of the individual when they seek to create a balance in meeting both organizational and individual learning needs.

Training needs can also emerge as part of the appraisal process. Appraisals are cyclical (often annual) events. The appraisal process can generate high-quality data about a person in an organization. However, Leat and Lovell [11] counsel that the process tends to be used differently by different organizations with the result that, in some cases, the focus can be on summative performance for the appraisal period, in others it may reflect on the individual's performance for remuneration or progression, or the appraisal may try and equate diagnostic needs against summative judgements.

An effective appraisal will consider the individual, the team and the organizational needs in a balanced fashion so as to create an action plan. In this sense, a more thorough analysis can create a complete and holistic overview. The organizational analysis will focus on the 'organization's goals, skills resources, indices of effectiveness, and the organizational climate' [11, p. 149]. The task analysis can reflect on the parameters for job roles that are typically identified through a job description and job specification. Finally, the person analysis can address the question about the individual's effectiveness in doing her or his job.

SKILLS DEVELOPMENT

Most jobs include a variety of skills that can be improved by practice, evaluated and developed through comparison with identifiable good practice or honed to near-perfection through engagement with those who seek to claim 'expert' status. A new crew member joining the food and beverage team in a service position is likely to spend a period of time working in the crew or officers' mess areas before progressing to serve in passenger buffet dining facilities. Thereafter the individual will proceed to restaurants in a support capacity before taking more responsibility for directing service. Progression is logical, allowing the individual to learn and develop skills through the use of a variety of training interventions and the involvement of key individuals. Learning is cumulative, building on basic skills and routines in order to establish standards that are recognized by the employee's supervisors, managers and the customers.

On many ships, employees are expected to converse in the language that is predominant for the cruise brand and the customers. This is as much to do with safety as it is concerned with communication to achieve high levels of customer service. Because the cruise industry is global, attracting a broad range of nationalities and cultures, language can present problems. New appointments may have rudimentary knowledge of, for example, English and their level of language skill may impede their progress from low customer contact areas to high customer contact areas. Language classes may be required onboard in order to support the employee in being operationally effective and to ensure the ship's company complies totally with safety regulations. Managers should recognize that learning on the job and conversing in a second language can be physically tiring for those who are seeking to develop language skills.

Many skills can be developed *in situ*, by creating a set of clear guidelines in the form of a reference manual or manuals that can include pictorial representations of the way a table is laid for meals, the presentation of dishes before they leave the galley or the standard presentation of toiletries in a guest's bathroom. Lists positioned strategically out of sight of the guests can also act as a useful *aide memoire* for practice. This approach can be supplemented by the use of posters or high-visibility signs to reinforce good practice for issues such as hygiene and food safety or customer service. On-the-job training can be supported by coaching or timely interventions to make adjustments during service routines. These can be acceptable if the routine is not impeded and service standards do not drop below acceptable levels.

Some skills are better developed away from the customer to allow the individual to achieve suitable levels of practice before utlizing these in operational areas. Off-the-job training can be practised in training areas or rooms away from the normal work location or within the usual work location but outside normal service times. This form of training can be beneficial: where the skills requires practice and development of technique; where demonstration may be of benefit; when larger groups can benefit from the practice or learning situation; where questions and answers can be helpful to confirm details and understanding; or where role-play can be used to simulate a situation. Invariably, off-the-job training removes risk from the workplace by introducing control features.

PLANNING A TRAINING SESSION

There are a number of key steps to follow when preparing to train a small group of staff. It is important to prepare in order to use time effectively and to achieve successful outcomes. The training must be for a purpose that is: relevant in order to achieve improvements that are required to meet set objectives; understandable in the eyes of the potential trainee; and be manageable within the time and place constraints that exist.

According to Reece and Walker [12], it is helpful to establish a plan that includes or takes into account:

- Knowledge of trainees – to be aware of levels of ability and likely orientation towards the training.
- Your objectives – what you expect the trainees to achieve. These should be SMART: specific (e.g. folding serviettes), measurable (to a set standard), achievable (the trainees have appropriate basic levels of dexterity), relevant (of direct importance to the job) and timely (to meet a timeframe or timetable).
- Timing – to fit in with, and be scheduled noting, operational constraints and to help the trainee and trainer to concentrate appropriately.

- Resources – in terms of condition and sufficiency that are essential to achieve the objectives (this can include equipment, materials and/or teaching aids).
- Training strategy – the approach you will use as a demonstrator or trainer.
- Assessment – the approach you will use to check the learning outcome.

Reece and Walker [12] believe that any training session will have, as basic components, an introduction, a main body and a conclusion. Each stage plays a part in, first, setting the scene, clarifying objectives and stating what will be achieved by the end of the session (introduction), second, delivering the training in a structured, carefully paced and systematic manner while paying attention to critical issues such as hygiene, quality standards, essential knowledge or customer service (main body) and third, revisiting the objectives, clarifying and stressing what has been covered, assessing learning and checking understanding (conclusion). The training session should encourage attentiveness, so location and conditions related to the place and time where training occurs are important, as are content and method of delivery. The trainer should raise expectations within the trainees about what they will learn and have high expectations about what they will learn. The trainees should see the benefit that arises from the training, both in terms of why they are doing it and how it can help them in their job. The trainees should understand what is expected from them in the session, such as the level of participation, any assessments that are required and rules that are in agreed to make the session work.

Training is a complex activity, which requires that the trainer develop a range of skills so she/he is confident, business like, enthusiastic, stimulating and clear. The relationship with the trainees is usually best when it is mature, professional and warm rather than aloof and cold. Many skills that are best trained off the job are known as 'psychomotor' skills [12]. That is, they require acting or doing. However, it is highly unlikely that a trainee will only learn psychomotor skills in isolation, as invariably the individual will also be expected to comprehend related theory and to understand why they are doing what they are doing.

When planning a psychomotor skill development session, the trainer should be able to analyse the skill and recognize key abilities, describe and demonstrate the skill to clearly portray correct sequencing, coordination and timing. More complex skills may need to be broken down to help understanding. The trainer should then be able to create conditions so the trainee can practise the skill and provide opportunities for feedback to be generated in relation to the learnt skill. In some cases the practice can follow the demonstration stage by stage before the trainee attempts the task independently. Feedback can be intrinsic (the trainee criticizes her/his own performance) or extrinsic (the trainer or a third party provides the criticism) or both. It is important to provide opportunities for trainees to continue to practise any learnt skill so as to increase levels of ability.

Assessment and evaluation can be undertaken through the use of observation and feedback, by asking questions to check understanding or by using a test (paper, electronic or practically based). The use of groups and peer assessment can add to this function by providing a support network that creates opportunities for discussion and problem solving. Coaching can be used as a follow-up in the workplace to provide individual support and attention using expert guidance to focus skills development.

MENTORING

New appointments or newly promoted appointees can benefit from the individual attention provided by a mentor in supporting and overseeing the employee's transition from novice in post to accomplished practitioner. According to Zey [13], the mentor provides a vital link as a teacher who helps the employee to interpret the complex organizational realities, as a counsellor to support the employee at times of difficulty, as a sponsor to provide information that can help the employee progress and as an intervener to get involved when necessary to provide protection. The complex environment onboard a cruise ship is, it would seem, a fitting place for the use of such a role.

The use of a mentor creates a bridge between the insecurity of a new setting and the social integration and effectiveness of the experienced crew or officer. Problems can arise from within the process if, for example, the wrong type of person is selected to be the mentor or if the mentor or the employee misinterprets the other party. It can be easy to forget that working in any environment creates a new hybrid language that can be unique to the setting. This may be to do with the notion of working at sea and the maritime jargon or the commonality of understanding about routines connected to the job. The mentor should take appropriate care and responsibility for the employee and not use the role as a form of power; equally the employee should take care to value the role of the mentor and to appreciate the benefits that are accrued from this type of support.

Zey [13] states that a mentor should be good at their job, be supported by the organization, be effective as a teacher and motivator and be secure in their position. Other factors are the ability to empathize with the employee and the accessibility of the mentor. In many respects these factors are also somewhat academic – as this is a partnership, the individual chemistry that exists is as important as any other element and managers should take care to consider this when aiming for best fit.

LEARNING AND MOTIVATION

It can be argued that as individuals we learn all the time and are constantly adding information and knowledge to our databanks [14]. What we learn will depend on our prior knowledge, learning and beliefs and the way we interpret our environment or socio-cultural setting [15]. Indeed, in many respects, what may be learnt by some individuals could be categorized by an observer as incorrect, inappropriate or apparently illogical. Learning is a highly personal act and what we learn is also a matter of our understanding about opportunities in conjunction with the potential to which we think we can aspire [16]. In making judgements about learning, the individual considers her or his needs and aspirations so as to rationalize the perceived options for possible action in order to meet a personal set of priorities that exist for the specific context.

The 'circumstantial curriculum' (Figure 11.1) encapsulates this theory and is a useful device for understanding learners and their motivation. The theory emphasizes the need to be aware of the way that individuals understand and relate to their setting [18]. This can help employers to appreciate that different employees may have a different or unique understanding or appreciation of their local environment because of who they are, what they know, how they perceive the realities onboard and their motivations. The model can also help to explain why individuals act as they do in respect of learning opportunities and can suggest ways for trainers to plan learning opportunities that address individual issues. Finally, the theory sug-

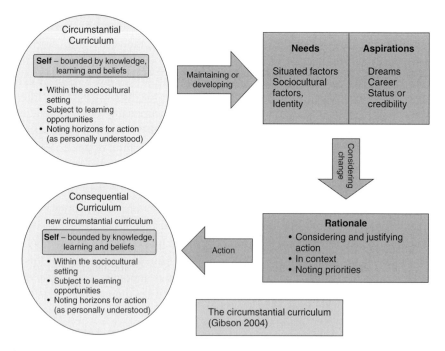

Figure 11.1 *The 'circumstantial curriculum': an integrated theory of learning (Gibson [17])*

gests that because learning is continuous and frequently unplanned, it is important to pay particular attention to the setting onboard. This enables the organization to create the best conditions for learning and learners and, in turn, the most appropriate professional outcomes to suit all parties.

It is useful to consider how this theory can be applied to practice. The following case study presents a training initiative called 'White Star Academy', which was introduced by Cunard Line. When reading this case study, reflect on the learning model and identify how good practice, which it is suggested can emerge from adopting the understanding implied by the circumstantial curriculum, is evident through the training initiative.

CASE STUDY: WHITE STAR ACADEMY (WSA)

Cunard introduced the White Star Academy as a College at Sea in 2000, partially in response to regulations requiring new seagoing staff to receive a comprehensive and compulsory safety induction programme. However, in introducing the WSA, Cunard enabled their training team to address skills and knowledge acquisition in a formal and structured manner so as to bolster quality control and provide a more supportive induction for new entrants to the industry. Essentially the WSA encompasses orientation, induction, diagnostic assessment, the establishment of basic operational skills (including customer service), product knowledge, company information, health, security and safety and contextual knowledge relating to working at sea.

The academy is structured to allow employees to be led through a process, incrementally and logically, developing their learning and preparing them for progression to full operational status. The programme is scheduled over four weeks. The various steps allow the employee to start by considering personal appearance, grooming and the appropriate use of uniforms. This is followed by training relating to the company, working onboard and the specific function the employee will perform. Objectives for each session are clearly stated so the employee knows what is expected to be achieved. The White Star Academy appears to create a powerful focus for training onboard that establishes an identity, clarity of purpose, a semblance that this is an entity for the protection of high standards, a body to differentiate the Cunard brand and a training regime which, despite a relatively short history, seems to have become an integral part of the Cunard way of doing things.

CASE STUDY: SAMAR KAMOLLAN, SENIOR HUMAN RESOURCE MANAGER (RCCL)

Samar is Senior Human Resource Manager onboard Royal Caribbean's Vision of the Seas. He is a hotel management graduate with considerable experience both in food and beverage operations and in corporate training. He has been a trainer with firstly Carnival Cruises and then, from 2004, with Royal Caribbean. He is responsible for training employees and for management development. Every new employee is trained for a month on the ship specific duties for a particular position. Samar delivers the 'soft skills' training while another trainer addresses job specific skills. Soft skills include guest service and interpersonal skills. Samar has been on seven different ships in the seven years he has worked with Royal Caribbean. On Carnival ships, crew members went to a training centre for prescribed language and skills development, but with RCCL Samar is responsible for designing training programmes and he finds that role more challenging. He has been involved in the pilots of performance management schemes, including the introduction of a 'balanced scorecard' as a management tool. Samar is a three and a half stripe officer and when he was promoted he was, at 34, one of the youngest Human Resource Managers in the fleet. Samar works very hard, he has clear ambitions and goals and has clearly enjoyed success and recognition in his job. He possesses self confidence and seeks new challenges. He hopes to target a job as Hotel Director in the future.

His job brings challenges. If there is a problem, the crew will bring that to him. He is involved in conflict resolution, which involves the crew and the division heads, where he acts as mediator. He recognizes he has to be consistent and a good communicator. This means he has to make sure he says the right thing at the right time. His experience helps him to prepare for his role and to aim to defuse difficult situations before they happen. His team looks at everything to do with the crew, including collecting and looking after passports, managing crew activities, coordinating crew travel, cabin allocation and immigration. He manages a team of four: a Training and Development Manager and a Crew Administration Manager, who in turn supervises a Crew Administrator and Crew Relations Specialist. His office is situated on the I.95 (the slang name for the main corridor that extends along the non-public part of the ship). He chairs the Crew Welfare Committee and guides the committee to help it create a purposeful crew activity programme.

Samar's advice to new employees is to start from the bottom in order to learn the job properly and to understand the complex world onboard a ship. He says it is a challenging career and you don't see the benefits in the beginning but they come through as time progresses. In his opinion, a person can really grow in this type of job and, with experience, the sky is the limit.

SUMMARY AND CONCLUSIONS

Training and development are serious challenges for cruise companies. The pace of growth is such that sourcing of staff becomes a problem. However, honing the ship's complement into an effective operational team is a further consideration. Growth creates opportunities for staff in terms of promotion and personal development but it can also dilute critical levels of competence. This chapter has examined training issues and reflected on learning issues. The very nature of a ship and the unique society onboard is well suited to developing a learning culture. However, in order for such a culture to survive and thrive, a company should consider creating mechanisms to support the individual in her/his search for learning opportunities. The final chapter will present research findings concerning planning for undergraduate work placements or internships. This is followed by a series of case studies, which will help the reader appreciate the range of roles that exist in the purser's department.

REFERENCES

1. Simmonds, D., *Designing and Delivering Training*. 2003, London: CIPD.
2. Wild, P. and J. Dearing, 'Growth Culture', *Lloyd's Cruise International*. 2004. p. 17–24.
3. Dickinson, R. and A. Vladimir, *Selling the Sea*. 1997, New York: Wiley.
4. Wood, R.E., 'Caribbean Cruise Tourism: Globalisation at sea', *Annals of Tourism Research*, 2000. 27(2): p. 345–370.
5. Honey, P., 'Learning Beliefs'. 2005 [accessed May 2005]; Available from: http://www. inspiringlearningforall.gov.uk.
6. Evans, N., D. Campbell and G. Stonehouse, *Strategic Management for Travel and Tourism*. 2003, Oxford: Butterworth-Heinemann.
7. Hofstede, G., 'Cultural Differences in Teaching and Learning', *International Journal of Intercultural Relations*, 1986. 10(3): p. 301–320.
8. Handy, C.B., *Understanding Organisations*. 4th ed. 1996, London: Penguin.
9. Miles, R.E. and C.C. Snow, *Organisational Strategy, Structure and Process*. 1978, New York: McGraw-Hill.
10. Chiu, W. and D. Thompson, 'Re-thinking Training Needs Analysis', *Personnel Review*, 1999. 28(1/2): p. 77–91.

11. Leat, M.J. and M.J. Lovell, 'Training Needs Analysis: Weaknesses in the conventional approach', *Journal of European Industrial Management*, 1997. 21(4/5): p. 143–154.

12. Reece, I. and S. Walker, *Teaching, Training and Learning*. 4th ed. 2000, Sunderland: Business Education Publishers.

13. Zey, M.G., *The Mentor Connection*. 1991, New Brunswick: Transaction Publishers.

14. Gibson, P., 'Learning, Culture, Curriculum and College: A social anthropology', (PhD) 2003, Exeter: University of Exeter.

15. Lave, J. and E. Wenger, *Situated Learning: Legitimate peripheral participation*. 1991, Cambridge: Cambridge University Press.

16. Bloomer, M. and P. Hodkinson, 'Learning Careers: Continuity and change in young people's dispositions to learning', *British Educational Research Journal*, 2000. 26(5): p. 583–597.

17. Gibson, P. 'Life and Learning in Further Education: Constructing the circumstantial curriculum', *Journal of Further and Higher Education*, 28(3): p. 335

18. Lave, J., *Cognition in Practice*. 1988, Cambridge: Cambridge University Press.

Managing integrated
12 operations

INTRODUCTION

By the end of the chapter the reader should be able to reflect on research undertaken to establish graduate internships, examine case studies or vignettes to reveal insights about working life onboard, reflect on the administrative role that the Purser's office plays onboard a contemporary cruise ship and consider the complex relationships that together establish integrated operations.

So far, this book has presented a series of chapters that have aimed to deconstruct the world of cruising from an operational perspective. In doing this it has considered the origins of cruising and charted the development of this fast-growing industry. It has reflected on the component parts of cruising to identify what makes a cruise both in terms of the itinerary, the range of services and facilities onboard and considered the mechanism for packaging and selling cruises as a product. The book has analysed the key operational functions for hotel services and the provision of revenue-generating services such as shore excursions. Finally an overview of security and safety was considered.

This penultimate chapter aims to round off the book by presenting a brief summary of research that was undertaken to plan for graduate internships or work placements onboard cruise ships. Thereafter, a series of vignettes, or case studies, are presented to consider the roles of a range of employees in the Purser's, or hotel, department on contemporary cruise ships. In conjunction with the findings from the research project, the vignettes provide the reader with an opportunity to reflect on the day-to-day reality of working for a contemporary cruise brand. The vignettes reflect the voice of the individuals concerned so as to convey authenticity.

RESEARCHING GRADUATE EMPLOYMENT ON CRUISE SHIPS

Following the introduction in 2003 of the BSc (Hons) Cruise Operations Management at the University of Plymouth in the United Kingdom, a research project was undertaken to investigate planning for establishing work placements onboard cruise ships. The BSc (Hons) Cruise Operations Management was designed as a result of collaboration and consultation between the former Institute of Marine Studies (now the School of Shipping and Logistics) at the university, representatives from cruise companies and members of the Tourism and Hospitality group at the university [1]. The programme was approved and identified as an important qualification for the expanding cruise industry.

This unique undergraduate qualification, with its module mix including cruise operations, management, tourism, maritime studies and hospitality, was designed to hold relevance for contemporary cruise companies and to prepare future cruise ship hotel services managers for the demands of employment in this context. An optional one-year industrial placement after stage two was seen as an important component, because students, who could secure such a placement, would be able to make an informed decision about selecting this type of work as a long-term career. Any student who subsequently rejected the lifestyle relating to this type of work could transfer to another degree qualification in the final year. Thus the cruise industry would be able to actively engage in offering work placements in

Figure 12.1 *University of Plymouth BSc Cruise Operations Management interns and graduates at work*

the knowledge that the programme aided their selection process to identify suitably motivated and prepared candidates. Students who successfully complete a placement and their degree become a secure investment for a cruise company because they are known commodities, will have undergone comprehensive professional development and be able to make the transition seamlessly from graduate to manager onboard.

In conjunction with the introduction of the degree, a research plan was formulated to inform the process of developing placement strategies. The project aimed to create a deep understanding of life onboard a contemporary cruise ship for officers and crew in the hotel services department, with a view to developing undergraduate work placements.

RESEARCH PLANNING

In order to achieve the depth of understanding associated with the research aim, the research adopted an interpretive stance with an anthropological focus [2]. Qualitative data collection techniques [3] were applied to the research setting, in order to examine the professional and social domain and to answer two primary research questions: what is it like to live and work on a large contemporary cruise ship and what are the implications for students studying on the recently introduced BSc (Hons) Cruise Operations Management, who may be seeking such a work placement?

In May 2004, a series of 24 interviews were undertaken over a seven-day period, with a range of hotel department employees onboard a cruise ship in the Mediterranean. The sample was carefully selected, in negotiation with senior personnel ashore and on the ship, to give a broadly representative range of hotel 'type' and service employees. Thus bars, restaurants, galley and buffet personnel; junior hotel managers; accommodation personnel; shops onboard and photography managers; the cruise director and senior managers, representing a range of nationalities, ranks and a mix of genders, were interviewed.

The ship that formed the focus for this research was built in 2002. This vessel is generally regarded as typifying a contemporary style of cruise ship [4], a style that is frequently replicated by other cruise brands. The ship carries 2,600 passengers and 1,100 crew and, while over the years this size of vessel has been eclipsed in terms of size, the ship, as a platform for replicating and constructing new cruise vessels, has become somewhat generic [5]. She is operated by a famous international cruise 'brand' and weighs in at 110,000 GRT.

The interviews were undertaken using a semi-structured interview schedule [6] with a view to constructing case studies [7] from the transcripts, so as to gain an insight into this complex world and to reflect on the implications for students on placement. The interviews were undertaken with due regard to the setting, the conditions, permissions and ethics [2]. The researcher adopted a friendly, encouraging style with open questions and occasional prompts. Interviews were conducted in locations where the interviewee felt comfortable and were scheduled at times that were convenient to the individuals involved. In all cases confidentiality was offered – the name of the vessel is withheld and, in line with respondents' wishes, individual names are disguised.

The transcripts were then transformed into case reports or case studies [8], so as to develop a series of individual narratives that accurately represented the data in an accessible format. The analysis of cases was undertaken using framework analysis within the context of a circumstantial curriculum model [9]. This device (see Figure 11.1, Chapter 11) helps to develop a sensitive interpretation of complex data within a specific setting and to explain motivation, decision making and action. The elements considered within the framework included: the self as a central factor; knowledge, learning and beliefs; the socio-cultural setting; options for learning; horizons for action; and needs and aspirations as understood by the individual. Finally, the case study data was scanned to highlight any pertinent issues that impacted upon placement planning.

RESULTS AND FINDINGS

A broad picture was produced from the data to throw light on the community onboard and the way individuals worked and lived in this unique setting. The findings help to describe the complex 'community of practice' [10] issues that exist for employees onboard this ship. The case subjects were selected in consultation with senior managers from the cruise company to be broadly representative of employees from the hotel department. Because of the link between the students on placement and the types of employment to which they aspired, more time was spent interviewing junior and assistant managers or pursers. Interviewees included departmental managers, APs, JAPs, accommodation supervisors, assistant headwaiters, senior chefs and assistant waiters.

The case subjects were originally attracted to work onboard for a variety of reasons. In most cases the decision to work on a cruise ship had been, in part, driven by a desire to travel in connection with the glamour implied by working within a luxury environment. In other cases the primary attractor had been to work in an environment that provided a good income and a desirable lifestyle. Very few subjects stated simplistic reasons for making the transition from being ashore to working at sea. In the main, responses were multidimensional and individually complex. Developing this, it was apparent that most subjects reassessed the working environment as time went by and formulated new reasons for remaining within this type of employment, in some cases stating that while the lure of travel remained, the powerful social context became more important: 'my friends are from all over the world and I can visit them in, for example, Canada or Mexico when I go on leave' said a JAP. 'I look forward to going home on leave but after a short time I find myself looking forward to coming back', stated an accommodation supervisor. For many subjects, working at sea provides a strong social context that becomes, for whatever reason, an increasingly important element.

The overall picture relating to life onboard that emerged was of a community that was considerably more diverse in make-up than had been predicted. There were 54 different crew nationalities onboard and a 2:1 male–female ratio. The average age of the crew was in the early 30s. The majority of the subjects were keen to emphasize the community as a model of good practice that existed onboard the ship: 'It is a lesson to the United Nations that people with different beliefs and different nationalities can live together' said one assistant restaurant manager. The description was apt, as it was easy to observe in passenger and crew areas a community in harmony. There were few signs of personal conflict and those limited occasions where a tension might arise were reported as being infrequent.

It appeared that the community operated at different levels or, that at any time there were different identifiable communities of practice. The professional level created a milieu, within which individuals undertook their role and interacted with supervisors, managers, subordinates and passengers. The working practices for a waiter were established by attending training sessions, observing colleagues, listening to supervisors, learning from mistakes and refining routines through practice. A JAP adopted similar approaches when establishing working practices, although in addition, this subject had access to online learning materials, had been provided with customized training and was periodically updated by line managers in relation to product knowledge and corporate practices. Senior managers adopted their routines relating working practices to cumulative learning, corporate missives, standard operational procedures and the need to respond to demands from head office. There was a sense that the working environment had changed because of electronic communication (emails, Intranet and Internet), which meant the professional community at sea was less isolated and subject to more external observation.

The subjects regarded the shared environment onboard in much the same way that residents view a village or town. There was a feeling of ownership presented by some ('This is a special ship to work on') or of loyalty and pride by others ('This ship is the best ship to be on, better than any other'). The time spent onboard was divided between 'on duty' and 'off duty'. Privileges afforded to some personnel, e.g. officers/managers, created an opportunity for them to socialize in uniform when they were not undertaking routine tasks. In other words they were still on duty but in a more relaxed mode. While crew, staff and officers or managers were not allowed in passenger areas out of uniform, in some cases, as long as the personnel wore a badge, this was identified as being sufficient. Working hours were long, reflecting the nature of the operation and the need to maintain continuity of services.

It appeared that the professional community of practice was directly impacted upon by the way that managers managed. In a sense this was a reflection of the management style adopted by individual managers. But at a more contemplative level, the 'mood' on the vessel indicated that a patterned approach to the way that the personnel onboard communicated with each other, while conducting professional duties, was in some way a derivative of the lead provided by senior managers. Managers and supervisors appeared to conform to their interpretation of the 'norm' in deciding how to treat people and how to communicate with their teams. There appeared to be evidence of two-way learning, in that managers actively learnt about the people they worked with and the staff actively learnt about their managers and their environment. In many respects this adds another dimension to a study undertaken by Testa [11], which implied that nationality and cultural background impact on leadership for the cruise industry. The case studies suggested that individuals were sensitive to the complex cultural differences that existed and that, at different times, decisions were made to subsume strong cultural beliefs or expectations so as to maintain the harmonious working balance.

This patterned approach carried forward to the social communities of practice within which members formed social alliances and networks. The networks were frequently, but not exclusively, formed according to hierarchical or national or cultural similarities. Occasional examples of what were described earlier as 'infrequent tensions', were sometimes glimpsed through the cases, when a member of a social community encroached on what was seen to be a territorial boundary, e.g. a table in the crew mess that was habitually claimed by a group of Mexican cabin stewards. It was noticeable that early contacts, when crew first joined the ship, were important in helping to orient the individual and help that person to settle in.

There was a sense that the community was self-aware; individuals stated their understanding about the complex make-up of this group of staff onboard, and that this was important in creating harmony. The hierarchy onboard was understood and yet, because of the American model of cruising, where the nautical is subsumed by the vacational, the pseudo-militaristic version of naval officers at sea was less prevalent. Rules and regulations play a significant part in setting societal parameters, but the subjects had clearly absorbed the meaning of regulatory life onboard. The ship operated effectively because there was a collective will to make sure the social and professional context met each individual's need. The subjects expressed an understanding that they were being paid to do a job and, if they were not successful, the job would disappear. It was in each person's best interest to maintain a balance. Individuals, who were unable to comply, appeared to be a minority and they were, it appeared, identified and repatriated very quickly. This ship appeared to be a perfect example of a self-righting society.

The numerical bias towards males onboard seemed to create certain issues for note. Firstly, a female joining the ship found that she soon became the focus of male attention. This focus was an exaggerated version of what might happen in a typical shoreside situation. Females in this position reported that the attention could be at various times a combination of flattering, irritating, annoying or exasperating. Subjects described how they found techniques to ward off unwelcome approaches and that eventually, after a period of time, the attention became less of an issue. There were many examples of couples working onboard. Sometimes they were married or in close partnerships. The company appeared to be flexible in meeting the needs of individuals to work and live with their partner. This included making arrangements for cabin accommodation. Social conditions were described as being very good. An assistant waitress said, 'I'm not allowed in passenger areas when I am not working. It sounds like I am something less than the passengers, but I don't care, the facilities are good. There is a pool, a jacuzzi, a gym, the crew bar. I like being with my friends. They are a mixture of Polish, Mexicans and Romanians.'

Subjects described the speed with which they found themselves settling into the community onboard. After a period of leave, rejoining a vessel or proceeding to a new vessel created few concerns because the contractual and employment patterns meant they inevitably met people with whom they had worked before. Friendships were quickly re-established. In many respects the communities on cruise ships were described in a manner that made them sound like university campus communities. The community members work in an environment where levels of interaction and communication are high. This means that individuals cannot become isolates and problems cannot be ignored. The success of the social community appeared to be important to enable success for the professional community.

It is apparent that the social communities onboard different cruise ships may well display similarities, but each ship is regarded as being unique. Indeed, as one senior assistant purser notes, 'The ships are different, the types of people, the passengers, the size, the itinerary – people want to be there for these reasons'. Her interpretation about the reasons why ships are popular from her and her colleagues' point of view, stresses that the uniqueness of the individual setting arises from the complexity of the variables relating to each setting. The dynamics onboard are impacted upon by: changing rotations (as contracts end and crew go on leave); the demographics of the passengers; the cruise itineraries; the way that individuals regard the physical environment of the ship; and the manner in which senior managers manage the ship.

IMPLICATIONS

Interns or placement students are in an interesting position when joining a cruise ship community. In some respects the community will be distinctly unsettling because it is likely to be a self-replicating, self-balancing and self-regulating environment quite unlike that experienced onshore. That said, with careful planning the individual can make a rapid transition to fit in and to feel comfortable.

It appears to be important that the placement student is provided with clear induction information relating to rules and regulations so that the environmental framework is clearly understood. Also, to facilitate the learning progression from new inductee to settled crew member, techniques should be considered to help create networks. These can include appointing appropriate mentors, holding group inductions with shared team orientation sessions and developing teambuilding activities. An orientation cruise that was offered to University of Plymouth students planning to join a cruise company, was an important element for the first group of placement students to achieve these ends.

The cultural context may be different to that which the individual has experienced, so some form of cultural induction should be considered to introduce factors for recognition. These can include awareness related to cultural differences, suggestions about settling in and what to expect, and directions about who to contact to get help or advice.

In the main, the study suggests that there are considerable strengths within this type of community and that the natural human predilection to learn is the critical element to note for achieving a successful integration. The organization is most likely to succeed in this task by considering how it is that they can create the best conditions to help the learner to learn. There is a counter-suggestion connected to the findings, which anticipates that the working dynamics may not be as successful on some ships and there are obvious implications in studying such communities to identify critical factors so as to make recommendations for good practice.

DEVELOPING AN UNDERSTANDING OF THE CRUISE ENVIRONMENT

According to Gibson [12], the work setting and professional and social realities onboard today's contemporary cruise ship are such that managers are placed in highly challenging positions when asked to make these complex business models work. Cruise ships grow larger and the communities at sea become more complex. Models for managing these communities that are based on the command structure, as required by international regulations, have been subject to change as the passenger demography gets younger, as the cruise product is refined and as more crew members are required onboard. Klein [13] highlights the types of concerns that arise from within larger ship communities when things go wrong, emphasizing that the quality of management is vital in ensuring staff and passengers are provided with a well-regulated and safe environment. More research is needed to reflect on the working environment and yet it is in the nature of cruise marketers to protect their brands.

The cruise industry has much to be proud of and the vignettes that follow show the calibre of professionals that are employed at sea. They are a professional community that any operator would be boastful of and yet the hotel-based cruise industry does not benefit from the formation and status that would be afforded by a professional association [14]. Millions of people enjoy cruise degrees and thousands of people enjoy cruise employment. It would appear to make sense for the cruise industry to recognize the value that presenting a professional face to their passengers and guests would provide.

THE PURSER'S OFFICE AND INTEGRATED PRACTICE

The Purser's Office onboard a cruise ship is the administrative hub for the vessel. The office is usually fronted by a reception desk, which is the focal point for passengers to interface with the cruise company onboard. The type of contact is unpredictable because, whilst a passenger may discuss food and wine with a restaurant manager or accommodation matters with an accommodation steward, the passenger sees this desk area as a shipboard version of Google. Any question may be asked and the answer will be expected promptly and accurately. The nature of the contact can range from the simple to the complex but throughout the service must remain consistent and the level of professionalism high. The first vignette considers a manager who oversees this area.

SENIOR ASSISTANT PURSER, FRONT DESK

In 1996 Donna McBride joined as a Junior Assistant Purser for Princess Cruises with the full intention of staying for six months. She had been working previously in travel agents and hotels but was attracted to the glamour of travel. Now she is a senior member of the administration team and is responsible for the front-line work at the Purser's Office managing a team of Assistant Pursers (Aps) and Junior Assistant Pursers (JAPs). The work is constant and demanding but she also describes it as incredibly rewarding. She reports to the Staff First Purser (Admin) and then to the Passenger Services Director. She controls a team that operates the Purser's Office and ensures the front desk is managed effectively.

Donna works closely with her APs to provide a 24-hour service. One AP acts as the Night Manager, another is Front Desk Supervisor and the 'Pratika' is an AP who facilitates administrative matters such as port clearance and dealing with port officials. The front desk also acts for the medical centre to cover the incoming phone calls for the ship's doctor. Donna's duties also mean she is in regular contact with the Accounts Manager and many other managers onboard. Her team includes 12 JAPs who are on rota to ensure the front desk is staffed. They also cover additional duties as may be required of them, including: assistant to the Night Manager; art track – administering the art auction; lost property; assist with work placement; captain's circle; casino, etc. There are usually four or five JAPs on the front desk at any time, depending on the itinerary and the volume of passengers seeking assistance. The office operates from 0800 to 1900 with a lunch break. The Assistant Night Manager covers the office 1900 through to 2300 and the Night Manager is on duty through to 0800. JAPs tend to be on-duty for 11 hours each day and 7 or 8 hours when in port. Turnaround days tend to be the busiest days.

Much of Donna's time is divided between coordinating the front office duties, ensuring passengers' problems are solved and training her staff to develop customer service skills, IT skills and product knowledge. Training can be one to one or in small groups. Training in product knowledge covers every aspect of front office operations, the Princess Product and systems training. Depending on whether it is the JAP's first contract there may also be a need for general refresher training, updating or familiarization. Additionally, Princess operates 'Princess U', with the U standing for 'university', which is an online training programme to help shipboard personnel improve their service skills, develop team-building strategies and deal with problem solving.

The front desk is a magnet for passengers who have something to say. On a ship with over 2,000 passengers there are many different types of people, some of whom may appear illogical or who are asking the impossible. Yet Donna's team must be consistent, friendly, passenger-focused and aim to satisfy the passenger. Frequently problems are presented that are easily solved. Sometimes the problem is more difficult. A focus file is a computer-generated report that tracks a recorded problem from the point it emerges through to the point when it is satisfactorily concluded. Different itineraries can create different problems. In the Caribbean, passengers can often be accompanied by large quantities of baggage and have problems if an item goes missing. In Europe, US passengers have flown long haul and there have been occasions when baggage fails to arrive with them at the ship. Focus files are sent ashore to the Passenger Relations Department to create a record in case a follow-up is required. The ship's staff are not empowered to make refunds: that is the domain of the corporate office.

Donna says that people can get very upset if they think their luggage has gone missing. She describes people wondering around in dressing gowns, swearing or crying. People can often be at their worst in these situations but the JAP helping the passenger must always do their very best to assist. Eventually passengers calm down and may even apologize if they have behaved badly. It can be that her team does its best but the customer does not always see it that way. If luggage is not located in time for sailing, the JAP working with the AP or SAP will follow the complaint through until it is resolved. Then arrangements will be made to get the luggage forwarded to the next port and the passenger will be helped with temporary solutions in terms of the provision of clothes to wear (including formal wear) and express laundry service. The intention will be to make the passenger as comfortable as possible.

Passengers can complete comment forms that go to a drop box to be collated by the Captain's secretary. In turn these are copied to the PSD and then sent to the corporate office. Every element of the cruise is reported on. The aim onboard is to keep customer satisfaction scores as high as possible, although these are not always reflective of real issues and can be a representative of the types of passengers, the weather or specific issues which arose that were out of the control of cruise personnel.

The diversity of customer complaints is worth considering. The front office team is often faced with making judgements about genuine complaints in sometimes rather unusual circumstances. For example, the Night Manager tends to have interesting situations to deal with. People seem to develop different personalities at night, possibly as a result of drinking too much alcohol. On one occasion the Night Manager was summoned to attend when a female passenger had collapsed outside a lift and her husband had refused to have anything more to do with her. Passengers have even been known to threaten suicide. Whatever the situation, it must be dealt with carefully, compassionately and effectively. The company has a strict policy that any passenger being violent or threatening will be sent off at the next port.

While passenger services are administered at the front desk, the 'Pratika' administers passenger records, deals with cabins that are empty because passengers have not arrived (or have cancelled) and ensures details are available for port authorities. The Night Manager prepares guest folios, ensuring they are up to date and records are maintained in case of a query.

Donna believes that cruise ships all 'feel' different in terms of the working and living atmosphere and the culture onboard. This may be because of the crew, the passengers, the size of the ship and/or the itinerary. She believes that people onboard have their own individual reasons for working on the ship but, irrespective of this, everyone will probably feel differently because of the particular ship they are on. The ship's dynamics are complex. The company tried to put together a team of like-minded people to set the ship up and, subsequently, they use teams to replicate the set-up. As contracts expire and people change, so the ship may change. Equally, the managers are important. They set a benchmark regarding the tone of the leadership style. On this ship there is a relaxed style; everyone appears to be happy in his or her work and life onboard and people are trusted to get on with their jobs. There appears to be an opposite potential in that those who are too strict may create a negative atmosphere that can affect passengers.

The CRUISE credo makes Princess different to all other cruise brands. While it has changed over time it has also become more and more important. Princess has developed competitions with prizes such as employee of month. The cruise committee review blue (generated by crew) or green (generated by passengers) feedback and award the accolade, complete with financial reward. Personnel who complete Princess U courses successfully can also be rewarded financially.

In Donna's view the cultural aspect of working in the Front Office does not really affect life onboard. The people in her office are multinational and represent a broad range of cultures. The only practical issue that can arise may relate to language and understanding. This is because some strong accents can affect understanding and some JAPs may also speak too quickly, thus inhibiting comprehension. In addition, passengers and crew may incorrectly interpret rudeness from the way someone says something. When the ship is cruising in the Mediterranean there are significant advantages in having an office team that is multilingual.

Donna's story includes a range of insights concerning the life and work onboard. Readers are prompted to reflect on the continuity of cover, the need to create a depth of cover for specific days and times, the importance of customer feedback forms and the subtle implications of the cultural milieu onboard. The next vignette considers the accounting function onboard.

SENIOR ASSISTANT PURSER (SAP), ACCOUNTS

Vince is a hotel management graduate from Italy. He started his employment career with the company as a Junior Assistant Purser five years ago and has found opportunities for promotion to be very good. He attributes this to the exceptional growth that the industry has experienced, coupled with the trend to construct large ships. He describes operations onboard these vessels as dynamic and he identifies the challenge faced by contemporary cruise companies to source and retain the right staff.

His position as an onboard Accounts Manager means he works closely with a number of senior personnel, including the SAP Front Office, the Crew SAP, the Staff First Purser (Administration) and the department managers for all revenue areas. On smaller ships the role of Accounts Manager and SAP Front Office are merged. He is located in a large office, which is dominated by a large and impressive safe that contains currencies that may be required on the voyage. The ship is virtually cash-free because the majority of passengers pay their folios or accounts by credit card, so the amount of money onboard is considerably lower than would otherwise be the case. Cash in the form of banknotes is used to pay the crew (US dollars) and to stock currency transaction machines (actual currencies will depend on the itinerary).

He has at his disposal a note counter and a coin counter, which he shares with casino staff.

His routines include managing the shipboard accounts: checking that guest folios are updated; posting or recording figures relating to all sales onboard (passengers and crew); reconciling the various financial records to balance the cruise; allocating floats for reception staff and any other cashiers who require a float; allocating cash for payment of crew wages; and allocating gratuities. He works with a shore-based accountant who has the responsibility of monitoring and checking the financial health of the vessel, cruise by cruise, and follows standard procedures using standardized documentation. He is also responsible for the various currencies that are carried onboard and for preparing and managing the automatic change machines.

The busiest day tends to be when the ship returns to the home port. Vince gets up at 0330 for a start time of 0430. He has to prepare all figures to 'close the cruise'. This term is used to identify that point when all transactions and records relating to the cruise are completed and the records are sent to head office. That morning final bills go to passengers (passengers can check folios halfway through so there is no shock). At 0600, passengers start disembarkation. Vince notes that the office can get hectic for the next hour or more as passengers visit the Purser's desk to query their folio. Passengers leave by 1000 and this creates a two-hour window when Vince completes the cruise closure routines and prepares to open the records for the next cruise by 1200.

While relatively rare, mistakes can happen. A sale may have been miscoded or allocated to the wrong passenger account. There can be computer errors but there is a technician onboard who can rectify that if called upon. Despite the large number of passengers onboard there may be 15–20 mistakes. Any error changes the cruise account and these must be handled with care. Refunds on errors are approved by senior staff and corroborated by the departmental manager who is responsible for the transaction. Vince takes the view that if a mistake cannot be found, the issue can become embarrassingly public, so it is, for him, a matter of pride to be accurate and timely.

Vince aims to prepare a document box that contains all accounting paperwork. This is sent to head office. During the day, cash may be offloaded using a contracted arrangement with a security firm. Money may also be ordered and delivered using the same method. The itinerary will determine the types of currencies that are to be carried onboard. The company provides a currency exchange service using automated machines. Some revenue may be generated in selling and buying back notes but the provision is primarily intended to be a service. During this stage of the day, Vince will balance his float. His experience has shown him that discrepancies can arise when closing the cruise because a number of individuals can input data onto the accounting software. This can sometimes lead to a data input error and as a result, Vince has to trace the source of any imbalance. Fraud is not a serious issue; credit cards are checked, cashiers are trained to identify forged notes and the system of using credit cards raises onboard security. Junior Assistant Pursers (JAPs) are meant to have cash handling training prior to appointment, but some training is done onboard and all receive training prior to joining. Usually 8–10 appointees spend two weeks onboard a ship going through theory, policy and product training prior to joining their first ship. Vince states that it is important for JAPs to possess as much knowledge as possible about the itinerary, practical matters such as the currency ashore and the products onboard.

Vince does not feel isolated in his job, as there is a lot of interaction. He emails head office frequently and he gives revenue managers the figures to show patterns and trends. For every cruise there is a revenue meeting to check targets relating to what is known as Passenger Berthing Daily (PBD) spend. Vince finishes his day in the afternoon prior to departure at around 1500 or 1600. The new cruise is ready, accounting systems are prepared and floats are allocated to all cashiers. It has been a long day but he is satisfied to have sent his documentation to head office on time and in the correct state of accuracy.

Vince's role is central within the administrative system and his remit means he deals with a wide variety of different managers and colleagues, both onboard and ashore. There are a number of officers on a cruise ship that act in this way, providing essential services to support operational effectiveness. This next vignette considers the role of the Crew Senior Assistant Purser, who undertakes a key role in undertaking aspects of the human resource management function.

CREW SENIOR ASSISTANT PURSER (SAP)

Tanya studied tourism marketing at a hotel school. She enjoyed her course but felt that it was too theoretical and didn't include enough practice or training from industry. She has come to this conclusion having worked in hotels, restaurants and in administration. Working at sea is very different to the equivalent hotel job. For example, at sea the reservation process is divorced from the hotel administration function while, if you work in a hotel, reservations are a significant element.

Tanya has worked for this company for five years. She has been a JAP and has experienced lots of different jobs: the crew office; working on the Purser's desk; shore excursions; and Assistant Night Manager. She was then appointed as AP for two contracts before being promoted to SAP. In the crew office she is responsible for tasks relating to the 1,100 personnel onboard. These tasks include wages, welfare, staffing, induction and administration.

She is supported in her job by an AP and a JAP. The crew office is located centrally in the crew area along a corridor colloquially known as the M1, which is the main service artery through the ship. Crew come to this office to find out information, to get help with personal matters, to collect items or wages, to arrange details for returning home and to liaise with the ship's personnel department. Most crew are paid in cash; some have money wired home, which Tanya and her staff can deal with. They can also supply debit cards for use by personnel in the crew bar or messes. The crew office role calls for the team to work closely together and to trust each other. This is the first place the crew will come to talk to the 'company' and this calls for the team to deal with each person with sensitivity, respect and tact. A recent situation occurred when a crew member's mother had died and the company arranged to repatriate him. The office had to organize, in consultation with other colleagues, to obtain the necessary visa and to arrange a flight.

All heads of department request new staff via the crew office. This is passed on in turn to head office. New personnel receive an induction pack from the crew office, are given induction information about life onboard and are then provided with a series of induction training sessions covering firstly, the use of watertight doors, secondly, conduct and regulations and thirdly, the use of fire extinguishers and lifeboat drills. The deck department undertakes all safety inductions. Every two weeks zone commanders or people in charge of stretcher parties train their teams.

The Crew Office team maintain a set of accounts and they act as a bank for the crew, dealing with all financial matters. In addition they sell phone cards that can be used on phones that are available for crew use only. There is a lot of paperwork connected to the job. Passports are held when the crew join and returned when they leave. A security system is employed, which is used to register when a crew member (or for that matter a passenger) leaves and then returns onboard a ship. This system generates a pass with a barcode that identifies the holder. A photograph is generated that can be checked by security personnel at the gangway. If crew do not return, Tanya has to ensure the passport is provided for the shoreside agent to hand on to the crew. The multi-national crew is interesting because of the way they view the onboard life, how they adapt to become culturally sensitive and integrated and how people can change as a result of working onboard. Dealing with problems can be difficult. The crew come to the Crew SAP expecting Tanya and her team to solve everything but unfortunately, as Tanya states, 'Life isn't always like that'. Tanya believes that the crew respect the officer's uniform but also expect the responsibility or authority of the uniform to solve their problems.

Tanya holds down a very responsible and extremely important job. She likes sea days because for her and her team there is less to go wrong. Every time the ship is in port there is a risk that a member of the ship's company will miss sailing and because each port can bring a new country, it can bring a new set of rules that can add complexity to the situation. Consider what you would do if there were 20 minutes to sailing and five crew members have not returned onboard. The next vignette examines the role of the 'Pratika'. This function is inextricably linked with the task of entering and leaving countries, crossing borders and dealing with the transportation of people and goods. The growth of cruising has increased the volume of passengers and crew who are travelling by cruise ship and has created the need to focus on the processes that occur to gain clearance for the ship's passengers and crew to leave a ship when the vessel arrives in port.

ASSISTANT PURSER: PRATIKA

David deals with all local authorities to get the ship cleared by both customs and immigration officials. Some itineraries are easier than others because of the rules and regulations they have in place and the way these rules and regulations can be interpreted. David believes that the US is strict in terms of their rules, which he believes are interpreted vigorously by officials. In Italy, ships may find that officials seek different types of information, not only if the ship visits different ports but also even when the ship returns to a previously visited port. In Europe a number of ports and countries are covered by the Schengen agreement (see Chapter 5).

The Pratika has an overview of everything that goes on and off the ship. David liaises with the ship's agent, customs officers and immigration officials. The work requires that preparation be done before the ship arrives in port and that lists of passengers and crew are sent to the ship's agent for processing the day before arrival. This inevitably means that the home port day, or turnaround day, is a particularly challenging time, especially if the ship arrives in a port the day after. Visas can cause problems as passengers can sometimes either fail to get a visa or get the wrong visa. There are many variables and if officials say the visa is invalid, the passenger cannot disembark.

Pratika is an Italian term, which, in the cruising world, means 'paperwork', and David notes that this is a big part of the job. In real terms, the phrase 'free pratique' is commonly understood to represent the condition which grants permission for people to leave the ship and this is the most likely derivation of the word 'Pratika'. David receives passenger lists from head office and he also has to deal with updates to these lists, special requests relating to reservations, upgrades or changes to cabins approved by head office and special information about specific groups of passengers. His role includes facilitating clearance by providing information to the relevant authorities and enabling embarkation by monitoring and assisting at check-in, dealing with cabin requests and assigning emergency cards for non-revenue passengers. He then supports disembarkation by assigning luggage tags to priority early flights and managing groups and by editing and distributing the internal routine and disembarkation schedule. He also looks after arrangements for transit passengers.

The role of the Pratika is a big responsibility. David says he has learnt a lot in his time doing this job. He has learnt to organize and, sometimes, to improvise. He has learnt how to nurture a partnership with port agents, port officials, customs and immigration. The hours of work can be long and the role can be stressful and unpredictable – things can be going well and something emerges at the last moment. His day starts on a port day after the ship docks and port officials come onboard, when the crew purser meets them. The Pratika lays out the necessary paperwork including passports in a lounge area. When the port official is satisfied he or she announces that the ship is clear.

The Pratika will supply passenger lists, lists about embarking and dis-embarking passengers, crew lists, bonded stores list, notices of any goods or supplies coming onboard, a list from Environmental Officer regarding any items being discharged or offloaded. The Pratika will make use of the shoreside agent to act as an intermediary in the proc-ess. The agent can be a cultural interpreter to facilitate the process. David is assisted in his job by a JAP who undertakes data input and administrative duties that help him to divide his time appropriately to ensure his targets are achieved.

Recently, a passenger had a severe heart attack and she had to be transported to a shoreside hospital immediately. David tried to arrange for an ambulance but when it did not arrive, he contacted an emergency helicopter service. He then had to undertake delicate negotiations with the passenger's travelling companion to find out what she wished to do. This resulted in the companion leaving the ship and moving into a hotel close to the hospital. David, working with the agent and colleagues, tried to make this traumatic event as stress free as possible. Carrying large numbers of passengers is also likely to mean that problems can emerge that must be dealt with instantly and appropriately so as to satisfy all parties.

The Pratika is a member of the Purser's department, and acts on infor-mation sent to the ship from head office and then processes that infor-mation to ensure the cruise operates to plan. The term Pratika is not common to all cruise companies and the reader should be aware that other job titles could be used. The person described in the final vignette also undertakes this type of activity, where the employee is an inter-preter and facilitator.

ASSISTANT PURSER HOTEL SERVICES

Cherie looks after special services onboard. This covers a variety of tasks, including family and friends who wish to send flowers or gifts to passengers, through to arranging weddings onboard or shoreside, and coordinating special celebration packages. She works almost independently reporting to the Staff First Purser and the Passenger Services Director (PSD). Requests for special services arrive from head office with the Pratika and they are then sent on to her. She creates a schedule to ensure the various requests are dealt with, any package that is ordered is organized and all departments are fully instructed in terms of requirements.

The role is relatively new and has been introduced in response to growing popularity for special services. The post is not essentially gender specific and the previous AP who undertook the role was a male officer. The job is rewarding and, in common with many of the JAP/AP/SAP jobs, very demanding. When the schedule becomes complex Cherie can call on the PSD's secretary to assist her.

Cherie has three events this particular day. She is at work just before 0800 and immediately starts double checking arrangements. Any event is a special event for Cherie and she wants to make sure it is perfect for those involved. There are two weddings and a renewal of vows scheduled. The timing is quite tight but by carefully coordinating reception venues, and with the support of her colleagues everything occurs to plan. Weddings are often individual, with the bride and groom requesting packages to suit their personal preferences. The bride can start her day by having her hair styled and being pampered in the beauty salon. Cherie makes sure the florist sends the appropriate flowers to the salon, checks that the bar, where the welcome reception is held, is prepared and checks the wedding chapel is in readiness.

When she is in her office she checks the certificates are prepared, confirms the arrangements with the captain, double checks that the photographer is prepared and starts to orchestrate events. Each wedding and event must flow seamlessly with the aim of ensuring that the focus is placed where it should be. The AP Hotel Services becomes a wedding planner and spends a lot of time leading the process, guiding all parties and ensuring the event progresses to time. There are many details to be noted and for that reason, the role suits the individual who is meticulous and who has particularly strong interpersonal skills.

More and more large cruise ships possess a wedding chapel that can be used for a variety of formal events, complete with live or recorded music and decorated appropriately. An added service is provided by the broadcast of pictures from the wedding ceremony to the company web page. This enables friends and family to be a virtual audience to the celebration. Cherie highlights the importance of the Captain's role in proceedings. The personal touch and the Captain's care, concern and professionalism help to add a special touch to the occasion. Cherie really gets into the day and admits to brushing the odd tear away. She stresses that she really enjoys what she does, attributing this to the nature of what is for all a happy and positive experience.

After the ceremony, which can be religious or secular, traditional or non-traditional, the wedding group will proceed to having photographs taken around the ship; this may include the tradition of cutting the cake. An onboard celebration can continue through the cruise if requested, with all sorts of opportunities for customization and the creation of special moments. At the end of the cruise, Cherie will send the paperwork to the head office for onward dispatch to the country where the ship is registered in order to formalize any wedding event. A card is sent to the happy couple in order to congratulate them and to pinpoint the location at sea where the event occurred.

On a port day, Cherie catches up with her other duties, which may include ensuring the delivery of gift vouchers and dealing with any ongoing requests for special items. In addition to her high-profile work she also acts on the PSD's behalf to help induct new crew members for Hotel Services. This includes allocating emergency cards and ensuring the crew know their emergency duties, orientation of the area and ensuring they sign the Captain's standing orders. Finally she also acts for the PSD to ensure all policies and procedures are updated and that these are then circulated and signed as read by the appropriate personnel.

JOHN RAE, RCCL HOTEL DIRECTOR

John came into the cruise industry relatively late on in his professional life. He actually started working in hotels when he was 13, doing typical weekend or holiday jobs and moving from back of house to front of house as time progressed. When he left school John gained an HND in Hotel Management from Napier University in Edinburgh, building on his experiences through his studies by holding down waiting and bar jobs. He found his qualification helped him to get his foot in the door but he is a firm believer that thereafter it is down to the individual to show their qualities. He also found that the theory he learnt while at college was only the start and it became clear early on he had much more to learn from practical experience. His career developed strongly, with experiences working for major hotel companies at first in the UK and then overseas, with a significant part of that being in Africa. His experiences are such that he is aware it isn't a 'free life' and to get the best return and to maximize your potential you have to work at it. Eventually, after accruing considerable managerial experience in four- and five-star properties, he became a highly successful General Manager and then Group Food and Beverage Manger for a major hotel company in Africa.

When John returned to the UK at the end of his contract in order to seek new challenges he found some UK hotel companies reluctant to recognize his international experience so he returned to Africa for a short time to help establish an independent luxury hotel and resort in Mozambique. Eventually he completed this contract and returned to the UK to find the job market had become more depressed. When scanning opportunities online he saw a vacancy with RCCL and, despite never having thought about this type of employment before nor having ever been on a cruise ship, he sent in his résumé. His application was successful. The company respected and recognized his career history and valued his multicultural experiences. He joined as Food and Beverage Manager and worked his way up to become Hotel Director, a post he has now held for five years. John talks warmly about his job. He is Hotel Director on *Rhapsody of the Seas*, a Vision class vessel. He oversees everything which a guest comes into contact with that isn't navigation, technical or security related. In house revenue areas onboard include the casino and explorations (tours ashore), while Steiner (beauty and hair), photographs and retail are concessions that pay a percentage of sales to Royal Caribbean for trading onboard.

He describes a significant challenge onboard being the dynamic that exists within this fast-paced environment. The ship is constantly changing out key members of team all the time. In a hotel shoreside the key personnel would work together around 48 weeks of the year and 80% would be on site and be available to each other at any given time. On a ship 15% of the crew can be changing on a turnaround day. When 100 crew are joining or rejoining the *Rhapsody of the Seas*, some are returning to the ship, some are arriving from another ship and some have never even been on a ship before. This can be problematic because the ship continues sailing, the passengers are expecting the best and if managed badly things can go wrong. The reason this doesn't happen is because the ship has well-worked routines that new crew can adopt quickly and quality control is high. John's ship is constantly going to new ports and that also presents new challenges when dealing the bureaucracy of international travel and managing the logistics of supply.

John's advice to students seeking a cruise job is:

> You will get information overload in the first month. It is a very fast-moving environment and it is alien to that which you are used to. Every person is there for a reason, there are no spare jobs so you will have to carry your weight. There will be some parachute time (time off) but initially it can be difficult. You have a new language to get used to, e.g. deck instead of floor, port for left and starboard for right, safety training to do; finding your way around can be tricky. Then there are Alpha drills (medical emergency training), Bravo drills (fire and safety training), and Charlie drills (security training). You need to know it all but won't be able to pick it all up straight away. Just ask questions if you are not sure. Everyone is busy so it is your responsibility to push yourself forward – everyone has been there themselves.

John acknowledges that it can be more difficult for people who join a ship when they have longer experience because they will be used to the patterns of life that exist shoreside and shipboard routines can potentially be outside their comfort zone. However, John notes that in reality RCCL's staff turnover rate is very low – 20% – so they must be doing the right thing. John says new appointees should also embrace the multicultural environment – it is an opportunity to make friends for life and those friends can come from all over the world. In his job he is fortunate to have seen all sorts of places in the world. He says that working at sea is not always a bed of roses but then asks what job is without its faults. John says he loves the pace and energy that comes with working on a cruise ship. He says his only regret in reflecting on his prior professional life is in not joining the cruise company 20 years earlier.

STEPHEN DANBURY, P&O CRUISES CREW LOGISTICS MANAGER

Stephen is a former student from the University of Plymouth and has been employed by P&O Cruises for five years. He is currently Crew Manager but will rejoin his next ship, the *Adonia*, as Crew Logistics Manager. The Administration Manager line manages the Front of House Manager and Crew Manager. Stephen deals with immigration and port authorities and the paperwork that is required for the crew (not the passengers). He says this is all-important and uses the phrase 'clearance', a condition which grants permission for people to leave the ship. This is related to port health and immigration and declares that all those carried onboard the ship are free of contagious disease and that all immigration and customs checks have been satisfactorily completed so as to allow free passage, or 'clearance', for passengers and crew to go ashore. Stephen's office hold passports, Seaman's Books, all visas, and keeps records for inspection by port authorities. Without a visa a seaman is not allowed into a country. In this case the individual will not be allowed ashore, and in some cases will be landed before the ship arrives into the country in question. Stephen also checks medical certificates for all crew and professional certificates for deck and engine officers. When the crew sign on, the first place they go is the crew office. They then sign the ship's articles to agree to the terms and conditions related to their job and to abide by the captain's standing orders. They cannot be signed on if the appropriate certificates, passports and visas are not held. Invariably crew will need a C1/D visa for the US and a MCV visa for Australia. Medical certificates are identified in various ways across the world. In the UK this is known as the ENG1. Masters tickets, Officers of the watch certificates, (known as certificates of competency or COCs) and Standards of Training, Certification and Watchkeeping (STCW) are all checked when the individual signs on, as is appropriate for the job. These various certificates allow the ship to sail. Every ship has a Safe Manning Certificate and that certificate lays out the qualifications that are required onboard (engineers, doctors, deck officers, etc). Without those certificates the ship cannot sail and at any time a port official can inspect the paperwork. The port official also checks for the right number of certified fire fighters and crew with appropriate safety certificates (including lifeboat certificates). If the ship does not have those it can be detained and subject to large fines. The crew office team looks after finance (crew wages, onboard accounts and currency exchange), logistics, customs, immigration and professional certification. Training is managed at departmental level and records are held by heads of those departments.

As Crew Logistics Manager onboard the comparatively smaller *Adonia*, Stephen will no longer be responsible for managing port authority requirements. This will instead be managed by the Administration Manager, who will become the only clearance officer for the ship for both crew and passengers, using the onboard IT database systems. Ports receive electronic copies of who is on the ship before arriving in the port; hard copies are then submitted and another electronic copy sent after departure. Stephen's job will be more complex when arriving in certain ports of call such as the US, because of the logistics of moving people and the paperwork connected to that. The other elements of the job will remain constant. Even finance stays the same, although Stephen will now deal with this alone, due to the smaller demand for the service from having a smaller ship's company.

SUMMARY AND CONCLUSIONS

The management and administration of hotel services on contemporary cruise ships are not easily understood when observed from the passenger's point of view. The ship's personnel engage in a range of activities and tasks that are designed to ensure that operations are continuous, that high levels of customer service are constant, that the passenger is the focus and that all services are available. In order to achieve these objectives, the individuals working onboard must function as a team. Moreover, emerging developments highlight the need for the onboard team and the shoreside team to share common aims and objectives so as to become congruous.

The research findings and the vignettes in this chapter stress the notion of integration in practice. Working at sea is not for those who cherish isolation. It is possible to steal moments of peace and solitude, but the environment is more suited to those who value human interaction and who empathize with others.

REFERENCES

1. Gibson, P. and J. Nell. 'Professional Development and Hotel Services on Cruise Ships', *Cruise and Ferry Conference 2003*. Earls Court, London: Informa Group.
2. Cohen, L., L. Manion and K. Morrison, *Research Methods in Education*. 5th ed. 2000, London: RoutledgeFalmer.
3. Denzin, N.K. and Y.S. Lincoln, eds. *Collecting and Interpreting Qualitative Materials*. 1998, Thousand Oaks, CA: Sage Publications.
4. Bjornsen, P., 'The Growth of the Market and Global Competition in the Cruise Industry', *Cruise and Ferry Conference 2003*. Earls Court, London: Informa Group.
5. Gibson, P. and D.M. Turner, 'Catering on Cruise Ships', *Essential FM Reports*, 2009: p. 4–7.
6. Bell, J., *et al.*, *Conducting Small-scale Investigations in Educational Management*. 1984, Milton Keynes: P-C-P Open University.
7. Bassey, M., *Case Study Research in Educational Settings*. 1999, Buckingham: Open University Press.
8. Yin, R.K., *Case Study Research*. 1994, Thousand Oaks, CA: Sage Publications.
9. Gibson, P., 'Life and Learning in Further Education: Constructing the circumstantial curriculum', *Journal of Further and Higher Education*, 2004. 28: p. 333–346).
10. Lave, J. and E. Wenger, *Situated Learning: Legitimate peripheral participation*. 1991, Cambridge: Cambridge University Press.
11. Testa, M.R., 'Leadership Dyads in the Cruise Industry: The impact of cultural congruency', *International Journal of Hospitality Management*, 2002. 21(4): p. 425–441.
12. Gibson, P., 'Cruising in the 21st Century: Who works while others play?', *International Journal of Hospitality Management*, 2008. 27(1): p. 42–52.
13. Klein, R.A., 'Sexual Crimes on Cruise Ships: A historical perspective on security issues for passengers and crew', *3rd International Cruise Conference*. 2010, Dubrovnik, Croatia: University of Zagreb.
14. Gibson, P., 'Credible Careers: Tomorrow's cruise hotel managers', *World Journal of Tourism, Leisure and Sport*, 2009. 3(1): p. 11–19.

Cruise management resources

13

INTRODUCTION

This final chapter provides guidance for students who are seeking to investigate the cruise industry further by identifying sources of information. Researchers who reflect on the cruise industry frequently comment on the scarcity of sources and, while this is true, there is a growing source of material available on the subject. The various sources are divided to create a logical overview of books, journals, trade publications and websites. In addition, wherever practicable, key topics are identified to help the reader focus in on specific resources. It would be an impossible task to identify every publication but this chapter seeks to help the researcher to make a start.

A CONSIDERATION OF SOURCES

The Cruise Research Society (CRS) was introduced to academics and industry professionals at the Second International Cruise Conference, which was held in Plymouth, England in 2010 [1]. The society aims to promote science and research in the field of maritime tourism and cruise management and as such is an essential vehicle for generating industry specific research by acting as a magnet for researchers working in this field and a catalyst for research ideas. The CRS has worked to support and promote three international cruise conferences to date, with further conferences planned in the future. The work that has been presented at the various conferences has been diverse and attracted much interest from industry-focused professionals and academics, and publications of proceedings are available [2].

Until this point, research into the cruise industry had been both *ad hoc* and individually motivated but the CRS provides a useful opportunity for more considered and applied research that can provide vital information for stakeholders [3]. This development helps to provide cruise industry researchers with a 'home' and it provides cruise companies with a useful source of information and a way of connecting with researchers in order to make best use of their skills.

However, the cruise industry possesses a number of qualities that have implications for the student or interested observer. In the first place, the business of cruising is somewhat reluctant to expose itself to scrutiny. This is probably because we live in a voraciously unforgiving, media-dominant world. A good media story is a bad human-experience story. Consumers have learnt that there are rewards to be had by joining a crowd and adding a voice to the many in the hope of extracting financial gain. Anecdotal evidence suggests that cruise managers note some passengers seem to count a good cruise experience as one where they have managed to accrue a financial advantage and this emerging social milieu presents problems in research terms because it does not promote transparency.

This lack of transparency means that engaging with research is more likely to be approached with a marketing manager's eye rather than an operational manager's eye. The result is that the question asked will be, 'Could this affect our image?', rather than, 'How can the research improve our business?'. The more the cruise industry engages with research and recognizes the importance of an educated workforce, the more these barriers will break down and dissolve.

Secondly, the industry is both international and has a broad outreach in terms of associated industries. Global realities mean that brands recruit internationally, language skills are critical in relation to the guests onboard and multiculturalism issues permeate all aspects of the business. The cruise industry operates in a setting where borders between countries are an inconvenience and mobility, flexibility and seasonality are both assets and liabilities. Assets, from the point of view that change is easy (world events are potentially critical for hotels in the face of a political or catastrophic event but can be avoided by a change of itinerary for a ship); and liabilities because control is often in the hands of the border gatekeepers rather than the cruise executives. Seasonality creates migratory trends where cruise ships follow the sun or rather, avoid adverse weather patterns.

The multiplier effect of businesses growing on the backs of the cruise industry has become of major importance to the supply companies concerned and to the areas they operate within. This is because of the spin-off of wealth and income generation and the impact on job creation. Each aspect of this set of realities creates a potential theoretical focus that has a cruise industry context. Identifying sources in this situation is made both more difficult, because of the need to identify best sources, and, paradoxically, more easy, because sources can sometimes be found within what might be considered unconventional subject areas.

GENERIC CRUISE TEXTBOOKS

A selection of textbooks that are related to this subject.

Cartwright, R., and C. Baird (1999). *The Development and Growth of the Cruise Industry*. Oxford: Butterworth-Heinemann. This textbook charts the history and development of cruises in the latter part of the twentieth century and provides useful support information for researching the industry.

Chin, C. (2008). *Cruising in the Global Economy: Profits, pleasure and work at sea*, Aldershot, Ashgate. An overview of the global economic issues relating to the cruise industry.

Dervaes, C. (2003). *Selling Cruises* (2nd ed.). New York: Thomson. *Selling Cruises* provides background information to give readers a good understanding of cruise travel: from freighters through to luxury cruising.

Dickinson, R., and A. Vladimir (1997). *Selling the Sea*. New York: Wiley. *Selling the Sea* offers a complete picture of the cruise line industry, along with step-by-step coverage of how businesses aim to market the cruising experience effectively.

Dickinson, R. and A. Vladimir (2007). *Selling the Sea: An inside look at the cruise industry*, Wiley. Second edition of the above.

Douglas, N., and N. Douglas (2004). *The Cruise Experience: Global and regional issues in cruising*. Frenchs Forest, Australia: Pearson Education. This book examines the cruise industry from various perspectives, paying particular attention to developments in the Asia-Pacific region.

Dowling, R.,ed. (2006). *Cruise Ship Tourism*. Wallingford: CABI Publishing. *Cruise Ship Tourism* explores the theory, issues, impacts and management considerations surrounding cruise tourism. It begins by giving an overview of the cruise industry, followed by chapters focusing on the increasing demand for cruising.

Gibson, P. (2006). *Cruise Operations Management*. Burlington: Butterworth-Heinemann. *Cruise Operations Management* provides a comprehensive and contextualized overview of operational and hospitality services for the cruise industry. The book provides a background to the cruise industry, considers cruise tourism from a planning and process point of view and looks deeper into the contextualized management issues, thus providing a practical learning guide for students and professionals.

Mancini, M. (2003). *Cruising: A guide to the cruise line industry* (2nd ed). Albany NY: Delmar. This guide presents comprehensive profiles of two dozen cruise lines, provides a study of cruises by their geographic itineraries, and considers an insider's view of cruise sales, marketing and operations.

Mancini, M. (2010). *The CLIA Guide to the Cruise Industry*, Delmar Publications. Marc Mancini's publication describing the cruise industry from a CLIA persepective.

Quartermaine, P. & B. Peter (2006). *Cruise: Identity, design and culture.* London: Laurence King Publishing. The interface between the sociology of cruising and the artefacts and aesthetics of the cruise ship.

Vogel, M., Papathanassis, A. and B. Wolber, eds. (2011). *The Business and Management of Ocean Cruises*, Wallingford: CABI. Comprehensive textbook covering a broad range of business and management topics that are cruise-industry relevant.

Ward, D. (2011). *Complete Guide to Cruising & Cruise Ships 2011.* London: Berlitz (published annually). This leading product-related textbook provides up-to-date and relevant data on cruise brands and cruise ships.

CRUISE CONFERENCE PROCEEDINGS

Papathanassis, A., ed. (2009). *Cruise Sector Growth: Managing emerging markets, human resources, processes and systems.* Wiesbaden: Gabler Verlag. Proceedings of the First International Cruise Conference in Bremerhaven.

Gibson, P., A. Papathanssis and P. Milde, eds. (2011). *Cruise Industry Challenges: Making progress in an uncertain world.* Wiesbaden: Springer. Proceedings of the Second International Cruise Conference in Plymouth.

CRUISE TOURISM AND PRODUCTS

Cartwright, R., & C. Harvey (2004). *Cruise Britannia: The story of the British cruise ship.* Stroud: Tempus.This book describes the evolution of cruising with a particularly British focus. The author has collected data to collate the first complete history of the British cruise ship, from the dawn of cruising through the glamorous thirties and beyond to the current fleets of dedicated cruise ships

Dawson, P. (1999). *Cruise Ships.* London: Brassey's Conway Maritime. This book provides an examination and explanation of the evolution of cruise ship design.

Lloyd, H. (2001). *Voyages: The romance of cruising.* New York: Dorling Kindersley. This guide provides an entertaining overview relating to ports of call and cruise ships.

CRUISE EMPLOYMENT

Bow, S. (2002). *Working on Cruise Ships*. Oxford: Vacation Work Publishing. Practical advice and guidance for those who want to find out more about working at sea and securing work onboard cruise ships is provided in this easy to read book.

Heitzmann, W. (2006). *Opportunities in Marine Science and Maritime Careers*, New York, McGraw-Hill.

Klein, R.A. (2002). *Cruise Ship Blues*. Gabriola Island: New Society Publishers. Ross Klein presents a hard-hitting exposé relating to his view of the cruise industry. The book has a predominantly negative viewpoint in relation to contextualized social, political and environmental factors.

CRUISE GEOGRAPHY, ITINERARY PLANNING AND ENVIRONMENT

Boniface, B. and C. Cooper (2005). *Worldwide Destinations*, 4th ed. Oxford: Butterworth-Heinemann. An easy-to-use compendium to world destinations.

Lück, M., P. Maher and E. Stewart (2010). *Cruise Tourism in Polar Regions: Promoting environmental and social sustainability?*, London: Earthscan/James & James. This book considers questions about environmental and social sustainability in sensitive areas.

MANAGING CRUISE SERVICES

Berger, A.A. (2004). *Ocean Travel and Cruising: A cultural analysis*. New York: Haworth Hospitality Press. A consideration of the experiences of cruise passengers from an informed observer's perspective.

Branch, A.E. (1996). *Elements of Shipping*, 7th ed. Cheltenham: Nelson Thornes. This book on shipping addresses all the components of this subject, embracing the economic, political, commercial technical and operating aspects. Particular emphasis is placed on current and future practices and trends within an efficient environment.

Branch, A.E. (1994). *Economics of Shipping Practice and Management*, 4th ed. London: Chapman and Hall. This book explains in simple terms the practical economic considerations involved in modern shipping management in changing legal and logistical environments.

Maclachlan, M. (2000). *The Shipmaster's Business Companion*. London: Nautical Institute. An authoritative practical guide on maritime laws affecting ship operations.

Parritt, B.A.H. (1991). *Security at Sea*. London: Nautical Institute. *Security at Sea* is a practical guide intended for both sea and shore staff. The chapters cover many security concerns, such as terrorism on passenger ships, anti-drug-smuggling protection measures, security in hostile war zones and piracy, and consider protective measures, official guidelines and legislation and contingency planning.

Parritt, B.A.H. (1994). *Crime at Sea*. London: Nautical Institute. A Nautical Institute publication intended to help ships' masters deal with, in a sensible and practical manner, any criminal problems that arise at sea and their subsequent consequences, including the minimization of risk, time loss and costs.

SELECTIVE GUIDE TO JOURNAL ARTICLES AND PERIODICALS

Brownell, J. (2008). 'Leading on Land and Sea: Competencies and context'. *International Journal of Hospitality Management*, 27: 137–150.

Busby, G. D. and P. Gibson (2010). 'Tourism and Hospitality Internship Experiences Overseas: A British perspective'. *Journal of Hospitality, Leisure, Sport and Tourism Education,* 9: 4–12.

Butt, N. (2007). 'The Impact of Cruise Ship-generated Waste on Home Ports and Ports of Call: A study of Southampton'. *Marine Policy*, 31: 591–598.

Chimonas, M.-A., G. Vaughan, Z. Andre, J. Ames, G. Tarling, S. Breard, *et al.* (2008). 'Passenger Behaviors Associated With Norovirus Infection On Board a Cruise Ship – Alaska, May to June 2004'. *Journal of Travel Medicine*, 15 (3): 177–183.

Dev, C. (2006). 'Carnival Cruise Lines: Charting a new brand course'. *Cornell Hotel and Restaurant Administration Quarterly*, 47 (3): 301–308.

Duman, T. and A. Mattila (2005). 'The Role of Affective Factors on Perceived Cruise Vacation Value'. *Tourism Management*, 26: 311–323.

Dwyer, L., D. Ngaire and L. Zelko (2004). 'Estimating the Economic Contribution of a Cruise Ship Visit'. *Tourism in Marine Environments*, 1(1): 5–16.

Erkoc, M., E. Iakovou and A. Spaulding (2005). 'Multi-Stage Onboard Inventory Management Policies for Food and Beverage Items in Cruise Liner Operations'. *Journal of Food Engineering*, 70: 269–279.

Forsyth, P. and L. Dwyer (1998). 'Economic Significance of Cruise Tourism'. *Annals of Tourism Research,* 25(2): 393–415.

Gabe, T., C. Lynch and J. McConnon (2006). 'Likelihood of Cruise Ship Passenger Return to a Visited Port: The case of Bar Harbor, Maine'. *Journal of Travel Research*, 44: 281–287.

Gibson, P., and M. Bentley (2007). 'A Study of Impacts – Cruise tourism and the South West of England'. *Journal of Travel & Tourism Marketing*, 20(3–4): 63–77.

Gibson, P. (2008). 'Cruising in the 21st Century: Who works while others play?' *International Journal of Hospitality Management*, 27(1): 42–52.

Gibson, P., and D.M. Turner (2009). 'Catering on Cruise Ships'. *Essential FM Reports*, 4–7.

Gibson, P. (2009). 'Credible Careers: Tomorrow's cruise hotel managers'. *World Journal of Tourism, Leisure and Sport*, 3(1): 11–19.

Gibson, P. and G. Busby (2009) 'Experiencing Work: Supporting the undergraduate hospitality, tourism and cruise management student on an overseas work placement'. *Journal of Vocational Education & Training*, 61: 467–480.

Gibson, P. and J. Watson (2011). 'e2c: Maximising electronic resources for cruise recruitment'. *Journal of Hospitality and Tourism Management*, 18: 57–65.

Goujard, B., A. Sakout and V. Valeau (2005). 'Acoustic Comfort On Board Ships: An evaluation based on a questionnaire'. *Applied Acoustics*, 66: 1063–1073.

Henthorne, T. L. (2000). 'An Analysis of Expenditures by Cruise Ship Passengers in Jamaica'. *Journal of Travel Research*, 38(3): 246–250.

Hritz, N. & A.K. Cecil (2008). 'Investigating the Sustainability of Cruise Tourism: A case study of Key West'. *Journal of Sustainable Tourism*, 16(2): 168–181.

Jaakson, R. (2004). 'Beyond the Tourism Bubble? Cruiseship passengers in port'. *Annals of Tourism Research*, 31(1): 44–60.

Johnson, D. (2002). 'Environmentally Sustainable Cruise Tourism: A reality check'. *Marine Policy*, 26(4): 261–270.

Kerstetter, D.L, I. Yin Yen and C.M. Yarnal (2005). 'Plowing Uncharted Waters: A study of perceived constraints to cruise travel'. *Tourism Analysis*, 10: 137–150.

Kester, J. (2003). 'Cruise Tourism'. *Tourism Market Trends: World overview and tourism topic*, (Madrid: WTO): 165–176.

King, J. (2005). 'The Security of Merchant Shipping'. *Marine Policy*, 29: 235–245.

Kwortnik, R.J. (2008). 'Shipscape Influence on the Leisure Cruise Experience'. *International Journal of Culture, Tourism and Hospitality Research*, 2(4): 289–311

Kwortnik, R. (2006). 'Carnival Cruise Lines: Burnishing the brand'. *Cornell Hotel and Restaurant Administration Quarterly*, 47(3): 286–300.

Lee Ross, D. (2004). 'Organisational Culture and Cruise Tourism – A "short life" occupational community'. *Hospitality Review*, 2004, 6(4): 46–53.

Lemmetyinen, A. (2009). 'The Coordination of Cooperation in Strategic Business Networks – the Cruise Baltic Case'. *Scandinavian Journal of Hospitality and Tourism*, 9(4): 366–386

Lester, J. and C. Weeden (2004). 'Stakeholders, the Natural Environment and the Future of Caribbean Cruise Tourism'. *International Journal of Tourism Research*, 6(1): 39–50.

Li, X. and J.F. Petrick (2008). 'Examining the Antecedents of Brand Loyalty from an Investment Model Perspective'. *Journal of Travel Research*, 47(1): 25–34.

Li, X. and J.F. Petrick (2008). 'Reexamining the Dimensionality of Brand Loyalty: The case of the cruise industry'. *Journal of Travel and Tourism Marketing*, 25(1): 68–85.

Lois, P., J. Wang, A. Wall and T. Ruxton (2001). 'Fundamental Considerations of Competition at Sea and the Application of Cost-benefit Analysis'. *Tourism Today* (1): 89–102.

Mak, J. (2008), 'Taxing Cruise Tourism: Alaska's head tax on cruise ship passengers'. *Tourism Economics*, 14(3): 599–614(16)

Marti, B. E. (2005). 'Cruise Line Logo Recognition'. *Journal of Travel and Tourism Marketing*, 2005, 18:1, 25–31.

Marti. B.E. (2007). 'Research Note: Trends in Alaskan cruising'. *Tourism Analysis*, 12: 327–334.

McCalla, R. J. (1998). 'An Investigation into Site and Situation: Cruise ship ports'. *Journal of Economic and Social Geography*, 89(1): 44–55.

Morais, D. B., D. Kerstetter and C. Yarnal (2006). 'The Love Triangle: Loyal relationships among providers, customers, and their friends'. *Journal of Travel Research*, 44(4): 379–386.

Morrison, A. M., C.H. Yang, J.T. O'Leary and N. Nadkarni (2003). 'Comparative Profiles of Travellers on Cruises and Land-Based Resort Vacations'. *Journal of Tourism Studies*, 14(1): 99–111.

Neri, A., E. Cramer G. Vaughan, J. Vinjé and H. Mainzer (2008). 'Passenger Behaviors During Norovirus Outbreaks on Cruise Ships'. *Journal of Travel Medicine*, 15 (3): 172–176.

Nilsson, P. (2008). 'Tourism in Cold Water Islands: A matter of contract? Experiences from Destination Development in the Polar North'. *Island Studies Journal*, 3 (1): 97–112.

Park, S.Y. & Petrick, J.F (2009). 'Examining Current Non-customers: A cruise vacation case'. *Journal of Vacation Marketing*, 15: 275–293.

Peisley, T. (1995). 'The Cruise Ship Industry to the 21st Century'. *Travel & Tourism Analyst*, 2: 4–25.

Pérez Arribas, F., and A. López Pineiro (2007). 'Seasickness Prediction in Passenger Ships at the Design Stage'. *Ocean Engineering*, 34: 2086–2092.

Perucic, D. (2007). 'The Impact of Globalization on Supply and Demand in the Cruise Industry'. *Tourism and Hospitality Management*. 13 (3): 665–680.

Petrick, J.F. (2003). 'Measuring Cruise Passengers' Perceived Value'. *Tourism Analysis*, 7: 251–258.

Petrick, J.F. and E. Sirakaya (2004). 'Segmenting Cruisers by Loyalty'. *Annals of Tourism Research*, 31(2): 472–475.

Petrick, J. (2005). 'Segmenting Cruise Passengers with Price Sensitivity'. *Tourism Management*, 26: 753–762.

Petrick, J.F., R. Li and S.Y. Park (2007). 'Cruise Passengers' Decision-making Process'. *Journal of Travel & Tourism Marketing*, 23 (1): 1–14.

Petrick, J., C. Tonner and C. Quinn (2006). 'The Utilization of Critical Incident Technique to Examine Cruise Passengers' Repurchase Intentions'. *Journal of Travel Research*, 44: 273–280.

Pizam, A., C. Mok and J.Y. Shin (1997). 'Nationality vs Industry Cultures: Which has a greater effect on managerial behaviour?'. *International Journal of Hospitality Management,* 16(2), 127–145.

Pizam, A. (2008). 'Space Tourism: New market opportunities for hotels and cruise lines'. *International Journal of Hospitality Management*, 27: 489–490.

Polydoropolou, A., and N. Litinas (2007). 'Demand Models for Greek Passenger Shipping'. *Research in Transportation Economics*, 21: 297–322.

Pratt, S. and A. Blake (2009). 'The Economic Impact of Hawaii's Cruise Industry'. *Tourism Analysis*, 14: 337–351.

Raub, S. ad E. Streit (2006). 'Realistic Recruitment: An empirical study of the cruise industry'. *International Journal of Contemporary Hospitality Management*, 18(4): 278–289.

Scantlebury, M. (2007). 'Cruise Ship Tourism'. *Annals of Tourism Research*, 34 (3): 817–818.

Seidl, A. , G. Fiorella and L. Pratt (2007). 'Cruising for Colones: Cruise tourism economics in Costa Rica'. *Tourism Economics*, 13(1): 67–85(19).

Shamsub, H., W. Albrecht and R. Dawkins (2006). 'Relationship Between Cruise-Ship Tourism and Stay-Over Tourism: A case study of the shift in the Cayman Islands' tourism strategy'. *Tourism Analysis*, 11: 95–104.

Shaw, G. and A.M. Williams (2004). *Tourism and tourism spaces*. London: Sage.

Shaw, M., and P. Leggat (2008). 'Illness and Injury to Travellers on a Premium Expedition to Iceland'. *Travel Medicine and Infectious Desease*, 6: 148–151.

Sobotta, B., M. John and I. Nitschke (2008). 'Cruise Medicine: The dental perspective on health care for passengers during a world cruise'. *Journal of Travel Medicine*, 15 (1): 19–24.

Stewart, E., V. Kirby and G. Steel (2006). 'Perceptions of Antarctic tourism: A question of tolerance'. *Landscape Research*, 31(3): 193–214.

Swain, R. A. and J.E. Barth (2002). 'An Analysis of Cruise Ship Rating Guides'. *International Journal of Hospitality and Tourism Administration,* 3(4): 43–60.

Szarycz, G. (2008). 'Cruising, Freighter-Style: A phenomenological exploration of tourist recollections of a passenger freighter travel experience'. *Int. J. Tourism Res.*, 10: 259–269.

Testa, M. R. (2002). 'Leadership Dyads in the Cruise Industry: The impact of cultural congruency'. *International Journal of Hospitality Management*, 21(4): 425–441.

Testa, M. (2009). 'National Culture, Leadership and Citizenship: Implications for cross-cultural management'. *Int. J. Hospitality Management*, 28: 78–85.

Thompson, E. A. (2004). 'An Orderly Mess: The use of mess areas in identity shaping of cruise ship workers'. *Sociological Imagination*, 40(1): 15–29.

Thompson, E. A. (200). 'Engineered Corporate Culture on a Cruise Ship'. *Sociological Focus*, 35(4) (Nov): 331–344.

Thurau, B.B., A.D. Carver, J.C. Mangun, C.M. Basman and G. Bauer (2007). 'A Market Segmentation Analysis of Cruise Ship Tourists Visiting the Panama Canal Watershed: Opportunities for ecotourism development'. *Journal of Ecotourism*, 6(1): 1–18.

Toh, R., M. Rivers and T. Ling (2005). 'Room Occupancies: Cruise lines out-do the hotels'. *Int. J. Hospitality Management*, 24: 121–135.

Weaver, A. (2005). 'Spaces of Containment and Revenue Capture: "Super-sized" cruise ships as mobile tourism enclaves'. *Tourism Geographies*, 7(2): 165–184.

Weaver, A. (2005). 'The Mcdonaldization Thesis and Cruise Tourism'. *Annals of Tourism Research*, 32(2) (April): 346–366.

Weaver, A. (2005). 'Interactive Service Work and Performance Metaphors – The case of the cruise industry'. *Tourist Studies*, 5: 5–27.

Whitney, G., S. Keith and I. Kolar (2005). 'Independent Mobility for Blind and Partially Sighted People Traveling by Large Passenger Ships'. *International Congress Series*, 1282: 1094–1098.

Wie, B.-W. (2005). 'A Dynamic Game Model of Strategic Capacity Investment in the Cruise Line Industry'. *Tourism Management*, 26: 203–217.

Wilkinson, P. (2005). 'Book Review of A.A. Berger, Ocean Travel and Cruising: A Cultural Analysis'. *Annals of Tourism Research*, 32 (2): 503–505.

Wood, Robert E. (2000). 'Caribbean Cruise Tourism: Globalization at sea'. *Annals of Tourism Research*, 27(2) (April): 345–370.

Vanem, E. and R. Skjong (2006). 'Designing for Safety in Passenger Ships Utilizing Advanced Evacuation Analyses – A risk-based approach'. *Safety Science*, 44: 111–135.

Véronneau, S., and J. Roy (2009). 'Global Service Supply Chains: An empirical study of current practices and challenges of a cruise line corporation'. *Tourism Management*. 30(1):128–139.

Vogel, M (2009). 'The Economics of US Cruise Companies' European Brand Strategies. *Tourism Economics*. 15(4): 735–751.

Yarnal, C., D. Kerstetter and I.-Y. Yen (2005). 'So Why Haven't You Taken a Cruise Lately? *Tourism Review International*, 8(3): 281–296.

Yarnal, C. and D. Kerstetter (2005). 'Casting Off: An exploration of cruise ship space, group tour behavior, and social interaction'. *Journal of Travel Research*, 43: 368–379.

USEFUL WEBSITES

Table 13.1 useful websites

Website	Content
http://www.british-shipping.org	Information on shipping regulations, environmental matters, webcams for all Princess cruise ships, links to International Maritime Organization's (IMO) website.
http://www.cdc.gov/nceh/vsp	Information on Vessel Sanitation Program (VSP), copies of ship reports and articles on shipboard health.
http://www.cruise.co.uk	Information on the history of cruising (from the 1970s), destinations, news, trends, life onboard, reviews, cruise ship overviews.
http://www.barbados.org/ cruise.htm	Information on Barbados as a cruise destination and facilities offered at cruise terminal plus a list of cruise lines visiting island. NB many cruise destinations produce this type of resource – this is just one example among many.
http://www.cruise-community.com	Website which provides daily information on the cruise industry and information on cruise lines and ports.
http://www.cruisedeckplans.com http://www.cruisingholidays.co.uk/ river/deckplans/deckplan.htm	Deck plans (some interactive) and cabin layouts of most major cruise lines (seagoing and river cruises).
http://www.cruiseexperts.org	Association of cruise experts. Training and information for cruise travel agents.
http://www.cruiseindustrynews.com	News about the industry, statistics and articles from their newsletters.

http://www.cruisejunkie.com	Controversial site that aims to reveal critical issues concerning cruising.
http://www.cruiseresearchsociety.com	Cruise research society home page with information for academics and industry professionals.
http://www.cruisebritain.org/consortia.php?c=3	Umbrella tourism group – part of Visit Britain/Cruise UK website
http://www.cruising.org	Cruise Lines International Association (CLIA) is the world's largest cruise association and is dedicated to the promotion and growth of the cruise industry.
http://www.cruising.org.au/general_pages/home.asp	The International Cruise Council Australasia is an association of leading cruise lines dedicated to the expansion of awareness of cruising worldwide.
http://www.cybercruises.com	Cruise news, links to cruise jobs and useful websites.
http://www.destinationsouthwest.co.uk	Website contains information on southwest England's ports, harbours and suggested excursions, and cruise ship calls to region.
http://www.discover-cruises.co.uk	UK passenger shipping association website.
http://www.europeancruisecouncil.com	Representing the leading cruise companies operating in Europe.
http://www.f-cca.com	The Florida-Caribbean Cruise Association (FCCA) is a non-profit trade organization composed of 12 member cruise lines operating more than 100 vessels in Floridian, Caribbean and Mexican waters. Created in 1972, the FCCA's mandate is to provide a forum for discussion on legislation, tourism development, ports, safety, security and other cruise industry issues. Downloadable magazine. Some research statistics available.

http://www.hardingbrothers.co.uk	The Harding Brothers group of companies was founded over 60 years ago and has traditionally offered a range of goods and services to the shipping industry. Areas of activity: The operation of onboard tax- and duty-free retail concessions and the provision of onboard health and beauty spa services.
http://www.imo.org	Website of International Maritime Organization whose main task is to develop and maintain a comprehensive regulatory framework for shipping. Its remit today includes safety, environmental concerns, legal matters, technical cooperation, maritime security and the efficiency of shipping.
http://www.lighthouse-foundation.org	Article by G. Robertson (2004) on 'Cruise Ship Tourism'.
http://www.marisec.org	Information on safety and regulation at sea including: Safety of life at Sea (SOLAS), marine pollution (MARPOL), International Ship and Port Facilities Security (ISPS). Environmental information and shipping stats.
http://www.maritimematters.com	Current news and ocean liner history.
http://www.mcga.gov.uk	The Maritime and Coastguard Agency is responsible throughout the UK for implementing the government's maritime safety policy, which includes coordinating search and rescue at sea through the Coastguard, and checking that ships meet UK and international safety rules.

http://www.nichecruise.com	The Niche Cruising Marketing Alliance (NCMA) is a collection of cruise lines that provide some of the finest travel experiences available in the travel industry today. Their purpose is to increase awareness of the concept of niche cruises. Links to specialist cruise lines.
http://www.nwcruiseship.org	North West Cruise Ship Association (NWCA) represents member lines throughout the Pacific Northwest - including Alaska, British Columbia, Washington State and Hawaii.
http://www.porthole.com	Porthole Cruise Magazine, is a one-stop connection to the cruising industry. Info on cruise news, jobs, links to cruise lines.
http://www.portsidetours.com http://www.portpromotions.com	Examples of shore excursion companies that allow cruise passengers to book their shore excursions in advance. Worldwide.
http://www.cruiseexperts.org/ http://www.the-psa.co.uk/	The Association of Cruise Experts (ACE), is the UK & Eire learning and development body – taking agents from cruise novice to cruise expert with unbiased guidance, advice and services.
http://www.rollingpincruise.com	Links to cruise industry news
http://www.shore-excursions.co.uk	Excursions Ltd is an inbound tour operator specializing in 'top end' touring throughout the UK and enjoy the custom of many of the world's leading cruise lines.
http://www.travelmole.com	Travel Mole is the largest global online community for the travel and tourism Industry with over 50,000 registered travel and tourism professionals worldwide. Individuals can register for daily/weekly updates on their areas of interest.

http://www.worldcruise-network.com	Information source about the cruise industry
http://www.wttc.org	The World Travel & Tourism Council (WTTC) is the forum for business leaders in the travel and tourism industry. Research documents and search facility.

USEFUL CRUISE COMPANY/BRAND WEBSITES

Table 13.2 Useful cruise company and brand websites

Major cruise corporations and companies	Content
http://www.carnivalcorp.com **http://www.aida.de/** **http://www.carnival.com/** **http://www.costacrociere.it/** **http://www.cunard.com/** **http://www.hollandamerica.com/** **http://www.pocruises.com** **http://www.pocruises.com.au/html/** **http://www.princess.com/** **http://www.seabourn.com/** **http://www.iberocruceros.com/esp/**	Carnival Corporation: largest cruise corporation and owner of the following major brands: Carnival Cruise Lines, Holland America Line, Princess Cruises and Seabourn Cruise Line in North America; P&O Cruises and Cunard Line in the United Kingdom; AIDA in Germany; Costa Cruises in southern Europe; Iberocruceros in Spain and P&O Cruises in Australia.
http://www.royalcaribbean.com/ **http://www.azamaraclubcruises.co.uk/** **http://www.celebritycruises.com/** **http://www.pullmanturcruises.com/**	Royal Caribbean Cruises Ltd is the second largest cruise company, operating the Royal Caribbean International, Celebrity Cruises, Azamara and Pullmantur brands.

http://www.genting.com/ http://www.ncl.com/nclweb/home.html http://www.starcruises.com/	The Malaysian Genting group, owner of Star Cruises and part owner of NCL (with Prestige Cruise Holdings).
http://www.msccruises.co.uk/	MSC Cruises is the largest all-Italian-financed cruise company.
http://www.oceaniacruises.com http://www.rssc.com/	Oceania Cruises and Regent Seven Seas Cruises are owned and operated by Prestige Cruise Holdings.
http://www.americancruiselines.com/	American Cruise Lines
http://www.crystalcruises.com/	Crystal Cruises
http://disneycruise.disney.go.com	Disney Cruise Line
http://www.fredolsen.co.uk/	Fred Olsen
http://www.hlkf.de	Hapag Lloyd
http://hurtigruten.co.uk/norway/	Hurtigruten
http://www.louiscruises.com/	Louis Cruises
http://www.sagacruises.com/	Saga Cruises
http://www.silversea.com/	Silversea Cruises
http://www.thomson.co.uk/cruise/cruise.html	Thompson Cruises
http://www.tuicruises.com/	TUI Cruises
http://www.windstarcruises.com/	Windstar

CONCLUSION

The cruise industry is constantly changing and evolving to configure to the new global business order and customers' changing needs. In the same way, resources that are available to aid the student of the cruise industry will also be subject to constant change. This dynamic reality is a challenge but not an impossible task. The cruise industry is, like any other industry, subject to external scrutiny and the more it opens its doors to let the observer gaze beyond the porthole to see into the complex, but fascinating, multifaceted business world, the stronger it will become. The sources to illuminate this world may be relatively scarce but, inexorably, they are on the increase.

REFERENCES

1. Gibson, P. and A. Papathanassis, 'The Cruise Industry – Emerging issues, problems and solutions: Review of the 2nd International Cruise Conference, Plymouth, UK, 18–20 February 2010', *International Journal of Tourism Research*, 2010. 12(4): p. 405–407.
2. Gibson, P., A. Papathanassis and P. Milde, eds., *Cruise Industry Challenges: Making progress in an uncertain world*. 2011, Wiesbaden: Springer.
3. Vogel, M., 'Critical Cruise Research in the Age of Performativity', *Cruise Industry Challenges: Making progress in an uncertain world*, P. Gibson, A. Papathanssis and P. Milde, eds. 2011, Wiesbaden: Springer.

Index